T0181825

# Lecture Notes in Computer Science 14313

The series Lecture Notes in Computer Science (LNCS), including its subseries Lecture Notes in Artificial Intelligence (LNAI) and Lecture Notes in Bioinformatics (LNBI), has established itself as a medium for the publication of new developments in computer science and information technology research, teaching, and education.

LNCS enjoys close cooperation with the computer science R & D community, the series counts many renowned academics among its volume editors and paper authors, and collaborates with prestigious societies. Its mission is to serve this international community by providing an invaluable service, mainly focused on the publication of conference and workshop proceedings and postproceedings. LNCS commenced publication in 1973.

Shandong Wu · Behrouz Shabestari · Lei Xing
Editors

# Applications of Medical Artificial Intelligence

Second International Workshop, AMAI 2023
Held in Conjunction with MICCAI 2023
Vancouver, BC, Canada, October 8, 2023
Proceedings

 Springer

*Editors*
Shandong Wu
University of Pittsburgh
Pittsburgh, PA, USA

Behrouz Shabestari
National Institute of Biomedical Imaging
and Bioengineering
Bethesda, MD, USA

Lei Xing
Stanford University
Stanford, CA, USA

ISSN 0302-9743       ISSN 1611-3349  (electronic)
Lecture Notes in Computer Science
ISBN 978-3-031-47075-2       ISBN 978-3-031-47076-9  (eBook)
https://doi.org/10.1007/978-3-031-47076-9

This Springer imprint is published by the registered company Springer Nature Switzerland AG
The registered company address is: Gewerbestrasse 11, 6330 Cham, Switzerland

Paper in this product is recyclable.

# Preface

The Second Workshop on Applications of Medical Artificial Intelligence (AMAI 2023) was held as a hybrid event in Vancouver on October 8, 2023, in conjunction with the 26th International Conference on Medical Image Computing and Computer Assisted Intervention (MICCAI 2023). This continued event of the AMAI workshop followed its inaugural edition, AMAI 2022, which was held in Singapore on September 18, 2022 along with MICCAI 2022.

Along with the quick evolution of artificial intelligence (AI), deep/machine learning, and big data in healthcare, medical AI research goes beyond methodological/algorithm development. Many new research questions are emerging in the practical and applied aspects of medical AI, such as translational study, clinical evaluation, real-world use cases of AI systems, etc. The AMAI 2023 workshop created a forum to bring together researchers, clinicians, domain experts, AI practitioners, industry representatives, and students to investigate and discuss various challenges and opportunities related to applications of medical AI.

The aims of the AMAI workshop are to introduce emerging medical AI research topics and novel application methodologies, showcase the evaluation, translation, use case, and success of AI in healthcare, develop multi-disciplinary collaborations and academic-industry partnerships, and provide educational, networking, and career opportunities for attendees including clinicians, scientists, trainees, and students.

In this workshop, two submission tracks were included: full papers and abstracts (one page). The idea for the abstract track was to attract participation from researchers and clinicians primarily in the medical communities. AMAI 2023 received a strong response in submissions, including 26 full papers and 25 abstracts. All submissions went through double-blind review by the Program Committee and ad hoc reviewers, and each submission was reviewed by at least two qualified experts in the field. Finally, 17 full papers were accepted and included in this Springer LNCS volume. The 12 accepted abstracts were made publicly accessible on the workshop's website.

The organizers are grateful for the hard work of the Program Committee members and the ad hoc reviewers in undertaking their quality and timely reviews of the submissions. We thank all the authors for submitting their work to this new workshop. The collective efforts of all participants made this workshop successful.

September 2023

Shandong Wu
Behrouz Shabestari
Lei Xing

# Organization

## Program Committee Chairs and Workshop Organizers

Shandong Wu      University of Pittsburgh, USA
Behrouz Shabestari      National Institute of Biomedical Imaging and Bioengineering, USA
Lei Xing      Stanford University, USA

## Program Committee

Dooman Arefan      University of Pittsburgh, USA
Niketa Chotai      RadLink Imaging Centre and National University of Singapore, Singapore
Dania Daye      Massachusetts General Hospital/Harvard Medical School, USA
Douglas Hartman      University of Pittsburgh Medical Center, USA
Fabian Laqu      University Hospital Würzburg, Germany
Mireia Crispin Ortuzar      University of Cambridge and Cancer Research, UK
Chang Min Park      Seoul National University Hospital, Seoul Korea
Matthew Pease      Memorial Sloan Kettering Cancer Center, USA
Hong Peng      Shanghai Ninth People's Hospital, China
Nicholas Petrick      U.S. Food and Drug Administration, USA
Bhanu Prakash K. N.      Agency for Science, Technology and Research (A*STAR), Singapore
Parisa Rashidi      University of Florida, USA
Zaid Siddiqui      Baylor College of Medicine, USA
Tao Tan      Macao Polytechnic University, Macau
Zhiyong (Sean) Xie      Xellar Biosystems, USA
Qi Yang      Genentech, Inc., USA
Yudong Zhang      First Affiliated Hospital, Nanjing Medical University, China

# Contents

Clinical Trial Histology Image Based End-to-End Biomarker Expression
Levels Prediction and Visualization Using Constrained GANs .............. 1
  *Wei Zhao, Bozhao Qi, Yichen Li, Roger Trullo, Elham Attieh,*
  *Anne-Laure Bauchet, Qi Tang, and Etienne Pochet*

More Than Meets the Eye: Physicians' Visual Attention in the Operating
Room ................................................................ 11
  *Sapir Gershov, Fadi Mahameed, Aeyal Raz, and Shlomi Laufer*

CNNs vs. Transformers: Performance and Robustness in Endoscopic
Image Analysis ..................................................... 21
  *Carolus H. J. Kusters, Tim G. W. Boers, Tim J. M. Jaspers,*
  *Jelmer B. Jukema, Martijn R. Jong, Kiki N. Fockens, Albert J. de Groof,*
  *Jacques J. Bergman, Fons van der Sommen, and Peter H. N. de With*

Investigating the Impact of Image Quality on Endoscopic AI Model
Performance ........................................................ 32
  *Tim J. M. Jaspers, Tim G. W. Boers, Carolus H. J. Kusters,*
  *Martijn R. Jong, Jelmer B. Jukema, Albert J. de Groof,*
  *Jacques J. Bergman, Peter H. N. de With, and Fons van der Sommen*

Ensembling Voxel-Based and Box-Based Model Predictions for Robust
Lesion Detection ................................................... 42
  *Noëlie Debs, Alexandre Routier, Clément Abi-Nader, Arnaud Marcoux,*
  *Alexandre Bône, and Marc-Michel Rohé*

Advancing Abdominal Organ and PDAC Segmentation Accuracy
with Task-Specific Interactive Models .............................. 52
  *Sanne E. Okel, Christiaan G. A. Viviers, Mark Ramaekers,*
  *Terese A. E. Hellström, Nick Tasios, Dimitrios Mavroeidis, Jon Pluyter,*
  *Igor Jacobs, Misha Luyer, Peter H. N. de With, and Fons van der Sommen*

Anatomical Location-Guided Deep Learning-Based Genetic Cluster
Identification of Pheochromocytomas and Paragangliomas from CT Images .... 62
  *Bikash Santra, Abhishek Jha, Pritam Mukherjee, Mayank Patel,*
  *Karel Pacak, and Ronald M. Summers*

Video-Based Gait Analysis for Assessing Alzheimer's Disease
and Dementia with Lewy Bodies ........................................ 72
    Diwei Wang, Chaima Zouaoui, Jinhyeok Jang, Hassen Drira,
    and Hyewon Seo

Enhancing Clinical Support for Breast Cancer with Deep Learning Models
Using Synthetic Correlated Diffusion Imaging .......................... 83
    Chi-en Amy Tai, Hayden Gunraj, Nedim Hodzic, Nic Flanagan,
    Ali Sabri, and Alexander Wong

Image-Based 3D Reconstruction of Cleft Lip and Palate Using a Learned
Shape Prior ........................................................... 94
    Lasse Lingens, Baran Gözcü, Till Schnabel, Yoriko Lill,
    Benito K. Benitez, Prasad Nalabothu, Andreas A. Mueller,
    Markus Gross, and Barbara Solenthaler

Breaking down the Hierarchy: A New Approach to Leukemia Classification ... 104
    Ibraheem Hamdi, Hosam El-Gendy, Ahmed Sharshar, Mohamed Saeed,
    Muhammad Ridzuan, Shahrukh K. Hashmi, Naveed Syed, Imran Mirza,
    Shakir Hussain, Amira Mahmoud Abdalla, and Mohammad Yaqub

Single-Cell Spatial Analysis of Histopathology Images for Survival
Prediction via Graph Attention Network ............................... 114
    Zhe Li, Yuming Jiang, Leon Liu, Yong Xia, and Ruijiang Li

Ultrafast Labeling for Multiplexed Immunobiomarkers from Label-free
Fluorescent Images ................................................... 125
    Zixia Zhou, Yuming Jiang, Ruijiang Li, and Lei Xing

M U-Net: Intestine Segmentation Using Multi-dimensional Features
for Ileus Diagnosis Assistance ....................................... 135
    Qin An, Hirohisa Oda, Yuichiro Hayashi, Takayuki Kitasaka,
    Akinari Hinoki, Hiroo Uchida, Kojiro Suzuki, Aitaro Takimoto,
    Masahiro Oda, and Kensaku Mori

Enhancing Cardiac MRI Segmentation via Classifier-Guided Two-Stage
Network and All-Slice Information Fusion Transformer .................. 145
    Zihao Chen, Xiao Chen, Yikang Liu, Eric Z. Chen, Terrence Chen,
    and Shanhui Sun

Accessible Otitis Media Screening with a Deep Learning-Powered Mobile
Otoscope ............................................................. 155
    Omkar Kovvali and Lakshmi Sritan Motati

Feature Selection for Malapposition Detection in Intravascular Ultrasound
- A Comparative Study ............................................... 165
*Satyananda Kashyap, Neerav Karani, Alexander Shang,*
*Niharika D'Souza, Neel Dey, Lay Jain, Ray Wang, Hatice Akakin,*
*Qian Li, Wenguang Li, Corydon Carlson, Polina Golland,*
*and Tanveer Syeda-Mahmood*

**Author Index** ...................................................... 177

# Clinical Trial Histology Image Based End-to-End Biomarker Expression Levels Prediction and Visualization Using Constrained GANs

Wei Zhao$^{(\boxtimes)}$, Bozhao Qi, Yichen Li, Roger Trullo, Elham Attieh, Anne-Laure Bauchet, Qi Tang, and Etienne Pochet

Sanofi, Beijing, China
{wei.zhao,bozhao.qi,yichen.li,roger.trullo,elham.attieh,
anne-laure.bauchet,qi.tang,etienne.pochet}@sanofi.com

**Abstract.** The gold standard for diagnosing cancer is through pathological examination. This typically involves the utilization of staining techniques such as hematoxylin-eosin (H&E) and immunohistochemistry (IHC) as relying solely on H&E can sometimes result in inaccurate cancer diagnoses. IHC examination offers additional evidence to support the diagnostic process. Given challenging accessibility issues of IHC examination, generating virtual IHC images from H&E-stained images presents a viable solution. This study proposes Active Medical Segmentation and Rendering (AMSR), an end-to-end framework for biomarker expression levels prediction and virtual staining, leveraging constrained Generative Adversarial Networks (GAN). The proposed framework mimics the staining processes, surpassing prior works and offering a feasible substitute for traditional histopathology methods. Preliminary results are presented using a clinical trial dataset pertaining to the CEACAM5 biomarker.

**Keywords:** Histological staining · Biomarker expression · GAN Models

## 1  Introduction

Biomarkers are biological molecules that provide critical information about the presence, progression, or response to treatment of various diseases, including cancer. Some well-known biomarkers include Programmed Death-Ligand 1 (PD-L1), Human Epidermal Growth Factor Receptor 2 (HER2), etc. These biomarkers have proven to be essential in disease diagnosis, prognosis, and determining the most suitable treatment options for patients [19]. Biomarkers for early detection are urgently needed to improve patient prognoses.

CEACAM5 [12] (carcinoembryonic antigen-related cell adhesion molecule 5) is a molecular marker found in specific lung tumors, and it holds potential for early detection and prognosis of lung cancer [21]. Our research team is designing an investigational anti-CEACAM5 drug. The target CEACAM5 is a protein that

S. Wu et al. (Eds.): AMAI 2023, LNCS 14313, pp. 1–10, 2024.
https://doi.org/10.1007/978-3-031-47076-9_1

is more abundant on tumor cells than on normal cells. While the expression of this protein is limited in normal tissue, it is highly expressed in several tumor types, including colorectal, gastric, and breast cancer [10]. In fact, a significant proportion of patients with non-squamous non-small cell lung cancer have high CEACAM5 expression levels [21]. When the internalization rate is moderate, the anti-cancer drug can enter cells and trigger tumor-killing activity in cases where CEACAM5 expression is high [5]. Notably, there is a paucity of prior research on the application of machine learning-based staining techniques to CEACAM5.

The expression levels of these biomarkers are commonly assessed through IHC or fluorescence in situ hybridization (FISH) techniques [2]. However, these methods can be costly, time-consuming, and subject to inter-observer variability [4]. As a result, there is a growing interest in developing alternative approaches to predict biomarker expression levels based on H&E stained images, which are routinely used in histopathology laboratories.

**Contributions:** The contributions of this work can be summarized as follow:

- Our study addresses the gap in the current literature, which lacks previous investigations utilizing machine learning-based methodologies to predict CEACAM5 staining and expression levels, and its corresponding dataset.
- This study presents a novel end-to-end framework for predicting whole slide IHC staining images, leveraging H&E slide images along with corresponding predicted biomarker expression masks.
- Domain knowledge-based active learning is employed in the data annotation process, which effectively reduces the need for manual annotations.
- To showcase a comprehensive and intricate approach, we implement our framework based on a real dataset obtained from a Phase 1 clinical trial.

## 2   Clinical Trial Data

In our Phase 1 clinical trial, three cohorts of cancer patients (gastric cancer, colon cancer, and non-small cell lung cancer) underwent cross-sectional serial cuts from archived samples, fresh needle biopsies or other biopsies cut. H&E staining and CEACAM5 IHC staining were performed on the collected samples, which were then digitized at 20x magnification. Patient selection for the clinical trials was based on the extent of positive staining, defined as any partial or complete tumor cell membrane staining at an intensity of 2 or higher, as determined by board-certified pathologists. Tumor proportion score (details in Sect. 3.4), which denotes the proportion of CEACAM5-positive tumor cells among all tumor cells in a whole slide image (WSI), was also assessed by the pathologists. In total, we have collected H&E-stained tumor images from 317 patients, and corresponding sequential cut IHC staining images were sampled with pathologist's annotation with QuPath [1]. Patients can be grouped into two subgroups in two ways. One is by CEACAM5 positive or negative with positive defined as tumor proportion score (TPS) > 0 while negative as TPS = 0. Another way is by CEACAM5 high or low with high defined as TPS >= 50% while low as TPS < 50%. Note that the slides used for IHC staining images were cell-level different from those used for H&E images as they were cut sequentially.

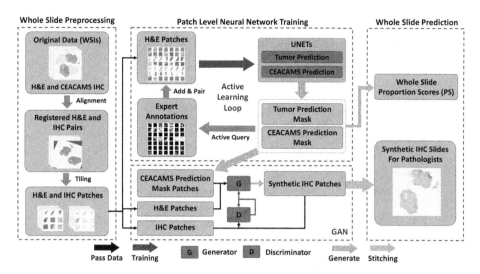

**Fig. 1.** The Active Medical Segmentation and Rendering (AMSR) framework.

## 3   Method

In this section, we present the Active Medical Segmentation and Rendering (AMSR) framework. As illustrated in Fig. 1, our proposed AMSR framework establishes a pipeline from raw H&E and IHC slides to predicted proportion scores and synthetic IHC slides. The AMSR leverages the advantages of active learning and maximizes the use of prediction masks results. First, the raw H&E and CEACAM5 IHC whole slide images are registered, aligned, and tiled to form a training dataset (left column of Fig. 1). Then, we treat tumor and biomarker expression prediction as segmentation tasks and only use H&E patches as inputs. In the upper of the second column, two neural networks are trained in an active learning loop, where active queries are applied to achieve efficient annotations from pathologists. Lastly, the GAN-based IHC image rendering is illustrated on the lower side of the second column. With the registered patch-level CEACAM5 prediction masks, H&E patches, and IHC patches, a constrained GAN model is trained to render two synthetic IHC images for CEACAM5 prediction positive areas and negative areas respectively, where they will be merged in accordance with the prediction mask, and subsequently stitched together.

### 3.1   Whole Slide Image Registration

The whole slide registration between H&E and IHC is done using Virtual Alignment of Pathology Image Series (VALIS) [6]. Dealing with whole slide images can pose certain challenges due to their diverse formats and large sizes. To overcome these challenges, OpenSlide is utilized to read each slide in small tiles, then merged to construct a single whole-slide image and registered between two slides. The slides that have been registered exhibit similarities at the tissue structure level, rather than aligning at the pixel level, due to the inherent cell-level differences that occur between slide-cuts.

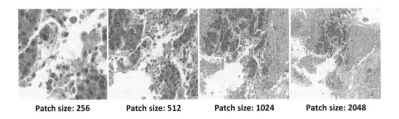

Patch size: 256       Patch size: 512       Patch size: 1024       Patch size: 2048

**Fig. 2.** A comparison of tissue morphology using various patch sizes.

## 3.2 Image Tiling and Pre-processing

It is often necessary to utilize smaller images due to the limitations of GPU memory and the complexity of deep learning models. In our study, we extracted patches that encompassed both partially extended areas beyond the edges of the WSI, as well as a set of coordinates identified by pathologists that were of particular interest. A comparison of tissue morphology with different patch sizes is shown in Fig. 2. The same center location on the same slide is used to extract four patches. Tumor areas are highlighted in green. A larger patch size yields improved tissue morphology in the designated regions of interest. Patch size of $2048 \times 2048 \times 3$ is selected with best performance after experiments with $D_x \times D_y \times 3$, where $D_x, D_y \in [256, 512, 1024]$. We also ensured a random distribution of patches with regards to morphology type balance and regional representation of the whole slide. Additionally, we also check patch-level registration performance and filtered out any paired patch (H&E with IHC) that did not align well.

## 3.3 Activate Learning (AL) for Semantic Segmentation

To mitigate the significant annotation requirements associated with supervised machine learning of our sizeable patch dataset $D(\sim 10k)$, collective outliers are applied for degrading pool-based active learning [11,13], as shown in Fig. 1.

Our initial balanced dataset $D_s$, containinf a list of image patchs and their annotated masks, denoted as $(x_i, y_i) \in D_s \subset D$. The remainder is denoted as $D_{pool}$. During the preparation of $D_s$, we considered domain knowledge including biopsy type $(Bt)$, organ location $(Or)$, cut type $(Ct)$, cancer cohort $(Co)$, etc.

We start the active learning loop by training a semantic segmentation model $S$ on $D_s$. The UNet architecture was selected based on a comparison study conducted with other architectures including Fully Convolutional Network (FCN) [15], MaskRCNN [8], and DeepLab Vx [3]. We combined a Sigmoid layer with a binary cross entropy loss and use it as the loss function.

With the trained network $S$, the subsequent step involves identifying the patches from $D_{pool}$ that are most likely to be informative given the network's current state. The average batch dice score $(D_i)$ and domain knowledge of the image source were employed to identify potential collective outliers during the training process. We assign domain knowledge information to the validation dataset for tracking dice score of different attributions.

The active learning loop conducted over a series of acquisition iterations, utilizing an acquisition function $A(x_i, S, D_i, Bt, Or, Ct, Co)$. The acquisition function takes dice score as well as domain knowledge into consideration, and calculates a score for each patch $x_i$. A new batch of patches $\widehat{x}$ is selected from $D_{pool}$ for annotation per $\widehat{x} = \arg\min_{x \in D_{pool}} A(x, S, D_i, Bt, Or, Ct, Co)$. The active learning iteration concludes with the retraining of the segmentation model $S$ with the updated dataset $D_s$. By utilizing active learning, we managed to label only 400 image patches instead of approximately 10,000.

### 3.4 Biomarker Expression Proportion Score (PS)

The CEACAM5 expression Proportion Score (PS) is defined as the percentage of tumor cells number that expressing CEACAM5 membrane staining at 2+ intensity in total amount of viable tumor cells. Here, we use the models in Sect. 3.3 and estimate PS as the ratio of the number of positive pixels in the CEACAM5 prediction mask $(C_p)$ to those in the tumor prediction mask $(T_p)$:

$$PS = C_p/T_p . \tag{1}$$

### 3.5 Constrained GAN for Virtual IHC Synthesis

The generative adversarial networks [7] include a generator (G) for synthetic data, and a discriminator (D) for estimating the probability of a sample originating from the training data versus G. The conditional GAN [17] is a variant of GAN that requires extra constraints, Liu et al. [14] applies it to IHC image synthesis via pathology consistency constraint, using segmentation masks. We further divide the generator's task as restaining the CEACAM5 positive and negative areas under the guidance of CEACAM5 prediction mask. We briefly list the enhancements made over Liu et al.'s work [14] as follows:

- We simplify the task of generator by branching out two upsampling image outputs. The two outputs in correspondence of CEACAM5 positive and negative areas are merged in accordance with the prediction mask.
- We concatenate H&E image with its corresponding CEACAM5 prediction mask as the generator's input, taking advantage of the intermediate results.
- We utilized VGG19 [20] to calculate the perceptual loss between synthetic and real IHC images. This step was taken as ground truth IHC images typically align with their corresponding H&E images at the tissue level.

We emphasis our contribution of generating separated upsampling branches to mimic the staining process, as discussed in Sect. 4.3.

## 4     Results and Discussion

In this section, we provide a comprehensive overview of our clinical trial dataset and demonstrate the effectiveness of our framework using the acquired dataset.

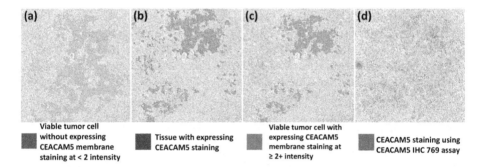

**Fig. 3.** An example of biomarker expression prediction on the H&E slide and the corresponding area on the IHC slide.

### 4.1     Phase 1 Clinical Trial Dataset

For our evaluation, all 317 WSIs were utilized, with data from 268 patients employed for 5-fold cross-validation. Subsequently, an additional 49 patients' data was obtained later and treated as a distinct testing dataset. Annotations (tumor areas, CEACAM5 high areas) for each slides in the cross-validation dataset were generated and fine tuned using the active learning approach (discussed in Fig. 1 and Sect. 3.3).

### 4.2     Active Learning and PS Score Prediction

We partitioned the 268 patients' data into five folds based on patient IDs and evaluated the PS score prediction module using five-fold cross-validation. Within each fold, $C_p$ and $T_p$ in Eq. 1 are calculated by two separate UNET models respectively during the training and validation steps. The UNET models were trained and chosen based on the highest batch dice score. In each fold, the PS scores of the testing dataset were computed using Eq. 1 with the best model.

To assess the PS score prediction module, we converted the task into a binary classification problem by utilizing the PS score to predict whether it corresponds to CEACAM5 high or low. For the determination of CEACAM5 high or low, we established a threshold of 50%. If the PS score exceeded this threshold, the slide was classified as CEACAM5 high; otherwise, it was classified as CEACAM5 low. Evaluation results are presented in Fig. 4 and Table 1. Furthermore, to validate the results and mitigate potential biases in cross-validation, we assessed the best model from each iteration on the additional 49 patients' data.

An example of biomarker expression prediction from two UNET models is depicted in Fig. 3(a–c). The yellow shaded areas represent predicted viable tumor cell without expressing CEACAM5 membrane staining at < 2 intensity. The blue shaded areas indicate predicted tissue with expressing CEACAM5 staining, while the green shaded areas show viable tumor cell with expressing CEACAM5 membrane staining at 2+ intensity. Figure 3(d) displays the corresponding area on the IHC slide, which serves as the ground truth for comparison.

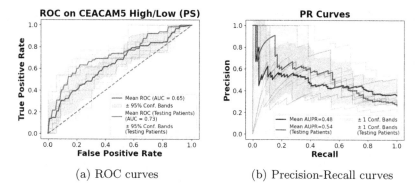

(a) ROC curves                    (b) Precision-Recall curves

**Fig. 4.** Biomarker expression level prediction results with predicted PS

Figure 4 provides an overview of the receiver operating characteristic (ROC) curves and Precision-Recall (PR) curves obtained from each fold across various testing sets. We calculated the average ROC, precision and recall values to better understand the trends. The grey region shows the 95% confidence bands of the mean value. Both figures demonstrate similar performance of the ROC and PR curves across different testing dataset on both the cross-validation testing data and the independent testing dataset. The blue lines shows the averaged results of 5-fold cross-validation, while the red lines remonstrates the results of our trained model on the distinct test set. We compared our results against a weakly-supervised baseline, CLAM [16], which has achieved success in multiple WSI classification tasks. It relies on a cross-attention between ResNet [9] features of patches and a class-token to identify the most informative patches and make accurate predictions at the slide-level (listed as MIL in Table 1). Our method performs generally better than this benchmark method. The area under curve (AUC) score (average 0.65 & best 0.76) and average precision (AP = 0.54 & best 0.83) achieved by our method surpass those of the MIL model. The MIL model yielded the AUC score (average 0.56 & best 0.62) and average precision values (AP = 0.47 & best 0.61). Our method demonstrated an average of 0.35 on the PR curves for recall values between 0.8 and 1, indicating that it effectively identifies a significant number of patients with high CEACAM5 expression during the pre-screening stage with high precision, which is better than current clinical trial practise. This discovery confirms the usefulness of our method and strengthens the reliability of the AUC result.

Table 1. 5-fold cross-validation evaluation results.

| (%) | Fold 1 | Fold 2 | Fold 3 | Fold 4 | Fold 5 | Testing Dataset |
|---|---|---|---|---|---|---|
| AUC (ours) | 0.54 | **0.76** | 0.60 | 0.71 | 0.62 | 0.73 |
| AP (ours) | 0.42 | **0.83** | 0.49 | 0.57 | 0.38 | 0.54 |
| AUC (MIL) | 0.61 | **0.62** | **0.62** | 0.46 | 0.57 | 0.48 |
| AP (MIL) | 0.37 | **0.61** | 0.55 | 0.40 | 0.46 | 0.43 |

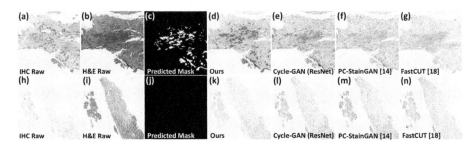

Fig. 5. Virtual synthetic IHC image results of different methods.

## 4.3   Constrained GAN Training and Testing

As demonstrated in Fig. 1, the generator in AMSR takes concatenated H&E patch and binary CEACAM5 prediction patch as input, and returns synthetic IHC patch by merging the outputs of the Generator. Our training set is composed of 885 sets of patches, with the CEACAM5 prediction mask distribution being 359 fully negative, 243 fully positive, and 285 more than half positive. Compared to the previous dataset used for segmentation, registered H&E and IHC patches are selected to generate the dataset, where we apply the segmentation model for CEACAM5 prediction on H&E patchs to generate corresponding binary prediction masks. The conditional GAN is trained on 8 Nvidia V100 GPUs with batch size 8 for both GAN train and pathology consistency train, where each training patch of size $504 \times 504$ is randomly cropped from the original $2048 \times 2048$ patch data. Samples of our testing results on 31 full slide patient after 200 iteration on the training set is shown in Fig. 5, where we compare with PC-StainGAN [14], FastCUT [18] and Cycle-GAN [22] under the same training parameters. The training patch of FastCUT [18] is resized $8\times$ smaller as suggested and results in low resolution. In Fig. 5, our model excels over previous works as it adheres strictly to the prediction mask, thereby eliminating the need to conjecture the CEACAM5 expression level in its outputs. Other models often inaccurately predict CEACAM5 high areas even when the mask indicates low values. For quantitative assessment, we use the pathologist's standard to review synthetic IHC slides and compare the diagnostic results with the ground truth from real IHC. Specifically, for each patient in the test set, we first assign binary high CEACAM5 expression label based on the real IHC slide, and obtain predicted labels following the pathologist's standard on fake IHC slides. The accuracy of different algorithms on the test set of 49 whole slides are listed in Table 2. Our method achieves 83.9% accuracy and demonstrates a significant advantage over other approaches.

**Table 2.** Synthetic IHC based biomarker expression level estimation performance.

| (%) | AMSR (ours) | Cycle-GAN [22] | PC-StainGAN [14] | FastCUT [18] |
|---|---|---|---|---|
| Accuracy | **83.9** | 61.3 | 54.8 | 51.6 |

## 5   Conclusion and Future Work

In this paper, we present Active Medical Segmentation and Rendering (AMSR), an end-to-end framework that translates H&E slides into Proportion Scores and synthetic IHC slides for pathologists. We further demonstrated the effectiveness of the AMSR with Phase 1 clinical trial data. Our initial findings shows that machine learning based techniques holds great promise for improving disease diagnosis. Though our method mainly focuses on a specific biomarker and cancer type, the results generally show promising potential for deep learning approaches to complement or even replace traditional IHC techniques in certain cases. Continued research and development in this area will help to further advance the field of digital pathology. Going forward, we aim to create AI-powered prescreening tools for clinical trial recruitment with quantitative comparison with standard clinical trial practise, following a structured progression in accordance with FDA guidelines.

**Prospect of Application:** This work accelerates clinical trial enrollment and acts as a pre-prescription screening tool, thereby alleviating patients' burden.

## References

1. Bankhead, P.: Qupath: open source software for digital pathology image analysis. Sci. Rep. **7**(1), 1–7 (2017)
2. Burge, C.N., Chang, H.R., Apple, S.K.: Do the histologic features and results of breast cancer biomarker studies differ between core biopsy and surgical excision specimens? The Breast **15**(2), 167–172 (2006)
3. Chen, L.C., Papandreou, G., Kokkinos, I., Murphy, K., Yuille, A.L.: Deeplab: semantic image segmentation with deep convolutional nets, atrous convolution, and fully connected crfs (2017)
4. Conklin, C.M., Craddock, K.J., Have, C., Laskin, J., Couture, C., Ionescu, D.N.: Immunohistochemistry is a reliable screening tool for identification of alk rearrangement in non-small-cell lung carcinoma and is antibody dependent. J. Thorac. Oncol. **8**(1), 45–51 (2013)
5. Decary, S., et al.: A novel anti-ceacam5 maytansinoid-antibody-drug conjugate for the treatment of colorectal, lung and gastric tumors. Cancer Res. **75**(15_Supplement), 1688–1688 (2015)

6. Gatenbee, C.D., et al.: Valis: Virtual alignment of pathology image series. bioRxiv pp. 2021–11 (2021)
7. Goodfellow, I., et al.: Generative adversarial networks. Commun. ACM **63**(11), 139–144 (2020)
8. He, K., Gkioxari, G., Dollár, P., Girshick, R.: Mask r-cnn (2018)
9. He, K., Zhang, X., Ren, S., Sun, J.: Deep residual learning for image recognition. In: Proceedings of the IEEE Conference on Computer Vision and Pattern Recognition (CVPR), June 2016
10. Huret, J.L., Ahmad, M., Arsaban, M., Bernheim, A., Cigna, J., Desangles, F., Guignard, J.C., Jacquemot-Perbal, M.C., Labarussias, M., Leberre, V., et al.: Atlas of genetics and cytogenetics in oncology and haematology in 2013. Nucleic Acids Res. **41**(D1), D920–D924 (2012)
11. Karamcheti, S., Krishna, R., Fei-Fei, L., Manning, C.D.: Mind your outliers! investigating the negative impact of outliers on active learning for visual question answering. arXiv preprint arXiv:2107.02331 (2021)
12. Kuespert, K., Pils, S., Hauck, C.R.: Ceacams: their role in physiology and pathophysiology. Curr. Opin. Cell Biol. **18**(5), 565–571 (2006)
13. Lin, X., Parikh, D.: Active learning for visual question answering: An empirical study. arXiv preprint arXiv:1711.01732 (2017)
14. Liu, S., Zhang, B., Liu, Y., Han, A., Shi, H., Guan, T., He, Y.: Unpaired stain transfer using pathology-consistent constrained generative adversarial networks. IEEE Trans. Med. Imaging **40**(8), 1977–1989 (2021)
15. Long, J., Shelhamer, E., Darrell, T.: Fully convolutional networks for semantic segmentation (2015)
16. Lu, M.Y., Williamson, D.F., Chen, T.Y., Chen, R.J., Barbieri, M., Mahmood, F.: Data-efficient and weakly supervised computational pathology on whole-slide images. Nature Biomed. Engi. **5**(6), 555–570 (2021)
17. Mirza, M., Osindero, S.: Conditional generative adversarial nets. arXiv preprint arXiv:1411.1784 (2014)
18. Park, T., Efros, A.A., Zhang, R., Zhu, J.Y.: Contrastive learning for unpaired image-to-image translation. In: Computer Vision-ECCV 2020: 16th European Conference, Glasgow, UK, August 23–28, 2020, Proceedings, Part IX 16, pp. 319–345. Springer (2020)
19. Simon, R.: Clinical trial designs for evaluating the medical utility of prognostic and predictive biomarkers in oncology. Pers. Med. **7**(1), 33–47 (2010)
20. Simonyan, K., Zisserman, A.: Very deep convolutional networks for large-scale image recognition. arXiv preprint arXiv:1409.1556 (2014)
21. Zhang, X., Han, X., Zuo, P., Zhang, X., Xu, H.: Ceacam5 stimulates the progression of non-small-cell lung cancer by promoting cell proliferation and migration. J. Int. Med. Res. **48**(9), 0300060520959478 (2020)
22. Zhu, J.Y., Park, T., Isola, P., Efros, A.A.: Unpaired image-to-image translation using cycle-consistent adversarial networks. In: Proceedings of the IEEE International Conference on Computer Vision, pp. 2223–2232 (2017)

# More Than Meets the Eye: Physicians' Visual Attention in the Operating Room

Sapir Gershov[1]([✉]), Fadi Mahameed[1,2], Aeyal Raz[2], and Shlomi Laufer[1]

[1] Technion - Israel Institute of Technology, Technion City, 3200003 Haifa, Israel
{sapirgershov,fadi.mahamee}@campus.technion.ac.il
[2] Rambam Health Care Campus, 3109601 Haifa, Israel

**Abstract.** During surgery, the patient's vital signs and the field of endoscopic view are displayed on multiple screens. As a result, both surgeons' and anesthesiologists' visual attention (VA) is crucial. Moreover, the distribution of said VA and the acquisition of specific cues might directly impact patient outcomes.

Recent research utilizes portable, head-mounted eye-tracking devices to gather precise and comprehensive information. Nevertheless, these technologies are not feasible for enduring data acquisition in an operating room (OR) environment. This is particularly the case during medical emergencies.

This study presents an alternative methodology: a webcam-based gaze target prediction model. Such an approach may provide continuous visual behavioral data with minimal interference to the physicians' workflow in the OR. The proposed end-to-end framework is suitable for both standard and emergency surgeries.

In the future, such a platform may serve as a crucial component of context-aware assistive technologies in the OR.

**Keywords:** Eye-tracking · Surgery · Anesthesia · Visual Attention · Operation Room · Webcams · Deep Learning

## 1 Introduction

While under surgery, there is a multitude of clinical information about the patient that the anesthesiologist and surgeon must monitor and oversee. Because most information is presented visually, the physicians' visual attention (VA) becomes vital. Furthermore, the distribution of said VA and the acquisition of signals at specific moments during the procedure may directly impact the ability to provide better care [12,13].

Several studies investigated the preoperative team members VA [1,6,11,12, 14,18] using a wearable eye-tracking device to record participants' gaze. Though these devices provide accurate data, they do not offer sustainable and ecological solutions for long-term data collection in the OR. These devices have limited

---

**Supplementary Information** The online version contains supplementary material available at https://doi.org/10.1007/978-3-031-47076-9_2.

S. Wu et al. (Eds.): AMAI 2023, LNCS 14313, pp. 11–20, 2024.
https://doi.org/10.1007/978-3-031-47076-9_2

battery life, require a calibration stage before use, and can become inconvenient for physicians after extended usage [16]. Our study presents an alternative approach that examines the physicians' monitor observation patterns. By placing a webcam on top of the relevant monitor and continuously recording video data with minimal interference, we can recognize scenes in which the physicians' gaze is directed at the camera (i.e., direct gaze at the monitor). Such a system will facilitate the collection of vast amounts of data, enabling in-depth analysis of the medical care provider's work. Furthermore, it may serve as a crucial component of context-aware assistive technologies in the OR.

Papers in the field of eye-tracking have tackled the task of Gaze Target Prediction - detecting the attended visual target in the scene and provided new datasets, challenges, and models that produce human-like results [2,4,15,17]. These new developments have not been implemented the medical domain, though they may significantly improve medical education, training, and patient safety.

Chong et al. [2] presented a state-of-the-art architecture for detecting attended visual targets. However, this model does not distinguish between a gaze directed toward an "out-of-frame" object and a direct gaze toward the camera. This requires a modified approach that will allow the model to recognize scenes in which the physicians' gaze is directed at the camera (i.e., screen). Therefore, we chose to address this challenge using "Onfocus" detection, which identifies whether the individual's focus is on the camera [21].

Onfocus detection in unconstrained capture conditions, such as the OR, presents multiple challenges due to the complex image scenes, unavoidable occlusion, diverse face directions, constant changes in the frame focus, the number of appearing objects, and imagery factors (e.g., blur, over-exposure). Zhang et al. [21] presented a model and a dataset to evaluate onfocus detection under these challenges.

Our study presents the implementation of a webcam-based eye contact recognition model. First, we improved both Chong et al. and Zhang et al. models and provided new SOTA results. We then evaluate our model on new data - webcam videos of physicians' gaze during medical simulations (MS) and in real-life OR settings. In the future, our methodology may be employed to assess the effect of VA on patient care.

The paper's contributions are as follows: (1) an improved deep learning model for detecting the attended visual target; (2) an end-to-end eye-contact tracking framework for analyzing the distribution of VA of preoperative team members.

## 2  Related Work

### 2.1  Face Detection

YOLO ("You Only Look Once") is a popular family of real-time object detection algorithms. The original YOLO object detector was published by Redmon et al. [10]. Since then, different versions and variants of YOLO have been proposed, each providing a significant increase in performance and efficiency.

Previously, Qi et al. [8] published a modification of the YOLO architecture, YOLO5Face, which treats face detection as a general object detection task. In their work, they designed a face detector model capable of achieving state-of-the-art performance in varying image sizes by adding a five-point landmark regression head into the original architecture and using the Wing loss function [5].

## 2.2   Facial Landmarks

Facial landmarks (FL) detection is a computer vision task in which a model needs to predict key points representing regions or landmarks on a human's face (i.e., eyes, nose, lips, etc.).

Dlib-ml [7] is a cross-platform open-source software library with pre-trained detectors for FL. The Dlib detector estimates the location of 68 coordinates $(x, y)$ that map the facial points on a person's face. Though newer algorithms leverage a dense "face mesh" with machine learning to infer the 3D facial surface from single camera input, these models fail to produce superior results when the acquired images have disturbances and motion [3].

## 2.3   Spatiotemporal Gaze Architecture

Most works that tackled the task of detecting gaze target prediction constructed 2D representations of the gaze direction, which fails to encode whether the person of interest is looking onward, backward, or sideward. Chong et al. [2] proposed to use a deep-learning network to construct a 3D gaze representation and incorporate it as an additional feature channel. The input to their network was the video frame scene, the heads positions in the frame, and the reciprocal cropped head images. However, they did not provide a face-detection model to generate this input automatically. In addition, Chong et al.'s work applied $\alpha$ - a learned scalar that evaluates whether the person's object of attention is inside or outside the frame, with higher values indicating in-frame attention. Yet, when the person's object of attention was outside the frame, they did not examine the cases in which the object of attention was the camera itself.

## 2.4   Eye-Context Interaction Inferring Network

Zhang et al. [21] provided a novel end-to-end model for onfocus detection. The model, named "Eye-Context Interaction Inferring Network" (ECIIN), is a deep learning architecture incorporating the VGG architecture for feature extraction of the eyes region and a context capsule network (CAP) [9]. Inside the ECIIN, Zhang et al. applied several network modules that implicitly explore eye-context information cues by casting the whole learning problem as an image categorization task. As it shows, Zhang et al.'s model does not take advantage of Yang et al.'s [20] publicly available face detection dataset [20], which is rich with labeled data and suitable for training a model for such a task. Furthermore, they do not employ a well-known, state-of-the-art detection model that can be more accurate and robust using transfer learning techniques. Finally, their model was not trained for multiple object detection in the same image.

## 3   Materials

### 3.1   Benchmark Datasets

**WIDER FACE Dataset** [20]. This dataset is a subset of the publicly available WIDER dataset [19]. Currently, WIDER FACE dataset is one of the most extensive publically available datasets for face detection. It contains 32,203 images and 393,703 labels of faces with a wide range of scale, poses, and occlusion variability. Each recognizable face in the WIDER FACE dataset is labeled by bounding boxes, which must tightly contain facial landmarks (FL) (e.g., forehead, chin, and cheek). In the case of occlusion, the face is labeled with an estimated bounding box.

**VideoAttentionTarget Dataset** [2]. This dataset was created specifically for video gaze target modeling and accommodated 1,331 annotated videos of people's dynamic gaze behavior in diverse situations. The videos, which were gathered from YouTube, are of various domains, and they were trimmed to contain dynamic gaze behavior in which a person of interest can be continuously observed. A trimmed video duration ranges from 1–80 s.

**OFDIW Dataset** [21]. The dataset has several unique characteristics: (1) the dataset contains videos of individuals during face-to-camera communication; (2) the data is collected from a single camera point-of-view, and most of the recorded faces are completely visible; (3) the camera is focused on the presented individual where there is very little change between frames. The dataset comprises 20,623 unconstrained images with good age diversity, facial characteristics, and rich interactions with surrounding objects and background scenes. Therefore, while the OFDIW dataset provides a great starting point, it lacks a few components crucial for onfcous detection in the OR settings. For that reason, we created our unique datasets.

### 3.2   Our Datasets

Our datasets consist of webcam video recordings from three different setups - one from medical simulations (MS) and two from real-life OR settings (See Fig. 1). The first OR dataset focuses on anesthesiologists' work (See Fig. 1-B), and the second on the surgeon's work during minimally invasive thoracic surgery (See Fig. 1-C).

   Our simulations combine two main components: a high-fidelity manikin that mimics the human body and its physiological responses and a patient monitor that presents the patient's vital signs. Data includes 31 simulations with 33 residents, and the setup was located inside the hospital's post-anesthesia care

**Fig. 1.** Illustration of the images in our dataset. (A) Simulated patient monitor point-of-view. The participants' faces are manually blurred; (B) Real patient monitor point-of-view; (C) Thoracic surgery setup. All shown subjects have given their consent to have their pictures featured.

unit (PACU), using real-life medical equipment and utilities. To document the resident's visual patterns during MS, we collected data using a single webcam above the patient monitor (See Fig. 1-A). The simulations dataset contains 31 videos, each approximately 20 min long.

Over 1200 frames of MS have been extracted from the videos. The appearing faces were manually labeled with bounding boxes suitable for the YOLO network, and an independent human observer marked the events of direct eye contact with the monitor. These events are classified as "Onfocus" or "Out of focus" while maintaining a class-balanced and diverse dataset (see Fig. 2).

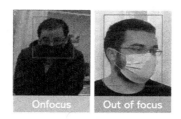

**Fig. 2.** The onfocus detection task labels. All shown subjects have given their consent to have their pictures featured.

To capture the anesthesiologist VA, we placed the webcams above two OR monitors - a patient monitor and a ventilator monitor. Ten different anesthesiologists (6 male, 4 female) were recorded during 11 surgeries.

Four thoracic surgeons (all male) were recorded by placing the webcams on top of a screen tower (See Fig. 1 - C). A board-certified thoracic surgeon and a resident executed each surgery. The OR dataset contains 11 videos, each approximately 2 h long.

The OR datasets comprise 1873 frames (1473 frames of anesthesiologists and 400 frames of surgeons) from the available OR videos. These frames were manually labeled as described for the MS dataset (see Fig. 2). Once again, we made sure that the dataset was balanced.

The Institutional Review Board of Rambam Health Care Campus approved the study.

## 4   Methods

### 4.1   Pipeline Construction

For face detection, we trained YOLOv7 on the WIDER FACE dataset [20]. For each detected bounding box prediction, an FL algorithm was applied. We used only the coordinates visible in the collected data - eyes, nose, and mouth.

The coupling of YOLOv7 trained for face detection with a FL detector is a suitable replacement for Zhang et al. [21] ECIIN-designed network modules. Our modifications harness the benefits of well-trained object detectors and large datasets and thus produce superior results. Then, once the region of interest is located, we apply the process described in Zhang et al. work to generate the onfocus detection.

Lastly, we modified Chong et al. work by adding the ECIIN. This modification has improved Chong et al. model performance in cases where the object of attention is "out-of-frame".

The complete end-to-end pipeline is depicted in Fig. 3.

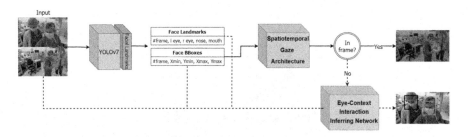

**Fig. 3.** End-to-end framework pipeline. The Spatiotemporal prediction is indicated by a bounding box over the allocated head and a heatmap over the object of attention. The ECIIN network classification confidence is indicated by color, where green is for high confidence and red is for low confidence. The score next to the bounding box is the prediction probability. (Color figure online)

### 4.2   Implementation

The training of the YOLOv7 for face detection was executed using AdamW optimizer with an initial learning rate of 1E-3 and weight decay of 5E-3. The training procedure ran for 250 epochs with a batch size of 64, and the loss was calculated using the YOLO loss function. To avoid overfitting, we stopped training when the validation loss increased.

The ECIIN and the Spatiotemporal model have been fine-tuned based on their provided source code. The trained YOLOv7 was fine-tuned by training it for another 60 epochs. Again we stopped the training process when the generalization error increased.

The models are implemented in PyTorch 1.7.1 and trained using 2 NVIDIA RTX A6000 GPUs.

# 5    Results

## 5.1    Ablation Study of the End-to-End Pipeline

The following results are generated by utilizing the published models' weights and without fine-tuning the hyper-parameters:

**Table 1.** Results of the proposed modifications on different benchmarks and comparison to other architectures

| Model | Task | Dataset | Accuracy | F1-Score |
|---|---|---|---|---|
| YOLO5Face [8] | Face Detection | WIDER Face | 86.55% | - |
| YOLOv7 & FL | | | **87.03%** | 0.85 |
| ECIIN [21] | Onfocus Detection | OFDIW | 84.71% | 0.90 |
| ECIIN [21] with YOLOv7 & FL | | | **84.97%** | 0.90 |
| Spatiotemporal [2] | Gaze Target Prediction | VideoAttentionTarget | 86.12% | 0.85 |
| Complete pipeline | | | **87.2%** | **0.86** |

## 5.2    Evaluation of the Proposed Framework on Our Datasets

We fine-tuned the different models using the MS dataset and evaluated their performance on our labeled OR frames. We applied 5-fold cross-validation, dividing the dataset into 70% train, 10% validation, and 20% test. Throughout this procedure, we avoided using the same videos for both the training and testing of the model.

To assess the Spatiotemporal model [2] onfocus detection performance, we used our YOLOv7 model for face detection and addressed the Spatiotemporal model predictions as binary classification (i.e., the object of attention is inside the frame or outside) (Table 2).

**Table 2.** Models onfocus detection results on MS frames.

| Model | Train Dataset | Test Dataset | Accuracy | F1-Score |
|---|---|---|---|---|
| ECIIN | MS | MS | 63.98% ±2.53% | 0.64 ±0.03 |
| Spatiotemporal | | | 71.03% ±1.87% | 0.72 ±0.11 |
| Complete pipeline | | | **89.22% ± 1.26%** | **0.87 ± 0.02** |

Table 3 results are generated by testing the fine-tuned models on the OR datasets.

**Table 3.** Models onfocus detection results on real OR frames.

| Model | Train Dataset | Test Dataset | Accuracy | F1-Score |
|---|---|---|---|---|
| ECIIN | MS | OR-Anesthesiologists | 52.44% | 0.55 |
| Spatiotemporal | | | 76.44% | 0.77 |
| Complete pipeline | | | **86.43%** | **0.87** |
| ECIIN | MS | OR-Surgeons | 61.19% | 0.59 |
| Spatiotemporal | | | 75.88% | 0.73 |
| Complete pipeline | | | **90.01%** | **0.90** |

## 6   Discussion

In the field of surgery and anesthesiology, eye tracking became a popular methodology for investigating the visual behavior of physicians in their natural environment. However, most eye-tracking technology is intrusive, interferes with the participants' natural workflow, and is unsuitable for prolonged data collecting.

Therefore, we employ webcams, which are considered non-intrusive, and provide continuous visual behavior data in real-time without interfering with the medical personnel workflow. This work presents an end-to-end pipeline for processing and analyzing raw video recordings of preoperative team members' workflow in real-life OR settings. The data was collected via two webcams inside the OR and later processed with a deep-learning model for gaze target prediction. The first step in the pipeline is to locate the masked faces in a frame and, for each detected face, to extract the eyes region. To do so, we harnessed the potential of YOLOv7, a state-of-the-art object detection model, and a well-trained model for FL detection. After the faces and eye regions are allocated, Chong et al. [2] model deduces if the object of attention is located in the frame based on the $\alpha$ scalar value. In the last stage of the pipeline, we applied Zhang et al.'s [21] model for onfocus detection. These modifications have proven fruitful in making our model more robust and accurate than the original models (See Table 1) and suitable for real-life OR settings (See Table 3). In addition, our approach is not limited by the number of participants or their distance from the cameras.

It is important to note that although the complete pipeline was not fine-tuned using the public datasets it was tested on, it achieved better results. Furthermore, the complete pipeline has a significantly faster average inference speed, at 23 FPS, compared to other models. However, more thorough research is required to quantify the influence of each component on the framework performance.

We recognize that our small-scaled datasets are a limitation of this study. Indeed, further work is required to fully explore the applications of gaze target prediction in the OR settings. Another significant limitation is the camera field of view. There have been occasions in which the camera has not captured the participants while they had a clear view of the screen. This limitation can be overcome by adding more cameras to watch over different areas.

**Prospect of Application:** This unique approach for eye-tracking in a real-life OR setting may provide fresh and essential insight into surgery, anesthesia, and other fields. In the future, we trust that our non-intrusive framework could lay the groundwork for using gaze patterns, specifically onfocus detection, as an early alarm system to reduce clinical errors and as a metric to assess VA. In addition, gaze target prediction may facilitate developing an empiric metric for investigating medical personnel VA and evaluating its impact on patient outcomes.

# References

1. Chetwood, A.S.A., et al.: Collaborative eye tracking: a potential training tool in laparoscopic surgery. Surgical Endoscopy **26**(7), 2003–9 (2012). https://doi.org/ 10.1007/s00464-011-2143-x. http://www.ncbi.nlm.nih.gov/pubmed/22258302
2. Chong, E., Wang, Y., Ruiz, N., Rehg, J.M.: Detecting attended visual targets in video. In: Proceedings of the IEEE Computer Society Conference on Computer Vision and Pattern Recognition, pp. 5395–5405 (2020). https://doi.org/10.1109/ CVPR42600.2020.00544. https://github.com/ejcgt/attention-target-detection
3. Deng, J., Guo, J., Ververas, E., Kotsia, I., Zafeiriou, S.: Retinaface: single-shot multi-level face localisation in the wild. In: Proceedings of the IEEE Computer Society Conference on Computer Vision and Pattern Recognition, pp. 5202–5211 (2020). https://doi.org/10.1109/CVPR42600.2020.00525
4. Fang, Y., et al.: Dual attention guided gaze target detection in the wild. In: Proceedings of the IEEE Computer Society Conference on Computer Vision and Pattern Recognition, pp. 11385–11394 (2021). https://doi.org/10.1109/CVPR46437. 2021.01123
5. Feng, Z.H., Kittler, J., Awais, M., Huber, P., Wu, X.J.: Wing loss for robust facial landmark localisation with convolutional neural networks. In: Proceedings of the IEEE Conference on Computer Vision and Pattern Recognition, pp. 2235–2245 (2018)
6. Gil, A.M., Birdi, S., Kishibe, T., Grantcharov, T.P.: Eye tracking use in surgical research: a systematic review. J. Surg. Res. **279**, 774–787 (2022). https:// doi.org/10.1016/j.jss.2022.05.024. https://linkinghub.elsevier.com/retrieve/pii/ S0022480422003419
7. King, D.E.: Dlib-ml: a machine learning toolkit. J. Mach. Learn. Res. **10**, 1755–1758 (2009)
8. Qi, D., Tan, W., Yao, Q., Liu, J.: YOLO5Face: Why Reinventing a Face Detector (2021). https://www.github.com/deepcam-cn/yolov5-face. http://arxiv.org/abs/ 2105.12931
9. Ramasinghe, S., Athuraliya, C.D., Khan, S.H.: A context-aware capsule network for multi-label classification. In: Leal-Taixé, L., Roth, S. (eds.) ECCV 2018. LNCS, vol. 11131, pp. 546–554. Springer, Cham (2019). https://doi.org/10.1007/978-3-030-11015-4_40

10. Redmon, J., Divvala, S., Girshick, R., Farhadi, A.: You only look once: unified, real-time object detection. In: Proceedings of the IEEE Computer Society Conference on Computer Vision and Pattern Recognition, vol. 2016-Decem, pp. 779–788 (2016). https://doi.org/10.1109/CVPR.2016.91. http://pjreddie.com/yolo/

11. Roche, T.R., et al.: Anesthesia personnel's visual attention regarding patient monitoring in simulated non-critical and critical situations, an eye-tracking study. BMC Anesthesiology **22**(1) (2022). https://doi.org/10.1186/s12871-022-01705-6. https://doi.org/10.1186/s12871-022-01705-6

12. Schulz, C.M., et al.: Visual attention of anaesthetists during simulated critical incidents. British J. Anaesthesia **106**(6), 807–813 (2011). https://doi.org/10.1093/bja/aer087. www.anvil-software.de

13. Szulewski, A., Egan, R., Gegenfurtner, A., Howes, D., Dashi, G., McGraw, N.C., Hall, A.K., Dagnone, D., Van Merrienboer, J.J.: A new way to look at simulation-based assessment: the relationship between gaze-tracking and exam performance. Canadian J. Emergency Med. **21**(1), 129–137 (2019). https://doi.org/10.1017/cem.2018.391

14. Tien, T., Pucher, P.H., Sodergren, M.H., Sriskandarajah, K., Yang, G.Z., Darzi, A.: Eye tracking for skills assessment and training: a systematic review. J. Surgical Res. **191**(1), 169–178 (2014). https://doi.org/10.1016/j.jss.2014.04.032. https://linkinghub.elsevier.com/retrieve/pii/S0022480414004326

15. Tomas, H., et al.: GOO: a dataset for gaze object prediction in retail environments. In: IEEE Computer Society Conference on Computer Vision and Pattern Recognition Workshops, pp. 3119–3127 (2021). https://doi.org/10.1109/CVPRW53098.2021.00349. https://github.com/upeee/GOO-GAZE2021

16. Wagner, M., et al.: Video-based reflection on neonatal interventions during COVID-19 using eye-tracking glasses: an observational study. Archives of disease in childhood. Fetal Neonatal Edition **107**(2), 156–160 (2022). https://doi.org/10.1136/archdischild-2021-321806. https://fn.bmj.com/content/107/2/156 https://fn.bmj.com/content/107/2/156.abstract

17. Wang, B., Hu, T., Li, B., Chen, X., Zhang, Z.: GaTector: a unified framework for gaze object prediction. In: 2022 IEEE/CVF Conference on Computer Vision and Pattern Recognition (CVPR), pp. 19566–19575. IEEE, June 2022. https://doi.org/10.1109/CVPR52688.2022.01898. https://ieeexplore.ieee.org/document/9879784/

18. White, M.R., et al.: Getting inside the expert's head: an analysis of physician cognitive processes during trauma resuscitations. Ann. Emerg. Med. **72**(3), 289–298 (2018). https://doi.org/10.1016/j.annemergmed.2018.03.005

19. Xiong, Y., Zhu, K., Lin, D., Tang, X.: Recognize complex events from static images by fusing deep channels. In: Proceedings of the IEEE Computer Society Conference on Computer Vision and Pattern Recognition. vol. 07–12-June, pp. 1600–1609 (2015). https://doi.org/10.1109/CVPR.2015.7298768

20. Yang, S., Luo, P., Loy, C.C., Tang, X.: WIDER FACE: A face detection benchmark. In: Proceedings of the IEEE Computer Society Conference on Computer Vision and Pattern Recognition. vol. 2016-Decem, pp. 5525–5533 (2016). https://doi.org/10.1109/CVPR.2016.596, http://mmlab.ie.cuhk.edu.hk/projects/

21. Zhang, D., Wang, B., Wang, G., Zhang, Q., Zhang, J., Han, J., You, Z.: Onfocus detection: identifying individual-camera eye contact from unconstrained images. Science China Inf. Sci. **65**(6), 1–12 (2022). https://doi.org/10.1007/s11432-020-3181-9

# CNNs vs. Transformers: Performance and Robustness in Endoscopic Image Analysis

Carolus H. J. Kusters[1]([✉]) [iD], Tim G. W. Boers[1] [iD], Tim J. M. Jaspers[1] [iD], Jelmer B. Jukema[2] [iD], Martijn R. Jong[2] [iD], Kiki N. Fockens[2], Albert J. de Groof[2], Jacques J. Bergman[2], Fons van der Sommen[1] [iD], and Peter H. N. de With[1]

[1] Department of Electrical Engineering, Video Coding and Architectures, Eindhoven University of Technology, Eindhoven, The Netherlands
{c.h.j.kusters,t.boers,t.j.m.jaspers,fvdsommen,p.h.n.de.with}@tue.nl
[2] Department of Gastroenterology and Hepatology, Amsterdam University Medical Centers, University of Amsterdam, Amsterdam, The Netherlands

**Abstract.** In endoscopy, imaging conditions are often challenging due to organ movement, user dependence, fluctuations in video quality and real-time processing, which pose requirements on the performance, robustness and complexity of computer-based analysis techniques. This paper poses the question whether Transformer-based architectures, which are capable to directly capture global contextual information, can handle the aforementioned endoscopic conditions and even outperform the established Convolutional Neural Networks (CNNs) for this task. To this end, we evaluate and compare clinically relevant performance and robustness of CNNs and Transformers for neoplasia detection in Barrett's esophagus. We have selected several top performing CNN and Transformers on endoscopic benchmarks, which we have trained and validated on a total of 10,208 images (2,079 patients), and tested on a total of 4,661 images (743 patients), divided over a high-quality test set and three different robustness test sets. Our results show that Transformers generally perform better on classification and segmentation for the high-quality challenging test set, and show on-par or increased robustness to various clinically relevant input data variations, while requiring comparable model complexity. This robustness against challenging video-related conditions and equipment variations over the hospitals is an essential trait for adoption in clinical practice. The code is made publicly available at: https://github.com/BONS-AI-VCA-AMC/Endoscopy-CNNs-vs-Transformers.

**Keywords:** Barrett's Esophagus · CNN · Transformers · Robustness

C. H. J. Kusters—This work is facilitated by data/equipment from Olympus Corp., Tokyo, Japan.

# 1   Introduction

Due to the increase in image quality of endoscopy devices, endoscopic image analysis by visual inspection has become an essential aspect in gastrointestinal endoscopy. The use of endoscopic procedures allows for non-invasive diagnosis and treatment of various gastrointestinal complications, such as cancer, ulcers and inflammatory diseases. However, the analysis of endoscopic imagery can be challenging due to operator dependence, low inter-observer agreement, variability in image quality, artifacts and subtle differences between normal and abnormal tissue. To address these aspects, CAD techniques have been developed to aid endoscopists in the diagnosis and treatment of gastrointestinal complications.

A recent technique that has emerged as a promising solution is deep learning-based AI. AI-based tools have the potential to attractively benefit the diagnostic accuracy and efficiency of endoscopic image analysis by endoscopists. Several AI-based tools have been proposed for the detection and classification of suspected neoplastic lesions in Barrett's esophagus (BE) [9–11,14], colorectal polyps [3,6] and gastric lesions [7,23]. For the aforementioned applications, Convolutional Neural Networks (CNNs) are considered the state-of-the-art solution.

Recently, the Vision Transformer (ViT) [8] adopted the Transformer [21] architecture originally developed for NLP tasks, in the field of Computer Vision (CV). The ViT and its derived instances [15,22,25] are able to directly capture long-range feature dependencies with the self-attention mechanism, unlike CNNs which usually have a limited receptive field. Transformers have quickly gained popularity in a wide variety of CV problems and are competing with CNNs for state-of-the-art performance in many CV tasks and applications.

The use of CNNs in endoscopic image analysis has been the state-of-the-art for several years. However, the increasing need for robustness in light of the posed challenges and the benefits of Transformers, raises the question whether Transformer-based networks are more suitable in this field. Therefore, in this paper, we evaluate and compare performance and robustness of CNNs and Transformers for endoscopic image analysis, particularly, neoplasia detection in BE. This study uses one high-quality test set, enriched with challenging subtle neoplasia cases, to evaluate clinically relevant performance. Furthermore, we selected three different robustness test sets to evaluate clinically relevant robustness against low-quality data and/or out-of-domain data. Additionally, the memory requirements of the architectures are assessed to determine their suitability for deployment in clinical practice.

This study is the first in its kind and aims to provide insights into the comparative efficacy of CNNs and Transformers for endoscopic image analysis, in terms of the performance, robustness and complexity in light of the posed challenges.

# 2   Methods

## 2.1   Data: Setting, Datasets and Preprocessing

**A. Setting:** This study uses private internal data collected both retrospectively and prospectively at 15 international centers using Olympus gastroscopes

(Olympus Corp., Tokyo, Japan), comprising of Barrett's neoplasia and non-dysplastic BE (NDBE) imagery (with histopathology confirmation), and curated for presence (neoplasia) or absence (NDBE) of a visible lesion, respectively.

**B. Datasets:** *1. Training, Validation and Test Sets:* The split between train/validation/test datasets is made in accordance with clinicians, to ensure representative training and validation sets, while the test set is enriched with more challenging subtle neoplasia cases. An example of a subtle neoplasia case from the test set can be observed in Fig. 1a. A strict split on patient basis is employed to avoid data leakage and intra-patient bias. Delineations of neoplasia are obtained from 14 Barrett's experts, where at least 2 experts delineated the same image. For each image, the experts delineated the largest area that is suspected to be neoplasia (LL) and the area within the LL that stands out more profoundly (HL). To achieve a minimal level of consensus, a third expert endoscopist is invited in case the two HL delineations obtained less than 30% agreement in terms of Dice Score. Subsequently, the two delineations among the three experts that achieved the highest overlap are used for further ground-truth (GT) processing. For training and evaluation purposes, a consensus GT mask is constructed by means of (1) union of HL delineations (2) intersection of LL delineations, and (3) the union of (1) and (2). A detailed summary of the datasets, in terms of images, patients and GT masks is presented in Table 1.

*2. Internal Robustness Test Sets:* For internal robustness evaluation, two different test sets are constructed from imagery that is excluded for training and validation. The image-quality robustness test set (QRT) consists of images that are excluded due to inferior subjective image quality, and can be used to evaluate robustness against subjective image quality. The quality exclusion criteria are defined as the distance to the lesion, illumination, blur, contraction of the esophagus, resolution of imagery and presence of mucus and bubbles. The image-criteria robustness test set (CRT) consists of images that are excluded based on the presence or absence of a visible lesion for NDBE and neoplasia, respectively, and can be used to evaluate robustness and generalization on data not matching the inclusion criteria of the training set. All patients included in QRT and CRT sets are excluded from the algorithm training and validation sets to avoid data-leakage and intra-patient bias and no GT masks are available. Example imagery of the QRT/CRT sets can be observed in Fig. 1c and 1d, while a summary of the data statistics is presented in Table 1.

*3. External Robustness Test Set:* For external robustness evaluation, a test set (BORN) is constructed from frames extracted from the BORN training module videos [1]. The data in this module was retrospectively collected at 3 international centers, with older generations Olympus (Olympus Corp., Tokyo, Japan) gastroscopes, compared to internal data collection, and Fujifilm (Fujifilm Corp., Japan) gastroscopes. The BORN set can be used to evaluate robustness against objective image quality, scope type and scope manufacturer. An example of a low-quality image of different scope manufacturer can be observed in Fig. 1b. Neoplasia delineations are obtained from 4 Barrett's experts, where at least

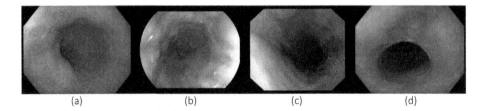

**Fig. 1.** (a) Test: high-quality subtle neoplasia case (b) BORN: low-quality image of different scope manufacturer (c) QRT: low-quality image (blur and presence of bubbles) (d) CRT: NDBE case with visible abnormality

3 experts delineated the same image. For evaluation purposes, a consensus GT mask is constructed by means of the intersection of the three individual delineations. A summary of data statistics is presented in Table 1.

**Table 1.** Description of datasets used for algorithm development and evaluation.

| Dataset | NDBE | Neoplasia | GT Masks |
|---------|------|-----------|----------|
| Train | 5,566 (948 pt) | 4,442 (1,038 pt) | 1,947 |
| Validation | 100 (36 pt) | 100 (58 pt) | 96 |
| Test | 300 (125 pt) | 100 (50 pt) | 100 |
| QRT | 109 (84 pt) | 463 (248 pt) | / |
| CRT | 150 (97 pt) | 637 (93 pt) | / |
| BORN | 1,601 (32 pt) | 1,301 (65 pt) | 1,301 |

**C. Data Pre-processing:** The central active region of raw endoscopic images is resized to 256×256 pixels, prior to normalizing the intensity values by channel-wise subtracting the mean and dividing by the standard deviation of the training data. Data augmentation techniques are applied during training to virtually increase the set size and to improve generalization. A random combination is employed of horizontal and vertical flipping, rotation by $\theta \in \{0°, 90°, 180°, 270°\}$, contrast/saturation/brightness enhancements, gray-scale conversion, Gaussian blurring, random affine and sharpness transforms, followed by random artificial Gaussian noise corruption. To obtain a reliable performance estimate of the model, validation evaluation is performed four times on a different randomly augmented internal validation set, by employing the first three augmentation techniques, to increase the sample size by a factor of four.

## 2.2 Network Architectures, Training and Evaluation

**A. Network Architectures:** In this study, four CNNs and three Transformer-based architectures are compared. The CNN selection includes the well-known

**Table 2.** Comparison of architectures used in this study, in terms of parameters, model size, multiply-add operations (M-A) and processing speed.

| Network (Backbone) | Param. | Mod. Size | M-A | Proc. speed |
|---|---|---|---|---|
| U-Net (ResNet-50) | 32.5 M | 130.1 MB | 127.6 G | 5.95 fps |
| U-Net (ResNet-152) | 67.2 M | 268.6 MB | 244.0 G | 3.23 fps |
| U-Net++ (ResNet-50) | 48.9 M | 196.0 MB | 689.3 G | 2.39 fps |
| U-Net++ (ResNet-152) | 83.6 M | 334.5 MB | 805.7 G | 1.78 fps |
| DeepLabV3+ (ResNet-50) | 40.3 M | 161.4 MB | 139.6 G | 5.96 fps |
| DeepLabV3+ (ResNet-152) | 74.9 M | 299.9 MB | 256.0 G | 3.08 fps |
| DeepLabV3+ (ConvNeXt-T) | 35.2 M | 134.4 MB | 75.8 G | 7.55 fps |
| DeepLabV3+ (ConvNeXt-B) | 96.8 M | 387.1 MB | 79.4 G | 2.96 fps |
| CaraNet (Res2Net-101) | 44.6 M | 172.7 MB | 143.4 G | 4.56 fps |
| ESFPNet-T (MiT-B0) | 3.5 M | 14.01 MB | 2.22 G | 22.97 fps |
| ESFPNet-L (MiT-B4) | 61.7 M | 245.5 MB | 20.6 G | 2.51 fps |
| FCBFormer-B0 (PVTv2-B0) | 11.3 M | 45.3 MB | 386.3 G | 1.65 fps |
| FCBFormer-B3 (PVTv2-B3) | 52.9 M | 211.2 MB | 536.6 G | 1.16 fps |
| Swin-T-UperNet (SwinV2-T) | 40.8 M | 137.4 MB | 30.9 G | 6.44 fps |
| Swin-B-UperNet (SwinV2-B) | 110.4 M | 357.9 MB | 55.3 G | 2.45 fps |

U-Net [18], U-Net++ [26] and DeepLabV3+ [5] architectures, with ResNet [12] and ConvNeXt [16] backbones. The more advanced CaraNet [17] is also included, which is based on context axial reverse attention. The Transformer-based architecture selection includes ESFPNet [4], FCBFormer [19] and UperNet [24], with Mix Transformer (MiT) [25], Pyramid Vision Transformer v2 (PVTv2) [22] and Swin Transformer V2 (SwinV2) [15] backbones, respectively. All backbones are initialized with ImageNet-pretrained weights, and extended with a simple classification head consisting of a downsampling stage and a single fully-connected layer with a Sigmoid activation function, after the final backbone feature extraction layer. Based on the endoscopic segmentation benchmarks (Kvasir-SEG [13], CVC-ColonDB [20] and CVC-ClinicDB [2]) performance, CaraNet, ESFPNet and FCBFormer are selected for comparison, while the other architectures are applied in generic segmentation problems. The original source codes of the architectures are adapted to fit our use case. A comparison of the architectures in terms of parameters, model size, multiply-add operations (M-A) and processing speed (measured on 12-Core Ryzen 9 5900X CPU) is listed in Table 2.

**B. Training Procedures:** All architectures are trained in a two-step procedure with batch sizes of 32 (16 for FCBFormer-B3) and learning rates in the range of $10^{-3}$ - $10^{-7}$, optimized by a maximum of three runs for each architecture, after which the best model is used for a single-evaluation iteration on the test sets. First, training with all available data for 150 epochs is performed, followed by training with prospectively collected data for 75 epochs. Early stopping is

**Table 3.** Performance on all test sets for all architectures

| Network (Backbone) | Test Set | | BORN Set | | QRT | CRT |
|---|---|---|---|---|---|---|
| | $AUC_{cls}$ | $mD_i$ | $AUC_{cls}$ | $mD_i$ | $AUC_{cls}$ | $AUC_{cls}$ |
| U-Net (ResNet-50) | 0.867 | 0.353 | 0.861 | 0.271 | 0.829 | 0.820 |
| U-Net (ResNet-152) | 0.938 | 0.529 | 0.849 | 0.313 | 0.878 | 0.782 |
| U-Net++ (ResNet-50) | 0.904 | 0.440 | 0.878 | 0.323 | 0.878 | 0.813 |
| U-Net++ (ResNet-152) | 0.898 | 0.451 | 0.860 | 0.308 | 0.868 | 0.780 |
| DeepLabV3+ (ResNet-50) | 0.860 | 0.410 | 0.825 | 0.308 | 0.799 | 0.784 |
| DeepLabV3+ (ResNet-152) | 0.926 | 0.456 | 0.885 | 0.296 | 0.854 | 0.789 |
| DeepLabV3+ (ConvNeXt-T) | 0.939 | 0.440 | 0.838 | 0.283 | 0.890 | 0.838 |
| DeepLabV3+ (ConvNeXt-B) | 0.909 | 0.453 | 0.862 | 0.291 | 0.871 | 0.820 |
| CaraNet (Res2Net-101) | 0.907 | 0.397 | **0.897** | **0.344** | 0.873 | 0.797 |
| ESFPNet-T (MiT-B0) | 0.908 | 0.424 | 0.850 | 0.209 | 0.872 | 0.806 |
| ESFPNet-L (MiT-B4) | 0.941 | 0.500 | 0.865 | 0.311 | 0.891 | 0.834 |
| FCBFormer-B0 (PVTv2-B0) | 0.896 | 0.470 | 0.861 | 0.283 | 0.877 | 0.828 |
| FCBFormer-B3 (PVTv2-B3) | **0.961** | **0.552** | 0.889 | 0.338 | 0.904 | 0.816 |
| Swin-T-UperNet (SwinV2-T) | 0.919 | 0.534 | 0.872 | 0.303 | **0.910** | **0.842** |
| Swin-B-UperNet (SwinV2-B) | 0.925 | 0.491 | 0.884 | 0.294 | 0.895 | 0.835 |

applied when the loss on the validation set has converged. The Adam optimizer with AMS-grad is used with $(\beta_1, \beta_2)=(0.9, 0.999)$ and a weight decay of $10^{-4}$, in combination with a learning rate scheduler that reduced the learning rate with a factor 10, when the validation loss stopped improving for 10 epochs with a maximum of 3 reductions. The classification loss of the algorithm is evaluated using the Binary Cross-Entropy (BCE) loss function, while the segmentation loss is evaluated with a compound BCE + Dice loss function, both with label smoothing of 0.01. To efficiently leverage images without a GT delineation, only the classification loss is used for backpropagation to improve training of the backbone encoder. Randomly sampling training images ensures an average 50-50% representation of classes in each iteration. Experiments are implemented in Python 3.10 using the PyTorch (Lightning) frameworks.

**C. Performance Evaluation Metrics:** The Area under the Curve (AUC) for the receiver operating characteristic (ROC), is used for evaluation of the classification ($AUC_{cls}$) performance. The metric is computed based on the classification branch output of the networks. The segmentation performance for neoplastic imagery is evaluated with the mean Dice Score ($mD_i$), by employing the segmentation mask, thresholded by 0.5, and the GT delineation.

# 3    Experimental Results and Discussion

The results on all test sets are presented in Table 3, while graphical illustrations of the comparison between the size requirements (Parameters and Model Size) and the performance metrics for each set are depicted in Fig. 2.

*1. General Performance on Test Set:*  The results indicate that FCBFormer-B3 outperforms other architectures on both classification and segmentation, with improvements of 0.02 and 0.018, respectively. As shown in Fig. 2a and 2b, the best performing classification and segmentation models are in the middle segment of parameter and model size, while the models in the low and high segment achieve similar performance. This suggests that having more parameters does not necessarily result in improved performance. Furthermore, a key observation is that Transformers achieve the top-2 scores for both classification and segmentation, and are well-represented in the top-5. These results suggest that Transformers generally perform better than CNNs on the classification and segmentation of challenging clinical cases of BE neoplasia, while requiring a comparable complexity in terms of parameters and model size.

*2. Robustness on BORN, QRT and CRT sets:*  The results on the BORN set indicate that CaraNet outperforms other architectures for both the classification and segmentation tasks, with margins of 0.008 and 0.006, respectively. As seen in Fig. 2c and 2d, the top classification and segmentation models are in the middle segment of parameter and model size, while models in the low and high segments achieve similar performance. This reinforces the conviction that having more parameters does not necessarily induce an improved performance. An important observation is that Transformers are well-represented in the top-5 of scores for both classification and segmentation. These findings indicate that Transformers achieve on-par robustness and generalization performance with CNNs on classification and segmentation of BE neoplasia in clinically realistic lower-quality data, obtained from older generation and different manufacturers' gastroscopes, while requiring a comparable model complexity. On the QRT and CRT sets, Swin-T-UperNet has the highest classification performance with margins of 0.006 and 0.004, respectively. As seen in Fig. 2e and 2f, the best performing models on the QRT set are found in the middle and high segments, which suggests that, in this case, having more parameters *is indeed* beneficial for performance, while the best performing models on the CRT set are found in all segments. It is noteworthy, that Transformers overshadow CNNs in the top-5 of scores for both the QRT and CRT sets, which indicates that Transformers show increased robustness compared to CNNs in clinically realistic data of lower subjective image quality or data that is not meeting the inclusion criteria of the training set, while requiring similar or less model complexity.

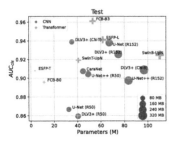

(a) Test: Size requirements vs. AUC$_{cls}$

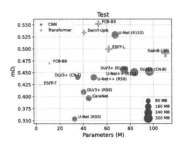

(b) Test: Size requirements vs. $mD_i$

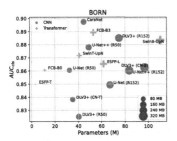

(c) BORN: Size requirements vs. AUC$_{cls}$

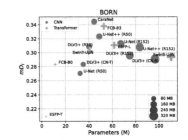

(d) BORN: Size requirements vs. $mD_i$

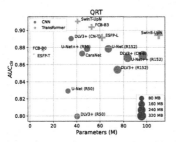

(e) QRT: Size requirements vs. AUC$_{cls}$

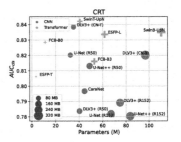

(f) CRT: Size requirements vs. AUC$_{cls}$

**Fig. 2.** Size requirements of all architectures, in terms of parameters and model size, versus the performance metrics on the Test, BORN, QRT and CRT sets.

## 4   Conclusions

Endoscopic image analysis is subject to several challenges, posing requirements on the performance, robustness and complexity of computer-based analysis techniques. These requirements and the benefits of the recently proposed Transformer-based architectures, raise the question whether Transformers are more suitable than state-of-the-art CNNs in this field. In this paper, we have evaluated and compared the performance, robustness and complexity of CNNs and Transformers for endoscopic image analysis, in this case Barrett's neoplasia detection. To this end, we have selected one high-quality test set and three different robustness test sets. The results show that Transformers generally outperform CNNs by a small margin on both classification and segmentation of challenging subtle clinical representative Barrett's neoplasia cases. Additionally, they exhibit on-par or increased robustness various to clinically realistic and relevant data variations, while requiring comparable complexity in terms of parameters and model size, for this specific application. These findings are overall promising for the deployment of Transformers into endoscopy clinical practice, as they show critical robustness and generalization traits in case of varying quality and equipment over hospitals. However, future research is required to generalize and strengthen these findings, which should focus on (1) extension to other endoscopic applications, (2) evaluating additional aspects, such as efficiency in training sample size, robustness to clinically realistic artificial image corruption and the comparison with expert endoscopist performance.

**Prospect of Application:** Providing valuable insights into the comparative efficacy of CNNs and Transformers in endoscopic image analysis, addressing domain-specific challenges and emphasizing essential traits such as robustness, generalization and complexity, crucial for reliable operation in the diverse and challenging imaging nature of endoscopy clinical practice. Future research is needed to generalize and reinforce the findings, ensuring applicability beyond the current scope.

# References

1. Bergman, J.J., de Groof, A.J., et al.: An interactive web-based educational tool improves detection and delineation of Barrett's esophagus-related neoplasia. Gastroenterol. **156**(5), 1299-1308.e3 (2019). https://doi.org/10.1053/j.gastro.2018.12.021
2. Bernal, J., et al.: WM-DOVA maps for accurate polyp highlighting in colonoscopy: validation vs. saliency maps from physicians. Comput. Med. Imaging Graph. **43**, 99–111 (2015). https://doi.org/10.1016/j.compmedimag.2015.02.007
3. Byrne, M.F., et al.: Real-time differentiation of adenomatous and hyperplastic diminutive colorectal polyps during analysis of unaltered videos of standard colonoscopy using a deep learning model. Gut **68**(1), 94–100 (2019)
4. Chang, Q., et al.: ESFPNet: efficient deep learning architecture for real-time lesion segmentation in autofluorescence bronchoscopic video. In: Gimi, B.S., Krol, A. (eds.) Medical Imaging 2023: Biomedical Applications in Molecular, Structural, and Functional Imaging, vol. 12468, p. 1246803. International Society for Optics and Photonics, SPIE (2023). https://doi.org/10.1117/12.2647897
5. Chen, L.C., et al.: Encoder-decoder with atrous separable convolution for semantic image segmentation. In: Ferrari, V., Hebert, M., Sminchisescu, C., Weiss, Y. (eds.) ECCV 2018. LNCS, vol. 11211, pp. 833–851. Springer, Cham (2018). https://doi.org/10.1007/978-3-030-01234-2_49
6. Chen, P.J., et al.: Accurate classification of diminutive colorectal polyps using computer-aided analysis. Gastroenterol. **154**(3), 568–575 (2018)
7. Cho, B.J., et al.: Automated classification of gastric neoplasms in endoscopic images using a convolutional neural network. Endosc. **51**(12), 1121–1129 (2019)
8. Dosovitskiy, A., et al.: An image is worth $16 \times 16$ words: transformers for image recognition at scale. ICLR (2021)

9.  Ebigbo, A., et al.: Real-time use of artificial intelligence in the evaluation of cancer in barrett's oesophagus. Gut **69**(4), 615–616 (2020)
10. de Groof, A.J., et al.: Deep-learning system detects neoplasia in patients with Barrett's esophagus with higher accuracy than endoscopists in a multistep training and validation study with benchmarking. Gastroenterol. **158**(4), 915–929 (2020)
11. Hashimoto, R., et al.: Artificial intelligence using convolutional neural networks for real-time detection of early esophageal neoplasia in Barrett's esophagus (with video). Gastrointest. Endosc. **91**(6), 1264–1271 (2020)
12. He, K., et al.: Deep residual learning for image recognition. In: 2016 IEEE Conference on Computer Vision and Pattern Recognition (CVPR), pp. 770–778 (2016). https://doi.org/10.1109/CVPR.2016.90
13. Jha, D., et al.: Kvasir-SEG: a segmented polyp dataset. In: Ro, Y.M., et al. (eds.) MMM 2020. LNCS, vol. 11962, pp. 451–462. Springer, Cham (2020). https://doi.org/10.1007/978-3-030-37734-2_37
14. Kusters, C.H.J., et al.: A CAD system for real-time characterization of neoplasia in Barrett's esophagus NBI videos. In: Ali, S., van der Sommen, F., Papież, B.W., van Eijnatten, M., Jin, Y., Kolenbrander, I. (eds.) Cancer Prevention Through Early Detection, pp. 89–98. Springer, Cham (2022). https://doi.org/10.1007/978-3-031-17979-2_9
15. Liu, Z., et al.: Swin Transformer V2: scaling up capacity and resolution. In: 2022 IEEE/CVF Conference on Computer Vision and Pattern Recognition (CVPR), pp. 11999–12009 (2022). https://doi.org/10.1109/CVPR52688.2022.01170
16. Liu, Z., et al.: A convnet for the 2020s. In: 2022 IEEE/CVF Conference on Computer Vision and Pattern Recognition (CVPR), pp. 11966–11976 (2022). https://doi.org/10.1109/CVPR52688.2022.01167
17. Lou, A., et al.: CaraNet: context axial reverse attention network for segmentation of small medical objects. In: Medical Imaging 2022: Image Processing, vol. 12032, pp. 81–92. International Society for Optics and Photonics, SPIE (2022). https://doi.org/10.1117/12.2611802
18. Ronneberger, O., Fischer, P., Brox, T.: U-Net: convolutional networks for biomedical image segmentation. In: Navab, N., Hornegger, J., Wells, W.M., Frangi, A.F. (eds.) MICCAI 2015. LNCS, vol. 9351, pp. 234–241. Springer, Cham (2015). https://doi.org/10.1007/978-3-319-24574-4_28
19. Sanderson, E., Matuszewski, B.J.: FCN-transformer feature fusion for polyp segmentation. In: Yang, G., Aviles-Rivero, A., Roberts, M., Schönlieb, C.B. (eds.) Medical Image Understanding and Analysis, pp. 892–907. Springer, Cham (2022). https://doi.org/10.1007/978-3-031-12053-4_65
20. Tajbakhsh, N., et al.: Automated polyp detection in colonoscopy videos using shape and context information. IEEE Trans. Med. Imaging **35**(2), 630–644 (2016). https://doi.org/10.1109/TMI.2015.2487997
21. Vaswani, A., et al.: Attention is all you need. In: Guyon, I., Luxburg, U.V., Bengio, S., Wallach, H., Fergus, R., Vishwanathan, S., Garnett, R. (eds.) Advances in Neural Information Processing Systems, vol. 30. Curran Associates, Inc. (2017)
22. Wang, W., et al.: PVT v2: improved baselines with pyramid vision transformer. Comput. Vis. Media , 1–10 (2022). https://doi.org/10.1007/s41095-022-0274-8
23. Wu, L., et al.: Deep learning system compared with expert endoscopists in predicting early gastric cancer and its invasion depth and differentiation status (with videos). Gastrointest. Endosc. **95**(1), 92–104.e3 (2022). https://doi.org/10.1016/j.gie.2021.06.033

24. Xiao, T., et al.: Unified perceptual parsing for scene understanding. In: Ferrari, V., Hebert, M., Sminchisescu, C., Weiss, Y. (eds.) ECCV 2018. LNCS, vol. 11209, pp. 432–448. Springer, Cham (2018). https://doi.org/10.1007/978-3-030-01228-1_26
25. Xie, E., et al.: SegFormer: simple and efficient design for semantic segmentation with transformers. In: Neural Information Processing Systems (NeurIPS) (2021)
26. Zhou, Z., Rahman Siddiquee, M.M., Tajbakhsh, N., Liang, J.: UNet++: a nested u-net architecture for medical image segmentation. In: Stoyanov, D., et al. (eds.) DLMIA/ML-CDS -2018. LNCS, vol. 11045, pp. 3–11. Springer, Cham (2018). https://doi.org/10.1007/978-3-030-00889-5_1

# Investigating the Impact of Image Quality on Endoscopic AI Model Performance

Tim J. M. Jaspers[1]([⊠]) [ID], Tim G. W. Boers[1][ID], Carolus H. J. Kusters[1][ID], Martijn R. Jong[2][ID], Jelmer B. Jukema[2][ID], Albert J. de Groof[2], Jacques J. Bergman[2], Peter H. N. de With[1], and Fons van der Sommen[1][ID]

[1] Department of Electrical Engineering, Video Coding and Architectures, Eindhoven University of Technology, Eindhoven, The Netherlands
{t.j.m.jaspers,t.boers,c.h.j.kusters,p.h.n.de.with,fvdsommen}@tue.nl
[2] Department of Gastroenterology and Hepatology, Amsterdam University Medical Centers, University of Amsterdam, Amsterdam, The Netherlands

**Abstract.** Virtually all endoscopic AI models are developed with clean, high-quality imagery from expert centers, however, the clinical data quality is much more heterogeneous. Endoscopic image quality can degrade by e.g. poor lighting, motion blur, and image compression. This disparity between training, validation data, and real-world clinical practice can have a substantial impact on the performance of deep neural networks (DNNs), potentially resulting in clinically unreliable models. To address this issue and develop more reliable models for automated cancer detection, this study focuses on identifying the limitations of current DNNs. Specifically, we evaluate the performance of these models under clinically relevant and realistic image corruptions, as well as on a manually selected dataset that includes images with lower subjective quality. Our findings highlight the importance of understanding the impact of a decrease in image quality and the need to include robustness evaluation for DNNs used in endoscopy.

**Keywords:** DNN · Image degradation · Endoscopy · Robustness

## 1 Introduction

Deep neural networks (DNNs) have demonstrated state-of-the-art performance on numerous computer vision challenges [2,3,13,14]. As a result, DNNs are increasingly being used in safety-critical systems, such as self-driving cars and medical image analysis. However, the implementation of DNNs in real-world scenarios underscores the need for models that are inherently robust and can operate reliably under diverse and natural imaging conditions. Previous research in computer vision has already demonstrated that even small forms of image degradation can have a significant impact on the performance of DNNs [4,5,8,11,16] because DNNs are dependent on the input Image Quality (IQ).

© The Author(s), under exclusive license to Springer Nature Switzerland AG 2024
S. Wu et al. (Eds.): AMAI 2023, LNCS 14313, pp. 32–41, 2024.
https://doi.org/10.1007/978-3-031-47076-9_4

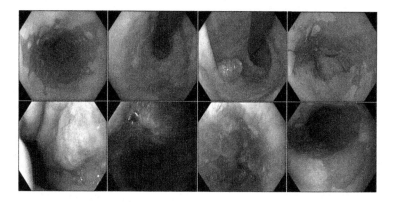

**Fig. 1.** Images with a high subjective quality, obtained from expert centers (top row), compared to lower quality images likely to encounter in clinical practice (bottom row)

This finding is particularly concerning in the context of Computer-Aided Detection and Diagnosis (CADe/CADx) models for gastrointestinal cancer screening, as the IQ heavily relies on the skill and experience of the endoscopist. Endoscopic CADe/CADx systems have gained considerable momentum in recent years, and an increasing number of AI systems have reached the market [6,20]. Such systems are typically trained on carefully selected pre-processed, high-quality images, while in clinical practice the IQ is considerably more heterogeneous. The IQ can be compromised by various factors such as inadequate lighting, motion blur, and compression. In contrast, manufacturers may apply post-processing filters to artificially enhance image appearance. If these models are unable to perform well under these heterogeneous clinical conditions, they become useless in clinical practice. Therefore, it is crucial to identify these blind spots and quantify their impact, to facilitate the development of robust DNNs delivering reliable performance under diverse imaging conditions.

In light of these challenges, our contributions can be summarized as follows: (1) We evaluate the performance of DNNs under image perturbation using clinically calibrated levels of severity, giving an indication of the quantitative performance loss in clinical practice. This assessment provides valuable insights into the performance of these models and their limitations for endoscopic applications. (2) By using a manually selected test set including lower subjective quality images, we demonstrate that peak performance and robustness are not necessarily correlated. It is important to note that achieving higher peak performance does not guarantee increased robustness, and conversely, higher robustness does not necessarily lead to lower peak performance (Fig. 1).

## 2 Methods and Materials

### 2.1 Network Training

**Training Data:** The dataset used for this study includes 2,752 images of Barrett esophagus neoplasia (NEO) (716 patients) and 7,595 images of non-dysplastic

Barrett esophagus (NDBE) (1,095 patients). The data is obtained in 17 different clinical centers using the Exera II, Exera III, and EVIS X1 production lines (Olympus Corp., Tokyo, Japan).

**Training:** All models evaluated in this study are based on the U-net architecture [17]. The training process for all models involves a 5 fold cross-validation on patient level of the training dataset. First, the encoder with ImageNet-1k-pretrained weights is frozen and the decoder is trained on all data [3]. After the initialization of the decoder in stage one, all weights of the encoder are unfrozen. During the second stage, the complete network is trained on all data. During training, the Adam optimizer is used with a learning rate of $1 \times 10^{-3}$ and $1 \times 10^{-5}$ for the first and second stage, respectively, while $(\beta_1, \beta_2) = (0.9, 0.99)$ remain constant during both stages [12]. The learning rate halves after 10 consecutive epochs without a decrease in validation loss. All input images are resized to a resolution of $256 \times 256$ pixels. A batch size of 16 images and the binary cross-entropy loss are used to train the network. Data augmentation is applied to the training frames, including translation, rotation, and horizontal and vertical flipping. The proposed methods are implemented in Python using the PyTorch framework and experiments are executed on a TITAN RTX GPU (NVIDIA Corp., CA, USA).

## 2.2    Experiments

This study primarily focuses on the effect of the encoder on model robustness, as the encoder is responsible for extracting features from an image. Five different encoders are evaluated in this study: VGG-19, ResNet-50, DenseNet-161, EfficientNet-b5, and Mixed vision Transformer (MiT)-B2 [1,7,9,18,19]. These encoders are selected based on their comparable complexity in terms of the number of parameters. Furthermore, the impact of model complexity is tested by using various sizes of the ResNet encoder: ResNet-18, ResNet-34, ResNet-50, ResNet-101, and ResNet-152 [7]. All of the encoders are incorporated into a U-Net architecture, using weights derived from initializing with ImageNet-1k [3,17]. All models are created and trained using PyTorch and the library PyTorch segmentation models [10,15]. Additionally, to investigate the impact of basic image augmentation techniques on the model's robustness, we have conducted an experiment that extends the basic augmentations with adjustments of hue, saturation, brightness, and contrast, as well as the addition of Gaussian blur and Gaussian noise.

## 2.3    Image Corruptions

During endoscopy, multiple forms of degradation occur, affecting the quality and appearance of the images and video captured by the endoscope. This study evaluates the robustness of AI models by applying eleven different types of synthesized corruptions grouped into three categories:

**(1) User-dependent:** Endoscopic IQ highly depends on the skill and experience of the endoscopist. Incorrect positioning, movement, or improper handling of the endoscope results in artifacts like motion blur, overexposure, and partial defocus blur.

**(2) Image acquisition and processing:** Image appearance also depends on the applied endoscopic system. Endoscopes of different manufacturers generally yield a slightly different image appearance. Furthermore, virtual chromoendoscopy methods are typically applied to improve the perceived IQ, which can also have unintended consequences on the performance of a CADe/x model. Three examples of such image enhancement techniques are shown in Fig. 2. The combination of the above results in different appearances of images in terms of contrast, brightness, hue, sharpness, and saturation.

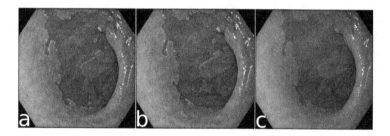

**Fig. 2.** Examples of different texture and color enhancement Imaging (TXI) enhancement settings on the Olympus Evis X1 system. (a) TXI 1, (b) TXI 2, and (c) standard white-light imaging.

**(3) Compression:** Image compression methods are used to reduce the file size of an image, making it easier to store and transmit it over multiple channels. This is especially useful for cloud-based solutions. These compression methods are typically based on lossy compression that results in several forms of information loss, which have usually an impact on the quality of the image. Information loss can occur in the form of coding noise along object borders, loss of detail in object or background, and block noise. In this study, we evaluate the effect of recording in lower resolution, JPEG compression, and JPEG2000 compression. Additionally, in order to draw a comparison between JPEG and JPEG2000 compression, the severity factor is based on the same compression factor.

**Severity:** To determine the severity of the corruption, ten levels are calibrated by two clinical experts. The first two levels simulate variations within high-quality endoscopic image datasets, while levels three to five are considered clinically relevant and reflect realistic real-world scenarios. The remaining levels (six to ten) are included to assess the model breaking point. The severity of the corruptions with respect to hue, saturation, brightness, and contrast, is categorized into both ten ascending and descending levels.

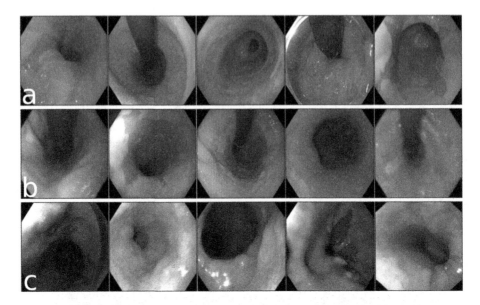

**Fig. 3.** Random examples included in the (a) original test set, (b) synthetic robustness test set (SR5T), and (c) the image quality robustness test set (QRT) robustness test set.

## 2.4   Evaluation

The models are evaluated using a detection-by-segmentation approach, where a detection label is assigned if the network's segmentation prediction exceeds a 0.5 threshold. To assess the classification accuracy, we use the Area under the Curve (AUC) of the Receiver Operating Characteristic (ROC) curve as the evaluation metric, which provides a comprehensive assessment of the model's sensitivity and specificity. The models' peak performance and robustness are assessed through evaluation on three datasets, examples are shown in Fig. 3.

**Original Test Set:** This test set consists of 100 images of NEO (58 patients) and 100 images of NDBE (36 patients), carefully selected on subtle neoplastic lesions. This dataset is regarded as a clean dataset, consisting of images that possess high subjective quality.

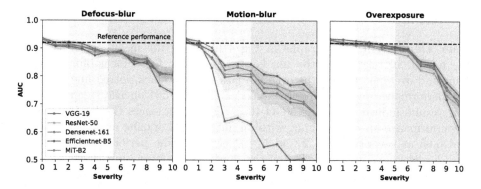

**Fig. 4.** Effects of user-dependent degradations on model performance. The white areas indicate the levels of severity expected to be present in expert datasets, while the light gray area indicates a clinically relevant amount of degradation. The black dotted line highlights the performance of the reference ResNet-50 encoder on the clean test set.

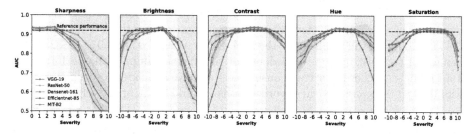

**Fig. 5.** Effects of changes in image acquisition and processing on model performance.

**Synthetic Robustness Test Set (SR5T):** Since multiple forms of image degradation can occur at once, the above-mentioned corruptions are used to create a new, more heterogeneous test set. Up to 5 random corruptions are applied to each image in the original test set, with the severity of each corruption selected at random from levels 1 to 5. This process is repeated five times for the entire test set. The code to generate the corruptions can be found on https:// github.com/BONS-AI-VCA-AMC/Robustness.

**Image Quality Robustness Test Set (IQRT):** We established an additional internal test set for our study, comprising 277 NEO images (115 patients) and 65 NDBE images (53 patients). These images were meticulously selected by two clinical researchers to ensure their inferior subjective image quality. The inclusion criteria for inferior quality were aspects such as illumination, blur, image resolution, as well as the presence of mucus and bubbles. Despite their lower subjective image quality, these images were deemed suitable for labeling.

## 3   Results

**User Dependent:** The graphs in Fig. 4 illustrate the mean performance of the models in relation to the ten levels of severity for defocus-blur, motion-blur, and overexposure on the original dataset. The black dotted line indicates the performance of the reference encoder (ResNet-50) on the clean test set. The results indicate that the VGG-19 encoder experiences the largest decline in performance for motion-blur, with an initial AUC of 0.95, decreasing to 0.84 and 0.65 at severity levels 2 and 5, respectively. The performance of the all encoder decreases with ±5% at severity level 5 for defocus-blur. However, when it comes to overexposure, the difference in model performance is only apparent at higher levels of corruption.

**Image Acquisition and Processing:** The effect of the corruptions related to image acquisition and processing on model performance can be observed in Fig. 5. Using a severity level of 5, the sharpness filter decreases the initial AUC of the ResNet-50 encoder from 0.93 to 0.86 (−7.5%). Limiting the contrast at severity level −5 results in the largest performance drop for the VGG-19 encoder (0.95 to 0.80) and the smallest for the MiT-B2 encoder (0.93 to 0.91). A synthetic increase of contrast up to level 5 does not significantly impact the performance of all models. A change in Hue causes the ResNet-50 encoder to drop the AUC from 0.93 to 0.91 and 0.87 at severity levels −2 and −5, respectively.

**Compression:** The graph in Fig. 6 illustrates that JPEG2000 compression has the highest impact on model performance at severity level 5. For the VGG-19 encoder, the AUC drops to 0.57 while the AUC of the other encoders stays within the range of 0.7–0.8. For JPEG compression up to severity level 5, there is no substantial decrease in performance. This may be due to the fact that the training data included JPEG-compressed images, but not JPEG2000-compressed images. A reduction of resolution does not result in notable changes in the AUC up to level 5 but decreases the AUC of the ResNet-50 encoder with 4% at level 6.

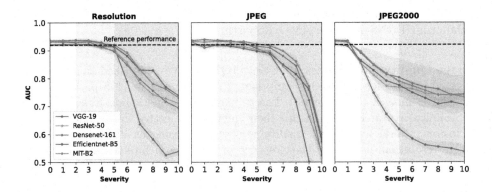

**Fig. 6.** Effects of artifacts from compression on model performance.

**Table 1.** Performance on the three test sets (mean±std).

| Encoder | Augmentation | Test Set $AUC\uparrow$ | SR5T $AUC\uparrow$ | IQRT $AUC\uparrow$ | Parameters | ImageNet $Top1ACC$ |
|---|---|---|---|---|---|---|
| VGG-19 | Light | **0.95 ± 0.01** | 0.82 ± 0.02 | 0.83 ± 0.03 | 20M | 72.6 |
| ResNet-50 | | 0.93 ± 0.01 | 0.83 ± 0.01 | 0.86 ± 0.02 | 23M | 76.1 |
| DenseNet-16 | | 0.94 ± 0.02 | 0.86 ± 0.01 | 0.88 ± 0.02 | 26M | 77.7 |
| EfficientNet-B5 | | 0.93 ± 0.01 | **0.88 ± 0.01** | 0.87 ± 0.00 | 28M | 83.6 |
| MiT-B2 | | 0.94 ± 0.01 | 0.87 ± 0.01 | **0.89 ± 0.02** | 24M | 81.6 |
| ResNet-18 | Light | 0.93 ± 0.01 | 0.83 ± 0.01 | 0.86 ± 0.02 | 11M | 69.8 |
| ResNet-34 | | 0.92 ± 0.01 | 0.85 ± 0.01 | **0.88 ± 0.01** | 21M | 73.3 |
| ResNet-50 | | 0.93 ± 0.01 | 0.83 ± 0.01 | 0.86 ± 0.02 | 23M | 76.2 |
| ResNet-101 | | **0.94 ± 0.01** | 0.84 ± 0.02 | 0.86 ± 0.04 | 42M | 77.4 |
| ResNet-152 | | 0.92 ± 0.00 | **0.85 ± 0.01** | 0.87 ± 0.03 | 58M | 78.3 |
| ResNet-50 | No | 0.89 ± 0.01 | 0.80 ± 0.01 | 0.85 ± 0.02 | 23M | 76.1 |
| ResNet-50 | Light | **0.93 ± 0.01** | 0.83 ± 0.01 | **0.86 ± 0.02** | 23M | 76.1 |
| ResNet-50 | Heavy | 0.91 ± 0.01 | **0.85 ± 0.01** | 0.82 ± 0.02 | 23M | 76.1 |

**Robustness Test Sets:** Table 1 presents the performance results of all trained models on the original test set, as well as the SR5T and IQRT test sets. Among the encoders evaluated, the VGG encoder demonstrates the highest AUC value on the original test set, albeit with a marginal difference compared to the worst performing encoders ($0.95 \pm 0.01$ versus $0.93 \pm 0.01$). Conversely, the VGG encoder exhibits the lowest performance on the SR5T and IQRT test sets. Notably, the EfficientNet-B5 encoder achieves the highest AUC ($0.88 \pm 0.01$) on the SR5T test set, while the MiT-B2 encoder outperforms the others on the IQRT test set with an AUC of $0.89 \pm 0.02$. Considering the complexity differences, the ResNet-101 encoder attains the highest AUC ($0.94 \pm 0.01$) on the test set, whereas the ResNet-152 and ResNet-34 ($0.85 \pm 0.01$) demonstrate better performance on the SR5T test set. On the IQRT test set, the ResNet-34 encoder achieves the highest AUC ($0.88 \pm 0.01$). Notably, the variance in performance between encoders with varying complexities is minimal ($<0.02$ AUC). Furthermore, incorporating additional data augmentation techniques leads to improved performance on the SR5T test set. However, no noticeable enhancement in model performance is observed on the original test set or the IQRT test set, indicating that the benefit of adding basic augmented data is limited to reduced image quality.

## 4 Conclusions and Future Work

In this study, we have examined the robustness of various deep neural networks against more heterogeneous endoscopic image quality, expected to be faced in clinical practice. To evaluate the robustness of the models, various types of image degradation are introduced and grouped into three categories. The results indicate that reference model performance decreased by 11%, 8%, and 18% within clinically calibrated boundaries, for user-dependent, image acquisition and processing, and compression, respectively.

Additionally, we show that models performing best on a clean high-quality test set do not necessarily perform better on test sets with lower subjective image quality (SR5T and IQRT). These observations emphasize the significance of including robustness evaluation for DNNs used in endoscopy, as other architectural designs may exhibit better performance under heterogeneous, clinical conditions. Furthermore, the influence of model complexity seems to be limited, since all models have a comparable sensitivity to IQ degradation. Lastly, the results imply that simply extending data augmentation may not result in improvements on lesser-quality test sets.

The insights gained in this study give a first demonstration of the robustness of DNNs against lower subjective image quality, however, it is important to note that the synthetic corruptions used in this study are relatively simple and may not fully encompass the heterogeneous and diverse data encountered in clinical practice. Future research can focus on incorporating even more realistic corruptions, or try to construct a paired low-quality/high-quality image dataset. Furthermore, an intriguing avenue for deeper exploration involves conducting a comparative pairwise evaluation between AI models and expert clinicians, on the sub-optimal image quality test sets.

**Prospect of Application:** Our study provides valuable insights into the robustness of DNNs for automated cancer detection in endoscopy that can be used to evaluate models intended to be used in clinical practice and help to develop models that can operate robustly and perform reliably under diverse and natural imaging conditions.

# References

1. Chen, J.-N., Sun, S., He, J., Torr, P., Yuille, A., Bai, S.: TransMix: attend to mix for vision transformers, June 2022. https://arxiv.org/abs/2111.09833
2. Cordts, M., et al.: The cityscapes dataset for semantic urban scene understanding, April 2016. https://arxiv.org/abs/1604.01685
3. Deng, J., Dong, W., Socher, R., Li, L.-J., Li, K., Fei-Fei, L.: ImageNet: a large-scale hierarchical image database. In: IEEE Conference on Computer Vision and Pattern Recognition (CVPR), pp. 248–255. IEEE (2009)
4. Dodge, S.F., Karam, L.J.: A study and comparison of human and deep learning recognition performance under visual distortions. CoRR, abs/1705.02498 (2017). https://arxiv.org/abs/1705.02498
5. Dodge, S.F., Karam, L.J.: Understanding how image quality affects deep neural networks. CoRR, abs/1604.04004 (2016). https://arxiv.org/abs/1604.04004
6. U.S. Food and Drug Administration. FDA authorizes marketing of first device that uses artificial intelligence to help detect potential signs of colon cancer (2021). https://www.fda.gov/news-events/press-announcements/fda-authorizes-marketing-first-device-uses-artificial-intelligence-help-detect-potential-signs-colon

7. He, K., Zhang, X., Ren, S., Sun, J.: Deep residual learning for image recognition. In: Proceedings of 2016 IEEE Conference on Computer Vision and Pattern Recognition, CVPR 2016, pp. 770–778. IEEE, June 2016. https://doi.org/10.1109/CVPR.2016.90, https://ieeexplore.ieee.org/document/7780459

8. Hendrycks, D., Dietterich, T.: Benchmarking neural network robustness to common corruptions and perturbations. In: International Conference on Learning Representations (2019). https://openreview.net/forum?id=HJz6tiCqYm

9. Huang, G., Liu, Z., van der Maaten, L., Weinberger, K.Q.: Densely connected convolutional networks. In: CVPR, pp. 2261–2269. IEEE Computer Society (2017). ISBN 978-1-5386-0457-1. https://dblp.uni-trier.de/db/conf/cvpr/cvpr2017.html#HuangLMW17

10. Iakubovskii, P.: Segmentation models pytorch (2019). https://github.com/qubvel/segmentation_models.pytorch

11. Karahan, Ş., Yildirim, M.K., Kirtaç, K., Rende, F.Ş., Bütün, G., Ekenel, H.K.: How image degradations affect deep CNN-based face recognition? vol. P-260. Gesellschaft fur Informatik (GI), November 2016. ISBN 9783885796541. https://doi.org/10.1109/BIOSIG.2016.7736924

12. Kingma, D.P., Ba, J.: Adam: a method for stochastic optimization (2014). arxiv:1412.6980Comment. Published as a Conference Paper at the 3rd International Conference for Learning Representations, San Diego (2015)

13. Krizhevsky, A.: Learning multiple layers of features from tiny images (2009)

14. Lin, T.-Y., et al.: Microsoft COCO: common objects in context, May 2014. https://arxiv.org/abs/1405.0312

15. Paszke, A., et al.: PyTorch: an imperative style, high-performance deep learning library, December 2019. https://arxiv.org/abs/1912.01703

16. Pei, Y., Huang, Y., Zou, Q., Zhang, X., Wang, S.: Effects of image degradation and degradation removal to CNN-based image classification. IEEE Trans. Pattern Anal. Mach. Intell. **43**, 1239–1253 (2021). ISSN 19393539. https://doi.org/10.1109/TPAMI.2019.2950923

17. Ronneberger, O., Fischer, P., Brox, T.: U-Net: convolutional networks for biomedical image segmentation, pp. 234–241, May 2015. https://arxiv.org/abs/1505.04597

18. Simonyan, K., Zisserman, A.: Very deep convolutional networks for large-scale image recognition. CoRR, abs/1409.1556 (2014). https://arxiv.org/abs/1409.1556

19. Tan, M., Le, Q.V.: EfficientNet: rethinking model scaling for convolutional neural networks. CoRR, abs/1905.11946 (2019). https://arxiv.org/abs/1905.11946

20. Yuba, M., Iwasaki, K.: Systematic analysis of the test design and performance of AI/ML-based medical devices approved for triage/detection/diagnosis in the USA and Japan. Sci. Rep. **12**, 16874 (2022). ISSN 20452322. https://doi.org/10.1038/s41598-022-21426-7

# Ensembling Voxel-Based and Box-Based Model Predictions for Robust Lesion Detection

Noëlie Debs[(✉)] [iD], Alexandre Routier [iD], Clément Abi-Nader [iD],
Arnaud Marcoux, Alexandre Bône [iD], and Marc-Michel Rohé

Guerbet Research, Villepinte, France
{noelie.debs,alexandre.routier,clement.abi-nader,alexandre.bone,
arnaud.marcoux,marc-michel.rohe}@guerbet.com

**Abstract.** This paper presents a novel generic method to improve lesion detection by ensembling semantic segmentation and object detection models. The proposed approach allows to benefit from both voxel-based and box-based predictions, thus improving the ability to accurately detect lesions. The method consists of 3 main steps: (i) semantic segmentation and object detection models are trained separately; (ii) voxel-based and box-based predictions are matched spatially; (iii) corresponding lesion presence probabilities are combined into summary detection maps. We illustrate and validate the robustness of the proposed approach on three different oncology applications: liver and pancreas neoplasm detection in single-phase CT, and significant prostate cancer detection in multi-modal MRI. Performance is evaluated on publicly-available databases, and compared to two state-of-the art baseline methods. The proposed ensembling approach improves the average precision metric in all considered applications, with a 8% gain for prostate cancer.

**Keywords:** semantic segmentation · object detection · ensembling · prostate cancer · liver cancer · pancreatic cancer

## 1 Introduction

Over the last 10 years, many deep learning methods have been proposed to identify objects in medical images, such as cancer lesions. These methods have the potential to assist radiologists by enhancing diagnostic accuracy and improving workflow efficiency. Two families of approaches can be distinguished in the literature. First, semantic segmentation methods such as the U-Net [1] perform voxel-level classification, thus providing precise dense contours of the lesion to be detected. Second, object detection methods like Feature Pyramid Networks (FPN) [2,3] propose to classify boxes within an image, which can be applied to medical images in order to localize and characterize lesions.

---

N. Debs and A. Routier—Contributed equally to this work.

S. Wu et al. (Eds.): AMAI 2023, LNCS 14313, pp. 42–51, 2024.
https://doi.org/10.1007/978-3-031-47076-9_5

Both semantic segmentation and object detection methods are calibrated in a supervised manner. However, they fundamentally rely on distinct data representations of the training annotations, which are typically encoded either as binary maps or box coordinates, and their respective optimization is therefore driven by distinct families of loss functions. These modeling differences result in different predictive performance patterns. For instance, semantic segmentation methods tend to be biased towards large-size objects, while object detection methods are less sensitive to variations in the target object sizes. On the other hand, object detection methods are less accurate than their semantic segmentation counterparts to describe lesion localization. Consequently, insofar as the two approaches are structurally different, they may lead to different levels of performances depending on the considered clinical application, thus raising the issue of choosing the right framework.

Some studies have attempted to build hybrid models in order to combine the respective strengths of semantic segmentation and object detection methods. For instance, the deep network architectures proposed in [4,5] are able to produce both voxel-based and box-based predictions. To do so, they rely on a hybrid cost function that aggregates semantic segmentation and object detection terms. The semantic segmentation term is viewed as a regularizer, and model selection is typically performed with respect to the object detection term. These loss-based hybridization approaches demonstrated solid performance on a wide range of applications in oncology imaging [6,7].

In this work, we propose an alternative hybridization approach, where semantic segmentation and object detection models are combined by ensembling their predictions. Because they fundamentally rely on distinct data representation, ensembling such models is not straightforward and was never proposed nor evaluated in the literature, to the best of our knowledge. Our approach can be divided in three steps: (i) semantic segmentation and object detection models are trained separately; (ii) voxel-based and box-based predictions are matched spatially; (iii) corresponding lesion presence probabilities are combined into summary detection maps. This proposed approach is generic and can be applied to any pair of architectures from the semantic segmentation and object detection families. We evaluate it on three different oncology applications: liver and pancreas neoplasm detection in single-phase CT, and significant prostate cancer detection in bi-parametric MRI. These applications are different in several key aspects such as physical nature of the medical images, organ shape and size, and the average number of lesions to be detected per case. Our contributions are the following:

1. two reference semantic segmentation and object detection methods are benchmarked on three oncology applications, with large training databases and public test sets;
2. we show that these baseline methods are outperformed by the proposed ensembling method across all three considered applications;
3. we propose and evaluate two possible variations for the spatial matching criterion.

## 2    Materials and Methods

### 2.1    Imaging Data

This section describes the different datasets that were leveraged for the three considered clinical applications.

**Liver.** An internal database of 1975 portal-phase Computed Tomography (CT) scans collected from multiple medical institutions was split with a 80%/20% ratio to form the training and validation sets. The 1975 cases included patients who had a variety of hepatic lesions, ranging from benign cyst or granuloma to malignant hepatocellular carcinoma or metastases. A separate test set of 65 cases, composed of 45 patients with liver cancer and 20 healthy liver donor candidates, was built by aggregating CT scans from the publicly-available LiTS [8], IRCAD [9] and CHAOS databases [10]. Due to corrupted image metadata, 20 LiTS cases were discarded. Furthermore, only cases with lesions smaller than 2cm in diameter were included in the test set, in order to focus the evaluation on the most arduous targets for detection. Manual volumetric lesion segmentation maps were available for all collected images.

**Pancreas.** A total of 2134 portal CT scans from our internal database was used for training. Images were collected from multiple manufacturers and medical institutions. Among the 2134 patients, 1692 had a pancreatic lesion and 442 were healthy controls. Each scan was reviewed by a radiologist who systematically contoured the pancreas and the lesion when it was visible. Data was split in a training and validation sets of 1707 and 427 cases, respectively. An independent test dataset was created by relying on publicly available data from the Medical Decathlon Challenge [11] and The Cancer Imaging Archive [12]. This led to a total of 361 independent test cases among which, 281 had a pancreatic lesion segmented by radiologists and 80 were healthy control subjects.

**Prostate.** A total of 1658 cases from the public PI-CAI [13] and Prostate158 [14] databases were used for training, validation and testing. Studies were guaranteed to be multi-center and multi-manufactures. Input MRI modalities available were T2-weighted (T2w) image, diffusion-weighted image (DWI) with highest b-value, and apparent diffusion coefficient (ADC) map. Among the 1658 cases, 509 were positive patients (425 from PI-CAI, 84 from Prostate158), *i.e.* patients with at least one clinically-significant lesion with ISUP $\geq$ 2. The other cases were negative, *i.e.* with benign tissue or indolent cancer. Data was split in 1398, 100, 160 cases for training, validation and test sets respectively.

### 2.2    Ensembling Method

The proposed ensembling method consists of three steps which are illustrated in Fig. 1.

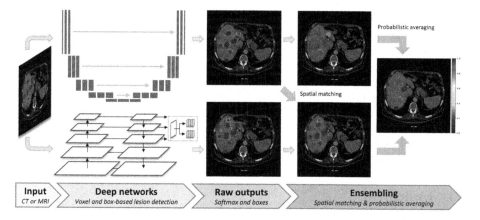

**Fig. 1.** Overview of the proposed ensembling method for voxel-based semantic segmentation and box-based object detection model predictions.

**Voxel-Based Semantic Segmentation Model.** For each clinical application, a deep convolutional network segmenting the organ of interest and potential lesions was learned from the training data previously described. Different input modalities were used depending on the clinical task: portal venous CT scans for liver and pancreatic cancer, and T2w, ADC, DWI MRI modalities for prostate cancer. Raw predicted softmax maps were post-processed into probabilistic lesion detection maps using the following approach: (i) voxel-level probabilites $\leq 0.1$ were set to 0; (ii) the resulting probabilistic map was decomposed into connected components, (iii) a single lesion-level probability was assigned to each connected component by averaging the corresponding voxel-level probabilities.

**Box-Based Object Detection Model.** Similar to the semantic segmentation model, an object detection model was trained for each clinical application. Each detection network took the same inputs as the segmentation model. A single output class was defined for target lesions. The detection algorithm returned scored bounding boxes around suspicious regions in the image.

**Spatial and Probabilistic Ensembling.** Voxel-based and box-based predictions were ensembled to create a final detection map in which each detected lesion was defined as a connected component with a single associated probability value. This was done in two steps: (i) spatial matching between lesions detected by the semantic segmentation and object detection models; (ii) combination of segmentation and detection models probabilities of matched lesions.

Two spatial matching criteria between the 0.1-clipped softmax maps and detection boxes were defined and tested.

- **Max-overlap matching** (MO): for each connected component of the 0.1-clipped softmax map, identify all overlapping boxes and associate with the one maximizing the overlap with respect to the tightest-fitting connected component bounding box.

- **Max-score matching** (MS): for each connected component of the 0.1-clipped softmax map, identify all overlapping boxes and associate with the one of maximal predicted lesion probability.

After the softmax components and box predictions were associated in pairs, the corresponding lesion presence probabilities were combined with a two-parameter logistic regression model calibrated. For each clinical application, the logistic regression models were calibrated on the validation sets.

### 2.3   Evaluation

**Baseline Semantic Segmentation and Object Detection Models.** Lesion segmentation and detection were performed using the nnU-Net [15] and nnDetection [16], respectively. Both methods present a standardized framework in order to reliably design and train networks, thanks to robust data preprocessing, optimal hyper-parameter choices, and large data augmentation. These approaches are adapted to different imaging modalities (CT, Magnetic Resonance Imaging: MRI) and have been successfully applied to identify lesions in many organs [17].

**Metrics.** The baseline methods and the two proposed ensembling approaches were similarly evaluated, both at the lesion and the patient levels. Lesion-level detection performance was evaluated using the Average Precision (AP) metric. Patient-level performance were evaluated using the Area Under Receiver Operating Characteristic (AUC) metric.

**Hit Criterion Between Predicted Lesion and Ground Truth.** Each predicted lesion was considered as a true positive if its 3D overlap with a ground truth lesion had an IoU $\geq 0.1$. Such a threshold value is in agreement with other lesion detection studies from recent literature [5, 16, 18, 19]. If not, the detected lesion was considered as a false positive. If several detected lesions matched the same ground truth lesion, then only the lesion with the largest overlap was retained, and the other detected lesions were discarded.

## 3   Results

Lesion detection performances are reported in Table 1. The proposed ensemble models outperformed the baseline methods across all clinical applications and metrics, at the exception of the patient-level AUC for cancer case detection. A maximum increase of 8.4% of AP was achieved for prostate cancer detection. On average across clinical applications, the max-overlap (MO) ensembling approach outperformed its max-score (MS) counterpart in terms of lesion-level AP, while the reverse observation can be made in terms of the patient-level AUC.

Precision-recall and sensitivity-specificity curves are shown in Fig. 2. The complementarity between the semantic segmentation and object detection models is particularly visible in the prostate application: the corresponding curves exhibit two distinct performance regimes (i.e. depending on the threshold, either nnU-Net or nnDetection show better performances) which are advantageously combined with the ensemble methods. While ensembling degraded the semantic segmentation baseline AUC performance in the case of pancreas cancer detection with a drop of 1.0%, it can be noted that the operating point maximizing the balanced accuracy (bACC) was reached by the MO ensemble. Maximum bACC was reached by the MS ensembles for the liver and prostate cancer applications.

Figure 3 provides an illustration of the proposed ensemble approach. Two healthy cases are shown (one for liver, one for prostate): in both cases, the voxel-based semantic segmentation model predicted a relatively high probability, while the box-based object detection model predicted a low probability. In the liver case, ensembling also allowed to filter out a false-positive box prediction. Therefore, ensembling was beneficial compared to relying on either one of the baseline models. Two lesion cases are also shown (pancreas and prostate cancer cases). For the pancreas case, the semantic segmentation model predicted a relatively low probability ($p \approx 0.5$), while the object detection model predicted a high-probability box ($p \approx 0.9$). Ensembling therefore increased the confidence associated with the detected lesion. For the prostate cancer case, it can be noted that the object detection model predicted two boxes very close to each other around the softmax connected component, illustrating the interest of the MS matching methods over its MO counterpart.

**Table 1.** Comparison of the proposed ensemble methods with baseline models (nnU-Net for semantic segmentation and nnDetection for object detection). Patient-level AUC and lesion-level AP are presented. "MS ensembling" stands for max-score matching; "MO ensembling" stands for max-overlap matching. Best result in each column is in bold, second best is underlined. Metric standard deviations were computed by using 100 000 bootstrapped samples.

| Method | Lesion-level AP (%) | | | Patient-level AUC (%) | | |
|---|---|---|---|---|---|---|
| | Liver | Pancreas | Prostate | Liver | Pancreas | Prostate |
| nnU-Net [15] | $\underline{73.3}_{\pm 0.08}$ | $\underline{66.1}_{\pm 0.02}$ | $49.0_{\pm 0.06}$ | $92.3_{\pm 0.04}$ | $\mathbf{92.0}_{\pm \mathbf{0.01}}$ | $80.6_{\pm 0.04}$ |
| nnDetection [16] | $58.6_{\pm 0.08}$ | $56.7_{\pm 0.04}$ | $48.8_{\pm 0.08}$ | $82.1_{\pm 0.04}$ | $76.3_{\pm 0.02}$ | $80.7_{\pm 0.05}$ |
| MS ensembling | $71.8_{\pm 0.07}$ | $66.0_{\pm 0.01}$ | $\mathbf{57.4}_{\pm \mathbf{0.06}}$ | $\mathbf{93.9}_{\pm \mathbf{0.04}}$ | $90.9_{\pm 0.01}$ | $\mathbf{81.6}_{\pm \mathbf{0.04}}$ |
| MO ensembling | $\mathbf{73.4}_{\pm \mathbf{0.07}}$ | $\mathbf{66.8}_{\pm \mathbf{0.01}}$ | $\underline{56.9}_{\pm 0.06}$ | $\underline{92.9}_{\pm 0.04}$ | $\underline{91.0}_{\pm 0.01}$ | $\underline{80.8}_{\pm 0.04}$ |

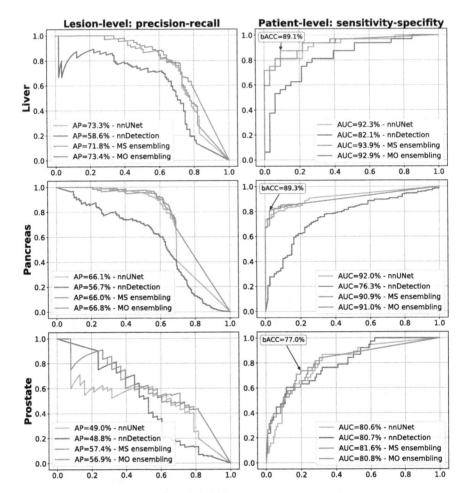

**Fig. 2.** Precision-recall and sensitivity-specificity curves computed on the test sets, for the two baseline methods (nnU-Net for semantic segmentation and nnDetection for object detection) and the two proposed ensemble approaches (max-score and max-overlap, noted MS and MO respectively). The operating points maximizing the balanced accuracy (bACC) are indicated with arrows. AP: Average-Precision. AUC: Area Under the Curve.

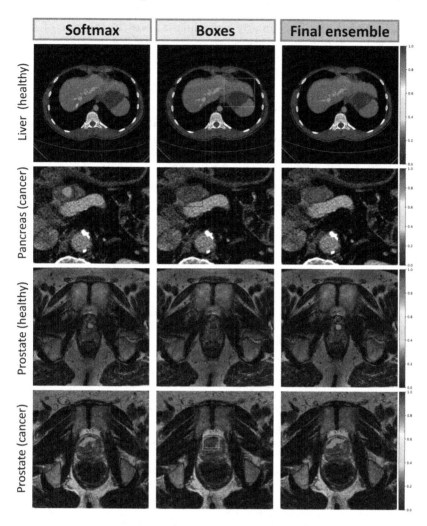

**Fig. 3.** Qualitative comparison of the proposed ensembling with stand-alone baseline methods: nnU-Net raw outputs (first column), nnDetection raw outputs (second column), proposed ensembling (last column).

## 4 Discussion and Conclusion

This work showed how combining off-the-shelf semantic segmentation and object detection models can boost lesion detection performance. The proposed approach makes no hypothesis over the internal architectural details of the ensembled network, but rather leverages complementary voxel-based and box-based predictions. Two variations in the ensembling approach were proposed and evaluated in three different oncology applications: liver, pancreas, and prostate cancer. Compared to state-of-the-art baseline models, our ensembling method improved the lesion detection AP across all considered applications.

Ensembling led to a particularly pronounced boost in the case of prostate cancer detection. Significant prostate cancer is particularly difficult to detect for radiologists, as illustrated by the typically low inter and intra-reader agreement with PI-RADS scoring [20,21]. For the liver and pancreas cancer application, performance improvement at lesion-level after ensembling was moderate with respect to the nnU-Net semantic segmentation baseline. We may hypothesize that the cancer cases in the public databases that defined our test sets were prototypical, presenting conspicuous lesions and therefore leaving little room for uncertainty for a well-calibrated baseline method.

Ultimately, we believe that ensembling different deep learning approaches improves the robustness and favors the generalization of lesion detection methods. Future work should focus on refining ensembling strategies and evaluate such approaches on other clinical applications.

# References

1. Ronneberger, O., Fischer, P., Brox, T.: U-Net: convolutional networks for biomedical image segmentation. In: Navab, N., Hornegger, J., Wells, W.M., Frangi, A.F. (eds.) MICCAI 2015. LNCS, vol. 9351, pp. 234–241. Springer, Cham (2015). https://doi.org/10.1007/978-3-319-24574-4_28
2. Lin, T.-Y., Goyal, P., Girshick, R., He, K., Dollár, P.: Focal loss for dense object detection. In: 2017 IEEE International Conference on Computer Vision (ICCV), pp. 2999–3007 (2017)
3. Lin, T.-Y., Dollár, P., Girshick, R., He, K., Hariharan, B., Belongie, S.: Feature pyramid networks for object detection. In: 2017 IEEE Conference on Computer Vision and Pattern Recognition (CVPR), pp. 936–944 (2017)
4. He, K., Gkioxari, G., Dollár, P., Girshick, R.: Mask R-CNN. In: Proceedings of the IEEE International Conference on Computer Vision, pp. 2961–2969 (2017)
5. Jaeger, P.F., et al.: Retina U-Net: embarrassingly simple exploitation of segmentation supervision for medical object detection. CoRR, abs/1811.08661 (2018)
6. Lei, Y., et al.: Breast tumor segmentation in 3D automatic breast ultrasound using mask scoring R-CNN. Med. Phys. **48**(1), 204–214 (2021)
7. Huang, Y.-J., et al.: 3-D ROI-aware U-Net for accurate and efficient colorectal tumor segmentation. IEEE Trans. Cybern. **51**(11), 5397–5408 (2020)
8. Bilic, P., et al.: The liver tumor segmentation benchmark (LiTS). Med. Image Anal. **84**, 102680 (2023)
9. Soler, L., et al.: 3D image reconstruction for comparison of algorithm database: a patient specific anatomical and medical image database. IRCAD, Strasbourg, France, Technical report, vol. 1(1) (2010)
10. Kavur, A.E., Selver, M.A., Dicle, O., Bariş, M., Gezer, N.S.: CHAOS - Combined (CT-MR) Healthy Abdominal Organ Segmentation Challenge Data, April 2019
11. Simpson, A.L., et al.: A large annotated medical image dataset for the development and evaluation of segmentation algorithms. CoRR, abs/1902.09063 (2019)
12. Roth, H.R., et al.: DeepOrgan: multi-level deep convolutional networks for automated pancreas segmentation. In: Navab, N., Hornegger, J., Wells III, W.M., Frangi, A.F. (eds.) Medical Image Computing and Computer-Assisted Intervention - MICCAI 2015–18th International Conference, Munich, Germany, 5–9 October 2015, Proceedings, Part I. LNCS, vol. 9349, pp. 556–564. Springer, Cham (2015). https://doi.org/10.1007/978-3-319-24553-9_68

13. Saha, A., et al.: The PI-CAI Challenge: Public Training and Development Dataset, June 2022
14. Adams, L.C., et al.: Prostate158 - an expert-annotated 3T MRI dataset and algorithm for prostate cancer detection. Comput. Biol. Med. **148**, 105817 (2022)
15. Isensee, F., Jaeger, P.F., Kohl, S.A.A., Petersen, J., Maier-Hein, K.H.: nnU-Net: a self-configuring method for deep learning-based biomedical image segmentation. Nat. Methods **18**(2), 203–211 (2021)
16. Baumgartner, M., Jäger, P.F., Isensee, F., Maier-Hein, K.H.: nnDetection: a self-configuring method for medical object detection. In: de Bruijne, M., et al. (eds.) Medical Image Computing and Computer Assisted Intervention-MICCAI 2021: 24th International Conference, Strasbourg, France, 27 September–1 October 2021, Proceedings, Part V 24, vol. 12905, pp. 530–539. Springer, Cham (2021). https://doi.org/10.1007/978-3-030-87240-3_51
17. Antonelli, M., et al.: The medical segmentation decathlon. Nat. Commun. **13**(1), 4128 (2022)
18. McKinney, S.M., et al.: International evaluation of an AI system for breast cancer screening. Nature **577**(7788), 89–94 (2020)
19. Hosseinzadeh, M., Saha, A., Brand, P., Slootweg, I., de Rooij, M., Huisman, H.: Deep learning-assisted prostate cancer detection on bi-parametric MRI: minimum training data size requirements and effect of prior knowledge. Eur. Radiol. **32**(4), 2224–2234 (2022)
20. Greer, M.D., et al.: Interreader variability of prostate imaging reporting and data system version 2 in detecting and assessing prostate cancer lesions at prostate MRI. AJR. Am. J. Roentgenol. **212**(6), 1197–1205 (2019)
21. Smith, C.P., et al.: Intra-and interreader reproducibility of PI-RADSv2: a multi-reader study. J. Magn. Reson. Imaging **49**(6), 1694–1703 (2019)

# Advancing Abdominal Organ and PDAC Segmentation Accuracy with Task-Specific Interactive Models

Sanne E. Okel[1], Christiaan G. A. Viviers[1(✉)], Mark Ramaekers[2],
Terese A. E. Hellström[2], Nick Tasios[3], Dimitrios Mavroeidis[3], Jon Pluyter[3],
Igor Jacobs[3], Misha Luyer[2], Peter H. N. de With[1], and Fons van der Sommen[1]

[1] Eindhoven University of Technology, Eindhoven 5612, AZ, The Netherlands
c.g.a.viviers@tue.nl
[2] Catharina Ziekenhuis, Eindhoven 5623, EJ, The Netherlands
[3] Philips Research, Eindhoven 5656, AE, The Netherlands

**Abstract.** Deep learning-based segmentation algorithms have the potential to expedite the cumbersome clinical task of creating detailed target delineations for disease diagnosis and prognosis. However, these algorithms have yet to be widely adopted in clinical practice, partly because the resulting model segmentations often fall short of the necessary accuracy and robustness that clinical practice demands. This research aims to make AI work in the real world, where domain shift is anticipated and inter-observer variability is inherent to medical practice. While current research aims to design models that can address these challenges, we propose an alternative approach that involves minimal user (clinician) interaction in the segmentation process. By combining the pattern recognition abilities of neural networks with the domain knowledge of clinicians, segmentation predictions can deliver the desired clinical result with little effort on the part of clinicians. To test this approach, we implemented, fine-tuned and compared three state-of-the-art (SOTA) interactive AI (IAI) methods for segmenting six different abdominal organs and pancreatic ductal adenocarcinoma (PDAC), an extremely challenging structure to segment, in CT images. We demonstrate that the fine-tuned RITM (Reviving Iterative Training with Mask Guidance for Interactive Segmentation) method can achieve higher segmentation accuracy than non-interactive SOTA models with as few as three clicks, potentially reducing the time required for treatment planning. Overall, IAI may be an effective method for bridging the gap between what deep learning-based segmentation algorithms have to offer and the high standard that is required for patient care.

**Keywords:** Interactive segmentation · Abdominal organs · Deep learning · Pancreatic tumor

S. E. Okel and C. G. A. Viviers—Contributed equally.

**Supplementary Information** The online version contains supplementary material available at https://doi.org/10.1007/978-3-031-47076-9_6.

# 1   Introduction

Increasingly more deep learning-based segmentation algorithms are being posed for computer-aided detection (CADe) and diagnosis (CADx) methods or supporting tools in the clinical workflow. Semantic segmentation is a method that has, arguably, received the most attention due to the highly detailed information derived from medical imaging modalities such as CT or MRI images. Obtaining the highly detailed segmentations required for improved disease treatment planning is currently still a manual and time-consuming task since current state-of-the-art (SOTA) methods do not yet meet this high accuracy.

Pancreatic cancer care is an example of such an application where CADx can support clinicians throughout the course of treatment. AI can be deployed to improve early detection of pancreatic ductal adenocarcinoma (PDAC), the most common form of pancreatic cancer, and consequently increase the patient survival rate [8]. Recent work [10, 24] employs a deep learning-based model to distinguish cancer tissue from non-cancerous tissue, resulting in a model sensitivity of 0.983 and 0.99, respectively. While detection is the first vital aspect of the problem, follow-up tasks such as tumor resection planning requires extremely detailed semantic segmentations of the tumor and surrounding anatomical structures, such as the vessels, to determine the extent of the tumor contact or involvement. Existing semantic segmentation approaches do not yet meet this high accuracy requirement, especially for the tumor.

Majority of deep learning-based semantic segmentation algorithms are trained on images and labels obtained from a single institute and often, even a single expert annotator. The models are then trained to match the provided annotations, which fails to impress when predictions do not perfectly match that of the annotator, does not align with a second readers opinion [28] or completely breaks down in a new setting. The current research trend is to design better deep models to adhere to these shortcomings, while it is possible that there will always be edge cases unaccounted for or different opinions on a correct segmentation. As such, the actual adoption into medical practice of AI-based CADx remains rather low [2].

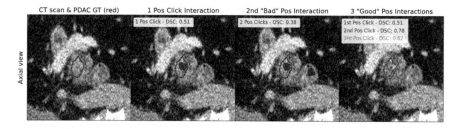

**Fig. 1.** Positive 1 radius click (5 pixels) interactions using the PDAC fine-tuned RITM framework for tumor segmentation.

We propose a novel use of interactive automated image segmentation, also known as Interactive AI (IAI), to include the user in the segmentation process of a specific structure of interest. In IAI, the user's preferences are encoded and supplied along with the query image to aid in the segmentation. The primary objective is to enable clinicians to achieve highly accurate annotations of the structures of interest in the shortest amount of time. IAI has multiple technological advantages over non-interactive AI. For example (1) when incorporating the user's knowledge, the result of the network will be flexibly accurate (incorporate user preference) and potentially robust [11]. This has follow-up advantages such as (2) speeding up the time to acquiring clinically relevant structure annotations and (3) potentially require less annotated data, since models can utilize an additional source of valuable information [20].

This research investigates the potential of click-based IAI for enhancing segmentation accuracy of abdominal structures (of various shapes, sizes and visibility). Additionally, we focus on PDAC, an extremely difficult structure to segment due to its limited contrast w.r.t. surrounding structures and often small size. Current SOTA approaches obtain a dismal 0.57 Dice Similarity Coefficient (DSC) [13], which is insufficient for follow-up resectability assessment. Although the focus of this study is abdominal structure segmentation, the approach is not limited to these structures and it is encouraged to investigate the potential of IAI for difficult and low segmentation accuracy structures, such as tumors. Our contributions are as follows:

1. The RITM with HRNet+OCR, CDNet and the SegFormer-B3 variant of FocalClick are implemented in an interactive segmentation framework and fine-tune for abdominal organ and PDAC segmentation from CT image slices.
2. We investigate the number of clicks required to achieve competitive organ segmentation results and show that the RITM implementation adapts well to the medical domain.
3. We show that it is possible to surpass prior methods' segmentation accuracy and present SOTA user guided segmentation performance (Tumor 0.61 mean DSC at 3 clicks and 0.75 mean DSC at 5 clicks) with minimal interaction.

Using IAI, the extremely high segmentation accuracies required for critical structures such as pancreatic tumor can be obtained with little interaction. With the accurate, fast and reliable description of the tumor obtained, assessment of follow up work and procedure planning can be accelerated.

## 2   Related Work

Automated and accurate segmentation of abdominal organs from CT images is of high value in CADx methods. The current best performing methods for the various abdominal structures (to the best of our knowledge) are: Aorta [3], SMA [13], CBD [6], Pancreas [17], PD [21] and PDAC [13]. These works reflect the significant research efforts dedicated to achieving high segmentation accuracies, driven by a compelling clinical demand for improved performance.

The field of interactive segmentation has explored several types of user input [19], including (1) bounding boxes as weak annotations for the segmentation of the fetal brain and lungs in MR images [18], (2) scribbles placed on both the foreground and the background of the image for improving the brain tumor segmentation [25] and user clicks, the most widely used input type for interactive segmentation are user clicks, where a plethora of variations exist [14, 22, 30]. Possibly the most important reason for implementing clicks over scribbles is the reduced difficulty in simulating the input for training the model [22].

Interactive segmentation is a very active research topic, but has only recently been investigated in a medical context due to the increasing requirements being posed for successful clinical adoption. For instance, recently, the Segment Anything Model (SAM) [9] was adjusted for the medical domain [15]. The approach shows impressive performance while not being trained on task-specific data, but ultimately still lags behind the task-specific expert models, indicating that limited interaction alone might not be sufficient to achieve the high segmentation accuracy required. Similarly, [16] showed that their interactive segmentation framework is flexible, but still requires many click interactions to achieve the desired level of accuracy. On the other hand, [30] developed a method where a user is prompted to click on the approximate center of the object of interest as a starting point for the AI. From the center point, a bi-directional ConvRNN neural network segments the kidney tumor or prostate. The interaction combined with task-specific fine-tuning results in improvement over non-interactive methods.

## 3   Method

### 3.1   Dataset

In this research, we collected and annotated contrast-enhanced CT scans of 148 patients from the Catharina Hospital Eindhoven. Patients (98 patients with and 50 patients without PDAC) older than 18 years who underwent surgical treatment at the Catharina Hospital, were eligible for this work when a complete pathology and surgical report were available. For some patients, multiple CT-scans at different phases were available, resulting in a total of 243 scans. Seven anatomical structures were selected and annotated by a resident supervised by an expert radiologist for IAI: the aorta, superior mesenteric artery (SMA), gastroduodenal artery (GA), pancreas, common bile duct (CBD), pancreatic duct (PD) and the pancreatic tumor (specifically PDAC). These were chosen to explore the feasibility of IAI on a variety of structures of different shapes, sizes and visibility. In this work we implement interactive segmentation on a 2D slice basis and as such, convert the 3D CT data to 2D axial slices, resulting in 42,558 slices with at least one of the targets present. The data was pre-processed in line with the steps employed in the nnU-Net [7].

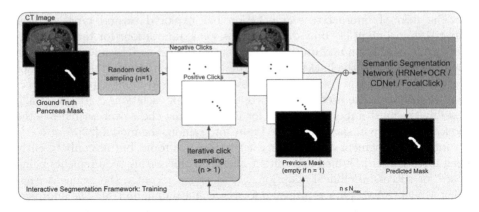

**Fig. 2.** Interaction framework employed for training, where $n$ is the iteration number and $\oplus$ indicates channel-wise concatenation of the four inputs.

## 3.2    Interaction Framework

In this research we adapt a click-based (binary disks) interactive segmentation framework for segmentation of a structure of interest in 2D slices from CT images. Although multiple other types of click representations were explored in literature (such as distance maps or Normal distributions [12]), binary disks generally resulted in the highest performance [1], therefore in this research the clicks are encoded as 2D binary masks with a fixed 1 radius (5 pixels). The proposed approach adopts two types of clicks. One click channel consists of the positive clicks, which are by definition placed on the structure of interest, while the negative click channel represents the background. The adapted pipeline for segmentation from CT images is visualized in Fig. 2. In the first iteration during training ($n = 1$), positive clicks and negative clicks are randomly sampled to initialize the click channels. The 2D CT image slice, the click channels and an empty mask are channel-wise combined and given as input to the segmentation model. The segmentation model then predicts a mask based on the provided input, according to the click sampling strategy described in [12]. We experiment with three segmentation models in this work: the HRNet+OCR model, the CDNet and the FocalClick model.   The first approach implemented is the Reviving Iterative Training with Mask Guidance for Interactive Segmentation (RITM) method [22] which is publicly available[1]. The HRNetV2+OCR model [23,26] was initialized with ImageNet pre-trained weights (HRNet-W64-C to be exact)[2] and a normalized Focal Loss (NFL) was used as the loss function during training. The second approach consists of the Conditional Diffusion Network (CDNet) [4] and the respective codebase is available *ClickSeg*[3]. The DeepLabV3+ with a ResNet-34 backbone was selected as the segmentation module in the network.

---

[1] saic-vul/ritm_interactive_segmentation.
[2] HRNet/HRNet-Image-Classification.
[3] XavierCHEN34/ClickSEG.

The model as initialized with pre-trained weights[4]. The more recent approach, FocalClick [5], was also implemented as a third method in this research. The network was trained with two different segmentation modules, namely HRNet and SegFormer-B3 [29]. The latter option yielded better results. Again, the network was initialized with pre-trained weights before our training commenced. In addition to the above mentioned experiments, we also optimize a 3D U-Net (based on the implementation by [27]) for all the same anatomical structures for comparison.

### 3.3 Training Details and Evaluation Criteria

In this early research we prepare the interactive framework for single class segmentation. For each of the anatomical structure in the dataset a new model is trained. The data subset is split into a patient specific 70%/15%/15% train/validation/test split. During training, for each batch a maximum number of click iterations is randomly chosen to prevent excessively long training time. In each iteration, the predicted mask is used to sample another click, concatenated with the image and the click channels and fed into the same model again. The same holds for the automated evaluation of the model, where random samples (positive and negative clicks) are taken from the difference between the ground-truth (GT) label and prediction. The performance of the model was evaluated using the mean DSC across our test set at click number $k$ ($DSC_{@k}$) and the mean number of clicks (NoC) required to obtain a specific mean DSC (for example, mean number of clicks per image to get 90% DSC - $NoC_{@90}$). Training is carried out on a V100-16GB GPU and model hyperparameters are kept as default in the respective repositories.

## 4 Results

The performance (expressed in DSC) of all three models for the seven structures acquired during automated evaluation on the test set is summarized in Table 1. In addition, we compare the performance with our non-interactive AI approach (3D U-Net). The RITM method with HRNet+OCR model outperforms the two other methods, FocalClick and CDNet, for all seven structures. The only exception is the $DSC_{@1}$ for the GA where the CDNet outperforms RITM. However, after an extra click, the CDNet model appears to collapse as performance deteriorates. Overall, IAI enables to the highest DSC results for the pancreas, aorta and CBD segmentations. To obtain an DSC of 0.8, approximately 2, 3 and 5 clicks are required, respectively. However, for a small increase in accuracy, a significantly higher NoCs are required, which sometimes still falls short of the 3D U-Net results. For the other structures, such as the PD and tumor, the model achieves an impressive 0.67 and 0.61 DSC at 3 clicks, outperforming our non-interactive 3D U-Net experiments, with minimal input.

---

[4] rwightman/pytorch-pretrained-gluonresnet.

**Table 1.** Performance (number of clicks (NoC) to obtain a DSC score (NoC$_{@DSC}$) and mean DSC after a specific number of clicks (DSC$_{@Clicks}$)) of the IAI models with a one radius click interaction on the seven different anatomical structures. A positive click (foreground) is followed by a negative click (background). The performance (2D DSC) of our 3D U-Net is added for comparison.

| Structure | ↓ NoC$_{@80}$ | NoC$_{@85}$ | NoC$_{@90}$ | ↑ DSC$_{@1}$ | DSC$_{@2}$ | DSC$_{@3}$ | DSC$_{@5}$ | DSC$_{@10}$ | DSC$_{@20}$ | 2D DSC |
|---|---|---|---|---|---|---|---|---|---|---|
| | | | | FocalClick | | | | | | |
| Aorta | 7.50 | 10.8 | 16.2 | 0.62 | 0.73 | 0.76 | **0.80** | **0.84** | 0.87 | |
| SMA | 37.0 | 42.8 | 47.8 | 0.42 | 0.20 | 0.20 | 0.20 | 0.25 | 0.39 | |
| CBD | 29.5 | 37.7 | 45.3 | 0.48 | 0.53 | 0.56 | 0.59 | 0.63 | 0.67 | |
| GA | 43.4 | 46.6 | 48.7 | 0.41 | 0.18 | 0.18 | 0.19 | 0.21 | 0.23 | |
| Pancreas | 12.9 | 16.4 | 23.5 | 0.55 | 0.56 | 0.58 | 0.62 | 0.72 | 0.84 | |
| PD | 46.6 | 48.2 | 49.3 | 0.43 | 0.26 | 0.27 | 0.27 | 0.26 | 0.25 | |
| Tumor | 46.5 | 48.3 | 49.6 | 0.38 | 0.12 | 0.10 | 0.11 | 0.13 | 0.20 | |
| | | | | CDNet | | | | | | |
| Aorta | 12.1 | 15.8 | 21.4 | 0.71 | 0.59 | 0.61 | 0.65 | 0.72 | 0.78 | |
| SMA | 31.8 | 39.8 | 48.2 | 0.42 | 0.25 | 0.29 | 0.34 | 0.36 | 0.31 | |
| CBD | 26.2 | 32.3 | 42.7 | 0.48 | 0.26 | 0.32 | 0.40 | 0.51 | 0.60 | |
| GA | 43.8 | 47.5 | 49.3 | **0.58** | 0.01 | 0.01 | 0.01 | 0.02 | 0.06 | |
| Pancreas | 28.2 | 34.6 | 41.4 | 0.61 | 0.35 | 0.24 | 0.22 | 0.32 | 0.46 | |
| PD | 42.0 | 47.7 | 49.6 | 0.65 | 0.02 | 0.02 | 0.01 | 0.01 | 0.02 | |
| Tumor | 49.5 | 49.9 | 50.0 | 0.43 | 0.01 | 0.02 | 0.01 | 0.01 | 0.02 | |
| | | | | RITM | | | | | | 3D U-Net |
| Aorta | **3.60** | **5.20** | **9.60** | **0.86** | **0.82** | **0.80** | 0.79 | **0.84** | **0.89** | **0.90** |
| SMA | **11.4** | **20.9** | **34.1** | **0.71** | **0.36** | **0.61** | **0.62** | **0.62** | **0.74** | **0.81** |
| CBD | **5.30** | **7.50** | **14.3** | **0.72** | **0.76** | **0.76** | **0.78** | **0.83** | **0.88** | 0.76 |
| GA | **21.4** | **28.5** | **38.3** | 0.47 | **0.44** | **0.54** | **0.60** | **0.69** | **0.78** | 0.56 |
| Pancreas | **1.80** | **2.60** | **5.70** | **0.86** | **0.86** | **0.87** | **0.89** | **0.92** | **0.94** | 0.87 |
| PD | **10.1** | **17.0** | **26.8** | **0.67** | **0.40** | **0.67** | **0.70** | **0.78** | **0.86** | 0.55 |
| Tumor | **6.40** | **10.0** | **17.6** | **0.57** | **0.48** | **0.61** | **0.75** | **0.86** | **0.89** | 0.41 |

## 5   Discussion

The RITM with HRNet methed is the best interactive segmentation method in the presented medical context of abdominal organ delineation. While model behavior is difficult to explain, the main hypothesis for the higher performance is that unlike the well-known encoder-decoder networks, where high-to-low resolution convolutions are implemented, HRNet retains high resolution representations to enable pixel-level clicks to propagate throughout the whole network. CDNet with a DeeplabV3+ with ResNet-34 backbone, which implements atrous convolutions to prevent downsampling of the input, presents results of lower quality. The local refinement module in the FocalClick network might be an explanation for the lower performance of the network. Upon clicking, a small crop around the click is taken and inserted into a local refinement module for further improvement of the segmentation. This process might not yield the required information for segmentation refinement since the CT slices might not contain enough contrast for clear delineation of the structure and a more global context is preferred. In addition, the authors already noticed that their approach has lower segmentation performance on smaller structures. Therefore, to successfully implement IAI for medical image segmentation, a model that preserves high resolution representations is a minimum requirement. This research employs a click interaction of 1 radius, which is the equivalent of 5 pixels. This implementation elucidates the segmentation performance upper-bounded limitations of certain structures. Our automated evaluation includes sampling a positive click followed by a negative click, which can include less informative samples (e.g., pixel differences at the segmentation border) or no need for negative clicks early during the evaluations. This explains the initial performance drop observed after the second click during segmentation. Employing a second positive click could be more informative and effective, as shown in Fig. 1. By exploring different clicking strategies, the total number of clicks needed to achieve high DSC can be further reduced. Comparing our 2D RITM method with the 3D U-Net (despite the inherent 2D vs. 3D discrepancy), valuable insights into the performance of the RITM approach are obtained as it outperforms the 3D U-Net in 5 out of 7 tasks within 5 or fewer clicks. However, for the Aorta and SMA, although an initial high segmentation accuracy is achieved after one click, we postulate that negative clicks and large disc sizes adversely affect the model's performance, hindering it from attaining the exceptionally high DSC scores observed with the 3D U-Net.

## 6    Future Work

This research applies 2D IAI for segmentation in images from 3D volumes, with potential for further improvements using 3D segmentation models from user clicks. Future work should investigate variable input size effects, utilizing larger discs for initial segmentations and smaller discs for refinements to speed up segmentation. The SAM [9] model shows promise for interactive segmentation, but initial results in the medical domain were underwhelming [15]. Therefore, fine-tuning these models for specific targets could unlock additional enhancements.

**Prospect of Application**: This work holds promise for CAD medical applications where current automated segmentation falls short of the high clinical performance required. It offers clinicians flexible and rapid control over resulting segmentations, addressing the need for improved accuracy and user control in medical imaging tasks, such as PDAC and other cancer resectability assessment.

## 7    Conclusion

This research is one of the first works to explore the potential of task-specific interactive image segmentation in CAD medical applications. We compare three different SOTA methods for interactive segmentation on a new abdominal organ and pancreatic tumor dataset. The dataset contains large, easier to segment structures, as well as the notably difficult PDAC, making it an ideal dataset to test the adaption of click-based IAI to the medical domain. The RITM framework outperforms FocalClick, CDNet and our 3D U-Net and is capable of segmenting the abdominal structures of interest at competitive accuracies with as little as three clicks on average. As expected, with more clicks the framework rapidly surpasses non-interactive segmentation methods in performance. This holds especially true for the pancreatic duct ($0.70$ $DSC_{@5}$) and tumor ($0.75$ $DSC_{@5}$) being segmented with notably high accuracy using minimal user input. These encouraging results reveal that IAI can help bridge the gap between what current deep learning-based segmentation algorithms have offer and the high standard that is required for patient care. Clinicians can rapidly express their segmentation preference, resolve ambiguities and obtain highly accurate segmentations for follow-up tasks.

# References

1. Benenson, R., Popov, S., Ferrari, V.: Large-scale interactive object segmentation with human annotators. In: Proceedings of the IEEE/CVF Conference on Computer Vision and Pattern Recognition, pp. 11700–11709 (2019)
2. Briganti, G., Le Moine, O.: Artificial intelligence in medicine: today and tomorrow. Front. Med. **7**, 27 (2020)
3. Chen, W., Huang, H., Huang, J., Wang, K., Qin, H., Wong, K.K.: Deep learning-based medical image segmentation of the aorta using xr-msf-u-net. Comput. Methods Prog. Biomed. **225**, 107073 (2022)
4. Chen, X., Zhao, Z., Yu, F., Zhang, Y., Duan, M.: Conditional diffusion for interactive segmentation. In: Proceedings of the IEEE/CVF International Conference on Computer Vision, pp. 7345–7354 (2021)
5. Chen, X., Zhao, Z., Zhang, Y., Duan, M., Qi, D., Zhao, H.: Focalclick: towards practical interactive image segmentation. In: Proceedings of the IEEE/CVF Conference on Computer Vision and Pattern Recognition, pp. 1300–1309 (2022)
6. Huang, L., et al.: Intelligent difficulty scoring and assistance system for endoscopic extraction of common bile duct stones based on deep learning: multicenter study. Endoscopy **53**(05), 491–498 (2021)
7. Isensee, F., Jaeger, P.F., Kohl, S.A., Petersen, J., Maier-Hein, K.H.: nnu-net: a self-configuring method for deep learning-based biomedical image segmentation. Nat. Methods **18**(2), 203–211 (2021)
8. Kikuyama, M., Kamisawa, T., Kuruma, S., Chiba, K., Kawaguchi, S., Terada, S., Satoh, T.: Early diagnosis to improve the poor prognosis of pancreatic cancer. Cancers **10**(2), 48 (2018)
9. Kirillov, A., et al.: Segment anything. arXiv preprint arXiv:2304.02643 (2023)
10. Liu, K.L., et al.: Deep learning to distinguish pancreatic cancer tissue from non-cancerous pancreatic tissue: a retrospective study with cross-racial external validation. Lancet Digit. Health **2**(6), e303–e313 (2020)
11. Luo, X., et al: Mideepseg: minimally interactive segmentation of unseen objects from medical images using deep learning. Media **72**, 102102 (2021)
12. Mahadevan, S., Voigtlaender, P., Leibe, B.: Iteratively trained interactive segmentation. arXiv preprint arXiv:1805.04398 (2018)

13. Mahmoudi, T., et al.: Segmentation of pancreatic ductal adenocarcinoma (PDAC) and surrounding vessels in CT images using deep convolutional neural networks and texture descriptors. Sci. Rep. **12**(1), 1–14 (2022)
14. Maninis, K.K., Caelles, S., Pont-Tuset, J., Van Gool, L.: Deep extreme cut: from extreme points to object segmentation. In: Proceedings of the IEEE Conference on Computer Vision and Pattern Recognition, pp. 616–625 (2018)
15. Mazurowski, M.A., Dong, H., Gu, H., Yang, J., Konz, N., Zhang, Y.: Segment anything model for medical image analysis: an experimental study. arXiv preprint arXiv:2304.10517 (2023)
16. Mikhailov, I., Chauveau, B., Bourdel, N., Bartoli, A.: A deep learning-based interactive medical image segmentation framework. In: Wu, S., Shabestari, B., Xing, L. (eds.) Applications of Medical Artificial Intelligence: First International Workshop, AMAI 2022, Held in Conjunction with MICCAI 2022, Singapore, September 18, 2022, Proceedings, pp. 98–107. Springer, Cham (2022). https://doi.org/10.1007/978-3-031-17721-7_11
17. Panda, A., et al.: Two-stage deep learning model for fully automated pancreas segmentation on computed tomography: comparison with intra-reader and inter-reader reliability at full and reduced radiation dose on an external dataset. Med. Phys. **48**(5), 2468–2481 (2021)
18. Rajchl, M., et al.: Deepcut: object segmentation from bounding box annotations using convolutional neural networks. IEEE Trans. Med. Imaging **36**(2), 674–683 (2016)
19. Ramadan, H., Lachqar, C., Tairi, H.: A survey of recent interactive image segmentation methods. Comput. Visual Media **6**, 355–384 (2020)
20. Sardar, M., Banerjee, S., Mitra, S.: Iris segmentation using interactive deep learning. IEEE Access **8**, 219322–219330 (2020)
21. Shen, C., et al.: A cascaded fully convolutional network framework for dilated pancreatic duct segmentation. IJCARS **17**(2), 343–354 (2022)
22. Sofiiuk, K., Petrov, I.A., Konushin, A.: Reviving iterative training with mask guidance for interactive segmentation. arXiv preprint arXiv:2102.06583 (2021)
23. Sun, K., Xiao, B., Liu, D., Wang, J.: Deep high-resolution representation learning for human pose estimation. In: CVPR (2019)
24. Viviers, C.G.A.., et al.: Improved pancreatic tumor detection by utilizing clinically-relevant secondary features. In: Ali, S., et al. (eds.) Cancer Prevention Through Early Detection: First International Workshop, CaPTion 2022, Held in Conjunction with MICCAI 2022, Singapore, September 22, 2022, Proceedings, pp. 139–148. Springer, Cham (2022). https://doi.org/10.1007/978-3-031-17979-2_14
25. Wang, G., et al.: Deepigeos: a deep interactive geodesic framework for medical image segmentation. IEEE TPAMI **41**(7), 1559–1572 (2018)
26. Wang, J., et al.: Deep high-resolution representation learning for visual recognition. In: TPAMI (2019)
27. Wolny, A., et al.: Accurate and versatile 3d segmentation of plant tissues at cellular resolution. eLife **9**, e57613 (2020)
28. Wong, J., et al.: Effects of interobserver and interdisciplinary segmentation variabilities on CT-based radiomics for pancreatic cancer. Sci. Rep. **11**(1), 1–12 (2021)
29. Xie, E., Wang, W., Yu, Z., Anandkumar, A., Alvarez, J.M., Luo, P.: Segformer: simple and efficient design for semantic segmentation with transformers. Adv. Neural. Inf. Process. Syst. **34**, 12077–12090 (2021)
30. Zhang, J., et al.: Interactive medical image segmentation via a point-based interaction. Artif. Intell. Med. **111**, 101998 (2021)

# Anatomical Location-Guided Deep Learning-Based Genetic Cluster Identification of Pheochromocytomas and Paragangliomas from CT Images

Bikash Santra[1]([✉]), Abhishek Jha[2], Pritam Mukherjee[1], Mayank Patel[2], Karel Pacak[2], and Ronald M. Summers[1]

[1] Imaging Biomarkers and Computer-Aided Diagnosis Laboratory, Radiology and Imaging Sciences, Clinical Center, National Institutes of Health, Bethesda, MD, USA
`bikashsantra85@gmail.com`, {`pritam.mukherjee,rms`}`@nih.gov`
[2] National Institute of Child Health and Human Development, National Institutes of Health, Bethesda, MD, USA
`mayank.patel@nih.gov`, `karel@mail.nih.gov`

**Abstract.** Pheochromocytomas and paragangliomas (PPGLs) are respectively intra-adrenal and extra-adrenal neuroendocrine tumors whose pathogenesis and progression are greatly regulated by genetics. Identifying PPGL's genetic clusters (*SDHx, VHL/EPAS1, kinase signaling,* and sporadic) is essential as PPGL's management varies critically on its genotype. But, genetic testing for PPGLs is expensive and time-consuming. Contrast-enhanced CT (CE-CT) scans of PPGL patients are usually acquired at the beginning of patient management for PPGL staging and determining the next therapeutic steps. Given a CE-CT sub-image of the PPGL, this work demonstrates a two-branch vision transformer (*PPGL-Transformer*) to identify each tumor's genetic cluster. The standard of reference for each tumor included two items: its genetic cluster from clinical testing, and its anatomical location. One branch of our *PPGL-Transformer* identifies PPGL's anatomic location while the other one characterizes PPGL's genetic type. A supervised contrastive learning strategy was used to train the *PPGL-Transformer* by optimizing contrastive and classification losses for PPGLs' genetic group and anatomic location. Our method was evaluated on a dataset comprised of 1010 PPGLs extracted from the CE-CT images of 289 patients. *PPGL-Transformer* achieved an accuracy of $0.63\pm0.08$, balanced accuracy (BA) of $0.63\pm0.06$ and F1-score of $0.46\pm0.08$ on five-fold cross-validation and outperformed competing methods by 2–29% on accuracy, 3–18% on BA and 3–14% on F1-score. The performance for the sporadic cluster was higher on BA ($0.68\pm0.13$) while the performance for the *SDHx* cluster was higher on recall ($0.83\pm0.06$) and F1-score ($0.74\pm0.07$).

**Keywords:** Pheochromocytoma · Paraganglioma · Genetic mutations · Transformer · CT images · Deep learning · Radiogenomics · PPGL

S. Wu et al. (Eds.): AMAI 2023, LNCS 14313, pp. 62–71, 2024.
https://doi.org/10.1007/978-3-031-47076-9_7

# 1   Introduction

Pheochromocytomas and paragangliomas (PPGLs) are tumors of the autonomic nervous system that originate from the chromaffin tissue in the adrenal medulla or extra-adrenal ganglia, respectively. PPGLs are rare and their occurrence is in two to eight per million humans [5]. 2–26 % of the PPGLs develop metastases while the rest are usually benign [18]. Since histopathology images are unable to differentiate benign and malignant tumors, the World Health Organization recommends the term metastatic instead of malignant. In case of PPGLs, metastatic is described by their presence in the locations (such as bones and lymph nodes) where paraganglia or chromaffin cells do not typically exist [18]. PPGLs are a special kind of tumor that is strongly associated with genetic pathogenic variants. In approximately 40% of PPGLs, a germline pathogenic variant is identified in one of the susceptibility genes; the remaining 60% are considered apparently sporadic. The genetic pathogenic variant of PPGL can be loosely divided into four genetic groups: cluster 1A (*SDHx*), cluster 1B (*VHL/EPAS1*), cluster 2 [*kinase signaling (KS)*], and sporadic. The most frequently encountered pathogenic variants are in *SDHx (A/B/C/D/AF2)*. *SDHx* and *VHL/EPAS1* are characterized by pseudohypoxia affecting the hypoxia-signaling pathway. *KS* includes the pathogenic variants *RET, NF1, TMEM127, MAX,* and *HRAS,* while sporadic represents the cluster for which the pathogenic variants are not identified yet [8].

Clinical management of patients with PPGL critically varies on the PPGL's genetic cluster type [16]. Therefore, for patient management, genetic testing is strongly recommended for all patients with PPGL [8]. But genetic testing is expensive and time-consuming. At the beginning of patient management, whole-body CE-CT scans are acquired to determine the tumor's location and staging and to decide the next therapeutic steps. CE-CT scans are inexpensive and time-efficient compared to genetic testing. Further in [8], it is described that the

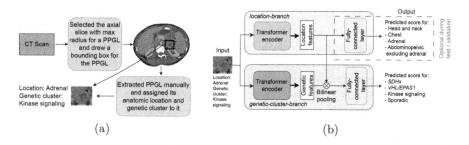

(a)                                    (b)

**Fig. 1.** (a) Process of extracting an axial slice containing maximum radius of a PPGL from a CE-CT scan, drawing 2D bounding boxes for the PPGL, assigning anatomic location and genetic cluster labels to the PPGL and cropping out of the 2D sub-image for the PPGL from the axial slice. (b) Work-flow of inference on the proposed two-branch *PPGL-Transformer*, where its *genetic-cluster-branch* identifies PPGL's genetic cluster utilizing PPGL's location representation obtained from its *location-branch*.

clinical, biochemical, and imaging phenotypes essentially represent the mutational status. Hence, the identification of PPGLs' genetic clusters from CE-CT scans will be a significant step in clinical advancement.

Recently the authors of [17] characterized PPGLs into three clusters using the radiomics [9] of FDG-PET/CT scans and the biochemical profile of a small cohort (n = 73). However, PET-CT [15] scans are also expensive. Hence, this motivates us to develop a deep learning-based approach to characterize PPGLs' genetic clusters from CE-CT scans of a larger cohort (n = 289), because to the best of our knowledge, no study has focused on this with CE-CT. We curated a dataset of PPGLs extracted from axial slices of CE-CT scans and then drew bounding boxes containing the PPGLs on the slices [Fig. 1a]. For each PPGL, a sub-image of the PPGL was cropped out from the axial slice and used for cross-validation of the proposed *PPGL-Transformer* [Fig. 1b]. For each tumor, the genetic cluster obtained from its genetic testing is considered the primary standard of reference. Later, each tumor's anatomical location (head and neck, chest, adrenal, and abdominopelvic excluding adrenal) was included as the auxiliary reference to provide the tumor's anatomical information for identifying its genetic type.

**Contributions.** Our contributions are three-fold: (a) The first is identifying genetic clusters of PPGLs, a disease rarely studied in the context of medical image analysis. (b) Though a few prior studies focusing on PET/CTs exist, to the best of our knowledge, we are the first to use CE-CT images. (c) We introduced a novel deep learning architecture – a location-embedded vision transformer – for the identification of PPGLs' genetic clusters.

## 2   Methods

### 2.1   Dataset

The dataset includes the portal venous phase CE-CTs of 289 PPGL patients screened for tumours at our institute between April 1999 and January 2022. The CE-CTs were acquired with a consistent protocol with a fixed delay of 70 s after administering contrast material intravenously. The slice spacing of the scans varies from 1 to 10 mm. 1010 PPGLs (584 *SDHx*, 107 *VHL/EPAS1*, 133 *KS*, and 186 sporadic) were extracted from the 300 CE-CT scans of 289 unique patients. The number of scans is greater than the patients because, for some patients, CE-CTs were separately acquired for head-neck and chest-abdomen-pelvis. The CE-CT images were viewed in ITK-SNAP [20] by setting the window level and window width to 50 and 450 HU, respectively. Subsequently, an axial slice presenting the maximum radius (visually determined) of a PPGL was extracted. Next, LabelImg [19] was used to draw a bounding box covering a tumor on the extracted slice and to assign the labels (genetic cluster from genetic test and anatomical location) to the tumor. Finally, we cropped out a 2D sub-image for each PPGL using bounding box annotations. The entire procedure is illustrated in Fig. 1a and a few examples of 2D sub-images of PPGLs from each of the four genetic clusters are shown in Fig. 2. The challenges of the machine learning-based identification of PPGL's genetic clusters can be seen in the images such as intra-class variance, inter-class similarity, and large tumor size variation.

## 2.2   PPGL-Transformer

This paper introduces a two-branch deep network (*PPGL-Transformer*) extending the ViT [6] for identifying PPGL's genetic cluster. The network takes the PPGL's anatomic location into account. As shown in Fig. 1b, for any CT sub-image of a PPGL, *PPGL-Transformer*'s *location-branch* recognizes the PPGL's anatomic location and its *genetic-cluster-branch* identifies PPGL's genetic cluster type. Both branches are comprised of the encoder module of the ViT (referred to as transformer encoder) that encodes the CT sub-image into a feature vector which is later fed to a fully-connected (fc) layer for classification. The *location-branch* or *genetic-cluster-branch* is essentially the ViT-Base [6] except the fc-layer for classification with 4 nodes for the 4-way classification of PPGL's anatomical location or genetic clusters. For any PPGL, the transformer encoder produces a 768-dimensional feature vector. The feature vector ($f_{al}$) obtained from *location-branch* represents the anatomical location information of a PPGL while the feature vector ($f_{gc}$) determined from *genetic-cluster-branch* encodes the genetic cluster features of the PPGL. The *genetic-cluster-branch* performs a bilinear pooling [14] by computing a matrix-matrix product between $f_{al}$ and $f_{gc}$ as:

$$f = f_{gc}f_{al}^T, \tag{1}$$

where $f$ is the ($768^2$-dimensional) resultant feature vector which embeds the location information of the PPGL into its genetic cluster identification pipeline [Fig. 1b]. Once the *location-branch* is trained, the classification of PPGL's anatomic location becomes optional during inference and can be discarded. For performing contrastive learning of the proposed network (see next section), in each branch, the encoded feature vector (i.e. $f_{al}$ or $f_{gc}$) was sent to a two-layered fc-projector network with 768 and 128 nodes respectively. ReLu non-linearity was applied to the input of the final layer. Once the training of the *PPGL-Transformer* was complete, the projector networks were removed during inference.

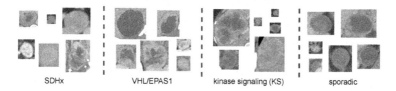

SDHx            VHL/EPAS1        kinase signaling (KS)        sporadic

**Fig. 2.** Examples of sub-images from each of the four PPGLs' genetic clusters. The examples clearly illustrate the challenges in classifying the sub-images due to high intra-class variance, and inter-class similarity, and large tumor size variation.

## 2.3 Supervised Contrastive Learning of PPGL-Transformer

*PPGL-Transformer* was trained in two successive stages. We trained the *location-branch* in the initial stage and the *genetic-cluster-branch* in the later stage by keeping *location-branch*'s trainable parameters untouched. In this way, we restricted the *PPGL-Transformer* to be dominated by the PPGL's anatomical location information in identifying the PPGL's genetic cluster. Both branches were trained in a supervised contrastive (SupCon) learning setting [12]. Thus, we implemented one projector network $(Proj(\cdot))$ for each branch to project 768-dimensional feature vectors $\mathbf{f}_{al}$ and $\mathbf{f}_{gc}$ into a (lower) 128-dimensional space. Let, $\mathbf{z}_{al} = Proj(\mathbf{f}_{al})$ and $\mathbf{z}_{gc} = Proj(\mathbf{f}_{gc})$ which were used for calculating the SupCon loss. However, both branches optimize joint loss:

$$\mathcal{L} = \mathcal{L}_{SupCon} + \mathcal{L}_{cl}, \tag{2}$$

where $\mathcal{L}_{SupCon}$ is SupCon loss and $\mathcal{L}_{cl}$ is classification loss (which is *cross-entropy loss* in this work). The addition of SupCon loss with classification loss essentially helped the *PPGL-Transformer* in determining the PPGL's features by minimizing the distances of the features from similar classes and maximizing the distances of the features from dissimilar classes. $\mathcal{L}_{SupCon}$ can be defined as the following.

Following [12], let us assume, we randomly sample $N$ pairs of CT sub-images of PPGLs and their labels (called image/label pairs) $\{\mathbf{x}^{(i)}, \mathbf{y}^{(i)}\}_{i=1,2,...,N}$ from the training set, and corresponding batch (which was used for training) comprises of $2N$ image/label pairs: $\{\tilde{\mathbf{x}}^{(j)}, \tilde{\mathbf{y}}^{(j)}\}_{j=1,2,...,2N}$, where $\tilde{\mathbf{x}}^{(2i-1)}$ and $\tilde{\mathbf{x}}^{(2i)}$ are two different views (or random augmentations) of $\mathbf{x}^{(i)}$ and $\tilde{\mathbf{y}}^{(2i-1)} = \tilde{\mathbf{y}}^{(2i)} = \mathbf{y}^{(i)}$. The set of $2N$ augmented samples is referred to as a "multiview batch". Assume the index of any arbitrary sample within the multiview batch is $k \in K \equiv \{1, 2, ..., 2N\}$, and the index of the other augmented sample generated from the same source sample is $l(k)$. Given this, the SupCon loss can be defined as:

$$\mathcal{L}_{SupCon} = \sum_{k \in K} \mathcal{L}_{SupCon}^{(k)} = \sum_{k \in K} \frac{-1}{|P(k)|} \sum_{p \in P(k)} \log \frac{\exp(\mathbf{z}^{(k)} \cdot \mathbf{z}^{(p)}/\tau)}{\sum_{a \in A(k)} \exp(\mathbf{z}^{(k)} \cdot \mathbf{z}^{(a)}/\tau)}, \tag{3}$$

where index $k$ is referred to as *anchor*, index $l(k)$ is called *positive*, $A(k) \equiv K \backslash \{k\}$, $P(k) \equiv \{p \in A(k) : \tilde{\mathbf{y}}^{(p)} = \tilde{\mathbf{y}}^{(k)}\}$ is the set of indices of all *positives* in the multiview batch different from $k$, $|P(k)|$ is the cardinality of $P(k)$, $\cdot$ represents inner products, $\mathbf{z}^{(j)} = Proj(\mathbf{f}^{(j)})$ is the projected feature vector of $\mathbf{f}^{(j)}$ obtained from transformer encoder for the image $\tilde{\mathbf{x}}^{(j)}$, $\tau \in \mathcal{R}^+$ is a scalar called temperature parameter. Note that, $\mathbf{z} \equiv \mathbf{z}_{al}$ and $\mathbf{f} \equiv \mathbf{f}_{al}$ for the *location-branch*, and $\mathbf{z} \equiv \mathbf{z}_{gc}$ and $\mathbf{f} \equiv \mathbf{f}_{gc}$ for the *genetic-cluster-branch* of *PPGL-Transformer*.

## 2.4 Implementation and Evaluation Details

The weights of the transformer encoder in the branches of *PPGL-Transformer* were initialized with the pre-trained weights of that of ViT-Base [6]. The weights of the classifiers and projector networks were randomly initialized following a normal distribution in $[-1, +1]$. Since the dataset is not balanced, we implemented a *weighted* version of *cross-entropy loss* [10] to get rid of data imbalance, where the weight of each class was inversely proportional to its prevalence.

The proposal was implemented using PyTorch 1.13.1. We used an NVIDIA A100 40GB GPU to carry out the experiments. PPGLs' CT sub-images were resized (or resampled) to $224 \times 224$ by applying the bilinear interpolation technique and standardized to zero mean and unit standard deviation. The mini-batch size was set to 64. The Adam optimizer [13] was used with the coefficients in $[0.5, 0.9]$ and initial learning rate $3 \times 10^{-6}$. Horizontal flipping and vertical flipping were used for data augmentations. We compared our method with the baseline methods support vector machine (SVM) [7], random forest (RF) [4], logistic regression (LR) with the radiomics [9] features extracted for each PPGL (referred to as Radiomics+SVM, Radiomics+RF, and Radiomics+LR, respectively), ResNet-101 [11], and ViT [6]. We utilized their publicly available implementations [1–3] for evaluation. Radiomics features included those characterizing shapes (including size) (n=14), and gray level histogram statistics (n = 18) and image texture (n = 68) extracted after applying 22 image filters for each by using the open-source Python package Pyradiomics (version 3.0.1). Our implementation of ViT, which optimized contrastive loss in addition to classification loss (ViT+CL), did not take PPGLs' anatomical locations into account in identifying their genetic clusters.

This study carried out five-fold cross-validation to use all PPGLs in evaluation. Patients were equally subdivided into 5 mutually exclusive groups. Then, the identification of PPGLs' genetic clusters was performed for each PPGL. The methods were evaluated using the metrics: accuracy (ACC) = $\frac{TP+TN}{TP+TN+FP+FN}$, recall (REC) = $\frac{TP}{TP+FN}$, balanced accuracy (BA) = $\frac{TPR+TNR}{2}$, and F1-Score (F1) = $\frac{2TP}{2TP+FP+FN}$, where TPR = $\frac{TP}{TP+FN}$, TNR = $\frac{TN}{TN+FP}$, TP = true positives, FP = false positives, TN = true negatives, and FN = false negatives.

## 3    Results

**Performance for PPGL's Genetic Cluster Identification.** Table 1 presents the PPGL's genetic cluster identification performance of various methods. The overall (see the rows for 'Overall' in Table 1) performance of *PPGL-Transformer* outperformed competitors by 2–29% on ACC, 3–19% on REC, 3–18% on BA, and 3–14% on F1. Overall performance (REC, BA, and F1) was computed by considering the average results of 4 genetic clusters in each fold. ViT+CL and *PPGL-Transformer* outperformed others in all three metrics by 3–10% except for REC and F1 in the case of *VHL/EPAS1* and *KS*, respectively. ViT+CL performed better than *PPGL-Transformer* in the case of all three metrics for the *KS* cluster type. Figure 3a shows the confusion matrix for *PPGL-Transformer*'s performance, where the numbers are the sum of the outcomes for five folds. Since the *SDHx* genetic cluster is so large, we carried out another experiment for *SDHx* versus others (*VHL/EPAS1, KS* and sporadic). We changed the #nodes in the

**Table 1.** PPGLs' genetic cluster identification performance (*mean ± standard deviation* over five folds) of various approaches in terms of REC, BA, and F1.

| Genetic clusters | Metrics | Methods | | | | | | |
|---|---|---|---|---|---|---|---|---|
| | | Radiomics+RF | Radiomics+SVM | Radiomics+LR | ResNet-101 | ViT | ViT+CL | PPGL-Transformer |
| SDHx | REC | 0.78 ± 0.08 | 0.58 ± 0.09 | 0.29 ± 0.06 | 0.80 ± 0.09 | 0.70 ± 0.10 | 0.83 ± 0.08 | **0.83 ± 0.06** |
| | BA | 0.50 ± 0.03 | 0.50 ± 0.16 | 0.42 ± 0.05 | 0.55 ± 0.04 | 0.57 ± 0.07 | 0.60 ± 0.04 | **0.62 ± 0.08** |
| | F1 | 0.68 ± 0.06 | 0.61 ± 0.09 | 0.38 ± 0.04 | 0.71 ± 0.08 | 0.69 ± 0.09 | **0.74 ± 0.07** | 0.74 ± 0.07 |
| VHL/EPAS1 | REC | 0.24 ± 0.06 | 0.33 ± 0.05 | **0.41 ± 0.19** | 0.15 ± 0.16 | 0.29 ± 0.15 | 0.23 ± 0.18 | 0.36 ± 0.22 |
| | BA | 0.59 ± 0.03 | 0.57 ± 0.02 | 0.48 ± 0.08 | 0.55 ± 0.07 | 0.59 ± 0.09 | 0.59 ± 0.08 | **0.63 ± 0.10** |
| | F1 | 0.30 ± 0.08 | 0.29 ± 0.04 | 0.23 ± 0.12 | 0.25 ± 0.15 | 0.31 ± 0.17 | 0.27 ± 0.17 | **0.34 ± 0.13** |
| KS | REC | 0.06 ± 0.03 | 0.19 ± 0.08 | 0.27 ± 0.12 | 0.23 ± 0.13 | 0.31 ± 0.09 | **0.25 ± 0.07** | 0.23 ± 0.14 |
| | BA | 0.48 ± 0.01 | 0.47 ± 0.02 | 0.44 ± 0.04 | 0.55 ± 0.06 | 0.57 ± 0.07 | **0.58 ± 0.05** | 0.58 ± 0.07 |
| | F1 | 0.07 ± 0.14 | 0.16 ± 0.07 | 0.20 ± 0.06 | 0.23 ± 0.11 | **0.29 ± 0.09** | **0.29 ± 0.09** | 0.28 ± 0.15 |
| Sporadic | REC | 0.25 ± 0.09 | 0.29 ± 0.20 | 0.31 ± 0.11 | 0.32 ± 0.22 | 0.40 ± 0.24 | 0.40 ± 0.22 | **0.44 ± 0.27** |
| | BA | 0.54 ± 0.06 | 0.53 ± 0.12 | 0.45 ± 0.06 | 0.58 ± 0.11 | 0.63 ± 0.13 | 0.64 ± 0.11 | **0.68 ± 0.13** |
| | F1 | 0.26 ± 0.11 | 0.30 ± 0.17 | 0.25 ± 0.10 | 0.32 ± 0.21 | 0.40 ± 0.25 | 0.42 ± 0.25 | **0.50 ± 0.29** |
| Overall | ACC | 0.53 ± 0.06 | 0.45 ± 0.07 | 0.34 ± 0.09 | 0.56 ± 0.07 | 0.55 ± 0.08 | 0.61 ± 0.08 | **0.63 ± 0.08** |
| | REC | 0.33 ± 0.02 | 0.35 ± 0.05 | 0.27 ± 0.05 | 0.37 ± 0.05 | 0.43 ± 0.06 | 0.43 ± 0.04 | **0.46 ± 0.09** |
| | BA | 0.53 ± 0.02 | 0.52 ± 0.04 | 0.45 ± 0.05 | 0.56 ± 0.03 | 0.59 ± 0.05 | 0.60 ± 0.03 | **0.63 ± 0.06** |
| | F1 | 0.33 ± 0.03 | 0.34 ± 0.04 | 0.32 ± 0.04 | 0.38 ± 0.03 | 0.42 ± 0.06 | 0.43 ± 0.05 | **0.46 ± 0.08** |

fc-layer of *genetic-cluster-branch* to 2. The overall ACC, REC, BA, and F1 were $0.71 ± 0.06$, $0.69 ± 0.05$, $0.69 ± 0.05$, and $0.69 ± 0.06$, respectively. The overall performance jumped by 8% on ACC, 23% on REC, 6% on BA, and 23% on F1 w.r.t. the 4-way classification of genetic clusters. In class-specific performance, REC, BA, and F1 were $0.78 ± 0.15$, $0.69 ± 0.05$, and $0.75 ± 0.10$, respectively (for *SDHx*) and $0.61 ± 0.14$, $0.69 ± 0.05$, and $0.63 ± 0.10$, respectively (for others).

**Ablation Study:** The removal of the *location-branch* from *PPGL-Transformer* (which utilizes PPGLs' anatomical location in identifying their genetic clusters) essentially produces the model ViT+CL. Thus comparing the performances of *PPGL-Transformer* vs. ViT+CL establishes the contribution of integrating anatomical location in PPGLs' genetic cluster identification. Table 1 depicts that the *PPGL-Transformer* improved the overall performance of ViT+CL by 3%

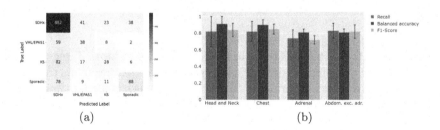

(a)                                                                    (b)

**Fig. 3.** (a) Confusion matrix of the *PPGL-Transformer*'s genetic cluster identification performance. The true label indicates the class-wise number of inputs to the system while the predicted label denotes the class-wise number of predictions w.r.t the number of inputs per class. (b) A bar chart with error bars for the *PPGL-Transformer*'s performance in recognizing PPGLs' anatomical location. "Abdom. exc. adr." represent the anatomic location abdominopelvic excluding adrenal. Bars and error bars represent the mean and standard deviation of the performance over five folds, respectively.

in the case of all metrics except ACC (2%). In the class-specific performance, sporadic increased its REC by 4%, BA by 4%, and F1 by 8% with the *PPGL-Transformer* compared to ViT+CL. The impact of the contrastive learning approach in our proposal can be assessed by comparing the performances of ViT versus ViT+CL (ViT with contrastive learning) in Table 1. Contrastive learning improved the ACC by 6%, overall BA, and F1 by 1%, and the performance for *SDHx* by 13% on REC, 3% on BA, and 5% on F1.

**Performance for PPGL's Anatomical Location Recognition:** Since *PPGL-Transformer* integrated PPGL's anatomical location in its modeling, we also present the *PPGL-Transformer*'s five-fold cross-validation results in recognizing PPGLs' anatomical location in Fig. 3b. The bar plot shows that all the PPGLs' anatomical locations were recognized with metrics exceeding 80% except adrenal (for which F1 and REC were within 0.7 and 0.8). The overall ACC, REC, BA, and F1 of the *PPGL-Transformer* were $0.81 \pm 0.04$, $0.80 \pm 0.06$, $0.86 \pm 0.04$, and $0.81 \pm 0.03$, respectively.

## 4    Discussion and Conclusion

This work introduces a two-branch vision transformer, *PPGL-Transformer* to determine the PPGLs' genetic cluster by analyzing CE-CT images. We utilized the PPGLs' anatomical location information to guide our network.

In comparison with the results of genetic testing, we found that *PPGL-Transformer* performed better for the *SDHx* cluster. One of the reasons is that *SDHx* had a larger number of samples than the other three clusters. Due to the poor performances of the other three clusters (specifically *KS*), the overall performance dropped. The confusion matrix showed that the other three clusters mostly got confused with the *SDHx* cluster. A similar thing happened with the competing methods; they did well in identifying *SDHx* but did not perform well in identifying other clusters. Thus, we posed the problem differently as a two-class problem: *SDHx* versus others (that included *VHL/EPAS1*, *KS*, and sporadic together). The comparison is meaningful because distinguishing *SDHx* from the other clusters is clinically relevant. For this binary classification, although the overall performance improved but *SDHx* was again dominant.

We found that the *PPGL-Transformer* was able to classify the anatomical location, based on the input CE-CT sub-images quite well. Also, an ablation study showed that integrating the location information led to improved performance for *SDHx*, *VHL/EPAS1*, and sporadic, but not for KS. The results suggest that *KS* lacks a strong relationship with anatomical location.

This work has limitations. We considered 2D sub-images of the CE-CT scans. In our future work, we will utilize the entire CE-CT scan. The ground truths generated by one of the authors were verified by only one radiologist. The methods were evaluated on the data that came from only one institution. In our future study, we plan to collect data from other institutions for a generalizability assessment of the methods.

In conclusion, we demonstrated a deep learning-based system that identifies PPGL's genetic clusters from CE-CT. We introduced a unique anatomical location-guided two-branch ViT. Results demonstrated the difficulty of determining PPGLs' genetic clusters from CE-CT images due to the challenges of intra-class variability, inter-class similarity, and large size variation. However, our method takes the first steps towards developing a cost-effective, faster, and more widely available genetic characterization of PPGLs.

**Prospect of Application.** This is a novel application of a deep learning-based system in the field of radiogenomics. To the best of our knowledge, an expensive genetic test is the only method to determine PPGLs' genetic clusters. We demonstrate that an inexpensive deep learning-based system may help to identify PPGLs' genetic clusters, offering timely personalized patient management.

**Acknowledgments.** This work was supported by the Intramural Research Programs of the NIH Clinical Center and NICHD.

# References

1. https://github.com/pwesp/random-forest-polyp-classification . Accessed Jun 2023
2. https://pytorch.org/tutorials/beginner/transfer_learning_tutorial.html . Accessed Jun 2023
3. https://github.com/lukysummer/VisionTransformer-PyTorch/blob/main/ViT_Iterative_Erasing.ipynb . Accessed Jun 2023
4. Breiman, L.: Random forests. Mach. Learn. **45**(1), 5–32 (2001)
5. DeLellis, R.A.: Pathology and genetics of tumours of endocrine organs. IARC Press, Lyon, World Health Organization classification of tumours (2004)
6. Dosovitskiy, A., et al.: An image is worth $16 \times 16$ words: transformers for image recognition at scale. arXiv preprint arXiv:2010.11929 (2020)
7. Drucker, H., Burges, C.J.C., Kaufman, L., Smola, A., Vapnik, V.: Support vector regression machines. Adv. Neural. Inf. Process. Syst. **9**(9), 155–161 (1997)
8. Fishbein, L., Nathanson, K.L.: Pheochromocytoma and paraganglioma: understanding the complexities of the genetic background. Cancer Genet. **205**(1–2), 1–11 (2012)
9. van Griethuysen, J.J.M., et al.: Computational radiomics system to decode the radiographic phenotype. Can. Res. **77**(21), E104–E107 (2017)
10. Guo, B., Chen, S., Hong, Z., Xu, G.: Pattern recognition and analysis: neural network using weighted cross entropy. J. Phys.: Conf. Ser. **2218**, 012043. IOP Publishing (2022)
11. He, K.M., Zhang, X.Y., Ren, S.Q., Sun, J.: Deep residual learning for image recognition. In: 2016 IEEE Conference on Computer Vision and Pattern Recognition (CVPR), pp. 770–778 (2016)
12. Khosla, P., et al.: Supervised contrastive learning. Adv. Neural. Inf. Process. Syst. **33**, 18661–18673 (2020)
13. Kingma, D.P., Ba, J.: Adam: a method for stochastic optimization. arXiv preprint arXiv:1412.6980 (2014)
14. Lin, T.Y., RoyChowdhury, A., Maji, S.: Bilinear CNN models for fine-grained visual recognition. In: Proceedings of the IEEE International Conference on Computer Vision, pp. 1449–1457 (2015)

15. Liu, L., et al.: Improved multi-modal patch based lymphoma segmentation with negative sample augmentation and label guidance on PET/CT scans. In: International Workshop on Multiscale Multimodal Medical Imaging, pp. 121–129. Springer, Cham (2022). https://doi.org/10.1007/978-3-031-18814-5_12
16. Nölting, S., et al.: Personalized management of pheochromocytoma and paraganglioma. Endocr. Rev. **43**(2), 199–239 (2022)
17. Noortman, W.A., et al.: [$^{18}$F]FDG-PET/CT radiomics for the identification of genetic clusters in pheochromocytomas and paragangliomas. Eur. Radiol. **32**(10), 7227–7236 (2022)
18. Turkova, H., et al.: Characteristics and outcomes of metastatic SDHB and sporadic pheochromocytoma/paraganglioma: An National Institutes of Health study. Endocr. Pract. **22**(3), 302–314 (2016)
19. Tzutalin: Labelimg. Free Software: MIT License (2015). https://github.com/tzutalin/labelImg
20. Yushkevich, P.A., et al.: User-guided 3D active contour segmentation of anatomical structures: significantly improved efficiency and reliability. Neuroimage **31**(3), 1116–1128 (2006)

# Video-Based Gait Analysis for Assessing Alzheimer's Disease and Dementia with Lewy Bodies

Diwei Wang[1], Chaima Zouaoui[1,2], Jinhyeok Jang[3], Hassen Drira[1], and Hyewon Seo[1(✉)]

[1] ICube laboratory, University of Strasbourg, Strasbourg, France
{d.wang,hdrira,seo}@unistra.fr, chaima.zouaoui@ept.ucar.tn
[2] Ecole Polytechnique, Carthage, Tunisie
[3] ETRI, Daejeon, South Korea
jjh6297@etri.kr

**Abstract.** Dementia with Lewy Bodies (DLB) and Alzheimer's Disease (AD) are two common neurodegenerative diseases among elderly people. Gait analysis plays a significant role in clinical assessments to discriminate these neurological disorders from healthy controls, to grade disease severity, and to further differentiate dementia subtypes. In this paper, we propose a deep-learning based model specifically designed to evaluate gait impairment score for assessing the dementia severity using monocular gait videos. Named MAX-GR, our model estimates the sequence of 3D body skeletons, applies corrections based on spatio-temporal gait features extracted from the input video, and performs classification on the corrected 3D pose sequence to determine the MDS-UPDRS gait scores. Experimental results show that our technique outperforms alternative state-of-the-art methods. The code, demo videos, as well as 3D skeleton dataset is available at https://github.com/lisqzqng/Video-based-gait-analysis-for-dementia.

**Keywords:** Gait impairment score · Dementia subtypes · Human 3D motion estimation · Geometric deep learning

## 1 Introduction and Related Work

Through many previous studies, it is now well understood that the quantitative gait impairment analysis is an established method for accessing neurodegenerative diseases such as Dementia with Lewy Bodies (DLB) or Alzheimer (AD) and gauging their severity, even in the prodromal phase [20]. In order to facilitate quantitative gait analysis, previous works have often relied on wearable sensors [6,12,17,27] or electronic walkways [19,22]. According to Merory et al.'s study [22], individuals with AD and DLB show comparable spatiotemporal gait characteristics that differ significantly from those of the normal population. Conversely, Mc Ardle et al. [19] demonstrate that the two subtype groups exhibit

S. Wu et al. (Eds.): AMAI 2023, LNCS 14313, pp. 72–82, 2024.
https://doi.org/10.1007/978-3-031-47076-9_8

distinct pathological gait signatures. Another study [18] has shown that the environment where walking takes place has an influence on the characteristics of gait impairment in different types of dementia. However, these studies do not aim to automatically estimate severity scores based on the measurement data.

Numerous efforts have been made to classify or estimate the severity of a patient's condition and even distinguish between different dementia subtypes, by using gait data. Muller [23] employed a decision tree [29] to analyse gait motions of individuals with AD and DLB, and showed that walking speed and the asymmetry in left-to-right step lengths were the two primary factors for distinguishing between dementia subtypes and estimating the disease severity. However, the reliance on wearable sensors equipped with tri-axial accelerometers or electronic walkways in such studies can be cumbersome in terms of wearability, calibration, and may not always be readily accessible.

The progress in deep learning has opened up new possibilities for vision-based severity assessment methods. Albuquerque et al. [1] have developed a spatiotemporal deep learning technique by producing a gait representation that combines image features extracted through Convolutional Neural Networks (CNNs) with a temporal encoding based on Long Short-Term Memory (LSTM) networks. Lu et al. [16] extract 3D body pose from videos, track them through time, and classify the sequence of 3D poses based on the MDS-UPDRS gait scores by using a temporal convolutional neural network. Similarly, Sabo et al. [25] have shown that ST-GCN models operating on 3D joint trajectories outperform alternative models. Motivated by the achievements of previous studies, we adopt a similar approach of extracting 3D pose sequences from gait videos with an aim to enhance pathological gait analysis. However, our work distinguishes itself in that we introduce a new dedicated model for 3D motion estimation from monocular gait videos. Additionally, we employ a geometric deep learning module specially crafted for 3D skeleton-based action recognition. Consequently, our method achieves superior performance compared to numerous state-of-the-art techniques.

## 2   Method

### 2.1   Our Patient Data

The videos of patients undergoing the MDS-UPDRS gait examination at a neurology clinic have been used in our study. The patient walks along a GAITRite (https://www.gaitrite.com/) electronic walkway with dimensions of $0.6m \times 8m$, from one end to the other end. Three views have been interchangeably chosen for the RGB camera, without calibration: a side view from the mid-way of the walkway, a front view as the patient walks towards the camera, and a back view as the patient walks away from the camera. In the two latter cases, the distance between the camera and the patient varied from 1 m to 9–10 meters. The recorded images had a resolution of $480 \times 640$ pixels, and the frame rate was set at 30 Hz. A total of 92 sequences have been recorded from 44 subjects, including 41 patients with AD and DLB. In addition, each video has been annotated with the personal data including the height and age of the person, dementia type and the severity, and the gait parameters measured by the GAITRite system, such as walk speed, step lengths of each leg, times of contact, etc. 3D joint positions were not available.

## 2.2   MAX-GRNet for 3D Pose Estimation

The first component of our work is the 3D human motion estimation from the 2D RGB video. Like many others, we base our 3D pose estimator on the SMPL [15] model, thus the estimated poses are represented in the form of a sequence of SMPL pose parameters [15]. Our proposed 3D gait reconstructor, named MAX-GRNet, is illustrated in Fig. 1.

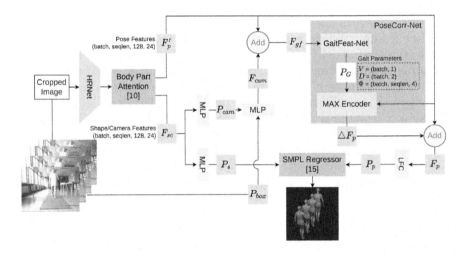

**Fig. 1.** The architecture of MAX-GRNet, the proposed 3D gait motion reconstructor. $P's$ denote the parameters whereas $F's$ denote the features. LFC stands for locally-connected linear layers. In LFC, pose parameter of each body joint is regressed by an individual linear layer [10].

In our patient video, challenging scenarios can arise due to truncations or reduced visual clarity. To mitigate the impact of truncation and enhance the overall accuracy, we employ the Part Attention mechanism [10], encouraging the model to focus on more credible visual features. As illustrated in Fig. 1, the visual features extracted by the HRNet-W32 [10] at each frame are fed into the Body Part Attention module, to generate joint-specific features. The subject-camera distance, frequently observed to be fairly long in our video (up to more than 10 m when the patient and the camera is at either ends of the walk-way), can also significantly decrease reconstruction accuracy, leading to unrealistic poses with distorted walking patterns, perturbed foot swings, and illogical step lengths. To tackle this issue, we introduce our Pose Correction Network

(PoseCorr-Net), which incorporates several gait characteristics as additional controls and employs the spatio-temporal encoding along with attention mechanism. To address different aspects of the gait motion, we combine average parameters and per-frame parameters as the gait characteristics. The average parameters ensure consistency in the reconstructed walking patterns, while the per-frame parameters accommodate the variations across different gait phases. To regress these parameters, we introduce a GRU-based module named as GaitFeat-Net. The gait parameters $P_G$ are subsequently mapped into a higher-dimensional feature space to enable the fusion with the pose feature $F_P'$. To further enhance the integration of estimated $P_G$ with $F_P'$, we introduce a Transformer-based encoder [28] which we refer to as MAX Encoder, to capture the intra-dependencies across different time steps and among the body joints, respectively, before their final merging.

**GaitFeat-Net.** We feed the pose feature $F_p'$ and camera feature $F_{cam}$ into an one-layer GRU to estimate a number of gait parameters. The effectiveness of gait parameter estimation using a GRU-based network from per-joint 3D position has been previously demonstrated in QuaterNet [24], in the context of generating plausible locomotion given previous poses and locomotive parameters as controls. Differently from Quaternet, our approach uses per-joint feature as the input, instead of per-joint 3D positions. This allows us to capture more detailed information and potentially improve the accuracy of gait parameter estimation. Additionally, we utilize $F_{cam}$ obtained from camera parameters $P_{cam}$ ($[s, t], t \in \mathbb{R}^2$ defined by a weak-perspective camera model) as additional input. As depicted in Fig. 1, we construct a patch of $224 \times 224$ pixels from each of the initial video frames based on the bounding box, before feeding the patch sequence into the reconstructor. By incorporating the parameters of the bounding box $P_{box}$, $F_{cam}$ can effectively capture the position of the patient within the original video frame, and the dynamic information regarding the motion in the video. Based on the available locomotive parameters in our patient data (Sect. 2.1), we have selected gait parameters $P_G = [V, D, \Phi]$, where $V = \|v\|$ is the speed amplitude averaged over the sequence, $D = [\bar{l}_{left}, \bar{l}_{right}]$ is the average left/right step lengths, and $\Phi = [cos(\phi_{left}), sin(\phi_{left}), cos(\phi_{right}), sin(\phi_{right})]$ encodes the phase of the left/right gait cycle.

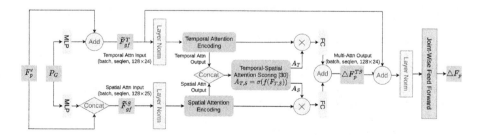

**Fig. 2.** Architecture of the MAX Encoder.

**MAXEncoder.** By developing this encoder based on a multi-head self-attention mechanism (MSA) [28], we aim to overcome the limitations of recurrent models that struggle to capture long-range relationships in the sequence. Figure 2 depicts its detailed architecture. We devise an attention-based block that builds upon the MSA variants MSA-T and MSA-S of Spatial-Temporal Encoder (STE) [30]. To incorporate the gait parameters $P_G$ obtained from GaitFeat-Net, and accommodate the joint-wise nature of the pose feature $F'_P$, we construct different inputs $\tilde{F}^T_{gf}$ and $\tilde{F}^S_{gf}$ for our temporal (TAE) and spatial attention (SAE) blocks. Unlike MSA-S, which focuses on modeling the intra-dependencies within each feature map, the proposed SAE explicitly captures the dependencies among each body joint while leveraging the corresponding gait feature. To merge the TAE and SAE blocks, we adopt the parallel connection method as described in [30]. Additionally, we replace the Feed-Foward Network (FFN) in the standard Transformer and the Vision Transforer (ViT) [3] with a Joint-Wise Feed Forward network (JWFF). JWFF employs separate linear layers for each joint, contrary to the global FC layers in FFN. Ablation studies in Sect. 3.3 clearly demonstrate the efficacy of such JWFF approach. The total loss of our proposed MAX-GRNet is:

$$L = w_1 \cdot L_{2D} + w_2 \cdot L_{3D} + w_3 \cdot L_{SMPL} + w_4 \cdot L_{GaitFeat}, \tag{1}$$

where $w_i$ is the weight assigned to each loss, more details on these weight values can be found in Sect. 3.2. $L_{SMPL}$, $L_{3D}$ and $L_{2D}$ denote respectively the loss term associated with the Euclidean distances calculated on SMPL parameters, 3D joint positions and projected 2D joint positions. $L_{GaitFeat}$ is designed to supervise the gait parameters regressed by the GaitFeat-Net.

## 2.3 Geometric Deep Learning for Severity Assessment

In the second part of our study, we employ the KShapeNet [5], a geometric deep learning model on Kendall's shape space specially developed for skeleton-based human action recognition. It has demonstrated favorable performances on the two large scale skeleton datasets NTU-RGB+D [26] and NTU-RGB+D120 [13] datasets. Initially, skeleton sequences are modeled as trajectories on Kendall's shape space by filtering out the scale and rigid transformations. Next, the sequences are mapped to a linear tangent space and the resulting structured data are fed into a deep learning model, KShapeNet. Notably, it includes a unique layer that learns the optimal rigid and nonrigid transformation to be applied to the 3D skeletons, thereby enhancing the precision of action recognition. This layer is followed by a Conv Block and an LSTM layer that captures the temporal dynamics of the sequences. A subsequent fully connected block generates the corresponding action class as the output. In this work we utilized only the optimization over the rigid transformation layer.

# 3  Experiments

## 3.1  Datasets

We utilized Human3.6M motion capture data [2,7] consisting of synchronized 3D joint positions, 2D joint positions, and RGB video frames recorded at 50 Hz. We selected 6 subjects to create a set of 79 sub-sequences of walking motions to train and validate the reconstructors. The GPJATK gait dataset [11] was used for the evaluation. It contains Vicon mocap data with video recordings of 4 calibrated RGB cameras. We estimated 3D poses from their videos, which have been time-aligned with the 3D poses computed from their marker data, allowing us to obtain consistent 2D-3D (video and the 3D pose sequence) pairs. To train and test the classifiers, we combine our patient data with a subset of the Toronto Older Adults Gait Archive [21], where we randomly selected 22 walking sequences from 5 subjects.

## 3.2  Implementation Details

**3D Pose Estimator.** We begin by training the GaitFeat-Net module separately on the gait sequences from Human3.6M, to enhance the stability of the overall MAX-GRNet training. Only $L_{GaitFeat}$ in Eq. 1 has been used in this pre-training stage, with gait parameters computed by analyzing the 3D joint positions. We apply L1 loss for $V$, $D$ and $\Phi$, with distinct weight assignments: $w_V=250$, $w_D=50$, $w_\Phi=100$. During the integral training of MAX-GRNet, we use distinct weights for the losses in Eq. 1, specifically $w_{2D}=100$, $w_{3D}=100$, $w_\theta=60$, $w_\beta=0.01$, where $\theta$ and $\beta$ denote the pose and shape parameters in SMPL. $L_{GaitFeat}$ is applied only for the initial 20 epochs with weights different from the previous training: $w_V=100$, $w_D=20$, $w_\Phi=50$, and the subsequent training continues without any supervision on the GaitFeat-Net. The metadata from the electronic walkway only provides the average locomotive parameters in the patient data such as the duration of the left/right gait cycle. Thus, we apply a fast Fourier transform to obtain the spectrogram from the reconstructed gait, to effectively supervise the estimated $\Phi$. Given the average frequency $\bar{f}$, the phase loss on the patient data is formulated as $L_\Phi = w_{\Phi'} \cdot (\frac{1}{\beta} \cdot A_{\bar{f}} + \beta \cdot \sum_{i=0}^{n} A_{f_i} |f_i - \bar{f}|)$, where $w_{\Phi'}=0.05$ and $\beta=0.2$ are weighting coefficients, and $A_f$ denotes the amplitude of $f$ in the spectrogram. The estimation of SMPL parameters on the Human3.6M dataset is performed by using MoSh [14] on the available 3D marker data, and each pose parameter is subsequently represented as a 6D vector [31]. The models were trained on 1 Nvidia RTX 3090 GPU using a batch size of 4 and an Adam optimizer with a learning rate of $5 \times 10^{-5}$. Optimal hyperparameters were chosen through grid search.

**Motor Severity Assessment.** As outlined in Sect. 3.1, we train the classifiers using the estimated skeleton sequences from both healthy and diseased older adults. To obtain the required number of frames for analysis, which has been set to 100 frames, we utilized a sliding window approach. It involved traversing the original video, extracting subsequences consisting of 100 frames each, and maintaining an overlap of 50 frames between adjacent subsequences. The last frames fewer than 50 frames were not used. We refrained from time-warping the sequences in order to preserve the velocity of the gait motion.

Each subsequence obtained by this way has been assigned the same label as the original video. This sliding window protocol was applied after dividing the dataset into training and testing sets to prevent the occurrence of subsequences from the same video being present in both sets. Note that this increases the total number of sequences used for training and testing, thereby augmenting the limited amount of our patient data.

### 3.3   Results

**Evaluation Criteria.** The reconstructor model has been validated and evaluated by measuring the 3D per-joint position error respectively on Human3.6M and GPJATK datasets. The classification accuracy has been used to evaluate the overall performance and to compare with other SOTA methods. Different variations of severity assessment tasks has been tested: normal/patient, 3-class diagnosis with normal/Alzheimer/DLB, and 3-class gait scoring (normal-0, moderate-1, and severe-2). All evaluations have used a 10-fold cross-validation scheme. Due to the limited size of the data, we opted to perform a train-test split.

**Table 1.** Comparison of performance with different model configurations, measured on mean per-joint position error (MPJPE) $(mm)$, and classification accuracy (%). Numbers in boldface indicate the top-1 performance, with the top-2 denoted as underlines.

| | MPJPE (valid) | MPJPE (test) | Normal /Patient | Normal /AD/DLB | Gait Score (0,1,2) |
|---|---|---|---|---|---|
| VIBE [9] | 70.40 | 131.52 | 94.60 | 71.37 | 63.69 |
| Baseline | 70.61 | 103.78 | 90.11 | 68.94 | 62.57 |
| + MAX Encoder /wo JWFF | 70.35 | 101.83 | 88.05 | 59.28 | 60.20 |
| + MAX Encoder /with JWFF | 68.90 | 106.40 | 86.76 | 58.03 | 65.24 |
| + Avg.+ MAX Encoder /wo JWFF | 71.13 | 102.43 | 85.54 | 57.74 | 58.43 |
| + Avg.+ MAX Encoder /with JWFF | 70.38 | 102.27 | 87.36 | 61.58 | 59.33 |
| + PoseCorr-Net /wo JWFF | **66.47** | **101.78** | 87.38 | 66.03 | 60.37 |
| + PoseCorr-Net /with JWFF (Ours) | 67.17 | 103.77 | **96.22** | **75.39** | **65.41** |

**Ablation Study.** We assessed six model configurations es well as VIBE model [9] based on the mean per-joint position error (MPJPE) and the classification accuracy. The design of MAX Encoder has been tested with and without joint-wise forward feedback (JWFF). To validate the design of the GaitFeat-Net, we performed three distinct configurations. First, we conducted tests without it, followed by tests using its estimation of only the average parameters $V$ and $D$ (referred to as Avg.), and finally, with the complete estimation $P_G$.

The results are shown in Table 1. In general, utilizing gait parameters by GaitFeat-Net and subsequently regularizing the 3D pose estimation improves the reconstruction on GPJATK dataset, which predominantly contains regular walking of young and normal people, but reduces the overall classification accuracy. This somewhat aligns with the observations by [19], who pointed out that gait asymmetry and variability are significant factors for differentiating between disease subtypes and the patient group from the normal one. JWFF tends to improve the classification accuracy both in gait scores and dementia subtypes, especially when gait parameters are used with it, indicating its efficacy of extracting informative features from the estimated locomotive parameters.

**Table 2.** Comparison of classification accuracy with state-of-the-art methods (% accuracy). Numbers in boldface indicate the top-1 accuracy, while the top-2 is denoted with underlines.

|  | Normal /Patient | Normal /AD/DLB | Gait Score (0,1,2) |
|---|---|---|---|
| VIBE [9] + OF-DDNet [16] | 89.60 | <u>72.78</u> | 60.43 |
| VIBE [9] + KShapeNet | <u>94.60</u> | 71.37 | 63.69 |
| MAX-GRNet + OF-DDNet [16] | 89.60 | 69.92 | 64.68 |
| MAX-GRNet + ST-GCN [25] | 94.24 | 66.67 | **72.31** |
| MAX-GRNet + FSA-CNN [8] | 93.02 | 72.19 | <u>66.74</u> |
| MAX-GRNet + PoseC3D [4] | 92.95 | 66.59 | 62.27 |
| Ours (MAX-GRNet + KShapeNet) | **96.22** | **75.39** | 65.41 |

**Comparison with the State-of-the-Art.** We compare our method with two closely related studies, which focus on vision-based gait analysis of parkinsonism severity in dementia [16,25]. Additionally, we include two state-of-the-art models proposed in the vision-based action recognition community [4,8] for further comparison. To evaluate the classifier based on a ST-GCN [25], we evaluate their classifier using solely skeletons as input, excluding the spatio-temporal gait features originally utilized in their work. This is due to the inability to compute these features from the skeleton data reconstructed with MAX-GRNet, as it does not provide the root.

Results shown in Table 2 demonstrate that our method achieves favorable performance compared to others, and remains competitive with the CNN-based action recognition approach, which demonstrates superior performance in differentiating dimentia subtypes.

**Limitations.** Our reconstructor struggles to estimate 3D poses in videos exhibiting severe cases where the patient's gait pattern is highly irregular. The classifier incurs an additional time cost and requires separate processing for the projection of skeleton data onto the tangent space, which hinders its seamless integration with the reconstructor in an end-to-end manner.

## 4   Conclusion

We have presented a new model aimed at evaluating gait impairment score for assessing the dementia severity using monocular gait videos. Our model features a gait motion reconstructor, which is specifically designed for 3D motion estimation from gait videos based on a gait parameter estimator and a multi-head attention Transformer. Additionally, we employ a geometric deep neural network tailored for the specific task of 3D skeleton-based classification. Our method improves the performance over state-of-the-art techniques in both 3D pose estimation and classification, thus demonstrating significant advancements in the field. In the future, we plan to improve the precision of both 3D pose estimation and classification by effectively leveraging image evidences and gait parameters, respectively.

**Prospect of Application.** In addition to its clear applications in clinical environments, where the computed gait scores from gait videos can be presented to clinicians, our research could also be used in the realm of care robots assisting elderly individuals in residential settings. Specifically, they could identify early signs or variations in the pathological condition through video analysis.

**Acknowledgements.** We would like to thank Dr. Candice Muller and Prof. Dr. Frédéric Blanc at the Robsertsau hospital for sharing patient data and theier valuable expertise. This work has been partially supported by the French national project ArtIC (Artificial Intelligence for Care, ANR-20-THIA-0006) and the binational project "Synthetic Data Generation and Sim-to-Real Adaptive Learning for Real-World Human Daily Activity Recognition of Human-Care Robots (21YS2900)" granted by the ETRI, South Korea. Chaima Zouaoui was supported by the ICube laboratory API project ShaGAI.

## References

1. Albuquerque, P., Verlekar, T.T., Correia, P.L., Soares, L.D.: A spatiotemporal deep learning approach for automatic pathological gait classification. Sensors **21**(18), 6202 (2021)
2. Catalin, I., Fuxin, L., Cristian, S.: Latent structured models for human pose estimation. In: International Conference on Computer Vision (2011)
3. Dosovitskiy, A., et al.: An image is worth $16 \times 16$ words: transformers for image recognition at scale. arXiv preprint arXiv:2010.11929 (2020)
4. Duan, H., Zhao, Y., Chen, K., Lin, D., Dai, B.: Revisiting skeleton-based action recognition. In: Proceedings of the IEEE/CVF Conference on Computer Vision and Pattern Recognition, pp. 2969–2978 (2022)
5. Friji, R., Drira, H., Chaieb, F., Kchok, H., Kurtek, S.: Geometric deep neural network using rigid and non-rigid transformations for human action recognition. In: Proceedings of the IEEE/CVF International Conference on Computer Vision, pp. 12611–12620 (2021)
6. Hsu, W.C., et al.: Multiple-wearable-sensor-based gait classification and analysis in patients with neurological disorders. Sensors **18**(10), 3397 (2018)

7. Ionescu, C., Papava, D., Olaru, V., Sminchisescu, C.: Human3.6M: large scale datasets and predictive methods for 3D human sensing in natural environments. IEEE Trans. Pattern Anal. Mach. Intell. (2014)
8. Jang, J., Kim, D., Park, C., Jang, M., Lee, J., Kim, J.: ETRI-activity3D: a large-scale RGB-D dataset for robots to recognize daily activities of the elderly. In: 2020 IEEE/RSJ International Conference on Intelligent Robots and Systems (IROS), pp. 10990–10997. IEEE (2020)
9. Kocabas, M., Athanasiou, N., Black, M.J.: VIBE: video inference for human body pose and shape estimation. In: Proceedings of the IEEE/CVF Conference on Computer Vision and Pattern Recognition, pp. 5253–5263 (2020)
10. Kocabas, M., Huang, C.H.P., Hilliges, O., Black, M.J.: PARE: part attention regressor for 3D human body estimation. In: Proceedings of the IEEE/CVF International Conference on Computer Vision, pp. 11127–11137 (2021)
11. Kwolek, B., Michalczuk, A., Krzeszowski, T., Switonski, A., Josinski, H., Wojciechowski, K.: Calibrated and synchronized multi-view video and motion capture dataset for evaluation of gait recognition. Multimedia Tools Appl. **78**, 32437–32465 (2019)
12. Li, H., Mehul, A., Le Kernec, J., Gurbuz, S.Z., Fioranelli, F.: Sequential human gait classification with distributed radar sensor fusion. IEEE Sens. J. **21**(6), 7590–7603 (2020)
13. Liu, J., Shahroudy, A., Perez, M., Wang, G., Duan, L.Y., Kot, A.C.: NTU RGB+D 120: a large-scale benchmark for 3D human activity understanding. IEEE Trans. Pattern Anal. Mach. Intell. **42**(10), 2684–2701 (2019)
14. Loper, M., Mahmood, N., Black, M.J.: MOSH: motion and shape capture from sparse markers. ACM Trans. Graph. **33**(6), 220–1 (2014)
15. Loper, M., Mahmood, N., Romero, J., Pons-Moll, G., Black, M.J.: SMPL: a skinned multi-person linear model. ACM Trans. Graph. (TOG) **34**(6), 1–16 (2015)
16. Lu, M., et al.: Vision-based estimation of MDS-UPDRS gait scores for assessing parkinson's disease motor severity. In: Martel, A.L., et al. (eds.) MICCAI 2020. LNCS, vol. 12263, pp. 637–647. Springer, Cham (2020). https://doi.org/10.1007/978-3-030-59716-0_61
17. Mannini, A., Trojaniello, D., Cereatti, A., Sabatini, A.M.: A machine learning framework for gait classification using inertial sensors: application to elderly, post-stroke and huntingtons disease patients. Sensors **16**(1), 134 (2016)
18. Mc Ardle, R., Del Din, S., Donaghy, P., Galna, B., Thomas, A.J., Rochester, L.: The impact of environment on gait assessment: considerations from real-world gait analysis in dementia subtypes. Sensors **21**(3), 813 (2021)
19. Mc Ardle, R., Galna, B., Donaghy, P., Thomas, A., Rochester, L.: Do Alzheimer's and Lewy body disease have discrete pathological signatures of gait? Alzheimer's Dementia **15**(10), 1367–1377 (2019)
20. McKeith, I.G., et al.: Research criteria for the diagnosis of prodromal dementia with Lewy bodies. Neurology **94**(17), 743–755 (2020)
21. Mehdizadeh, S., Nabavi, H., Sabo, A., Arora, T., Iaboni, A., Taati, B.: The Toronto older adults gait archive: video and 3D inertial motion capture data of older adults walking. Sci. Data **9**(1), 398 (2022)
22. Merory, J., Wittwer, J., Rowe, C., Webster, K.: Quantitative gait analysis in patients with dementia with Lewy bodies and Alzheimer's disease. Gait posture **26**, 414–419 (2007). https://doi.org/10.1016/j.gaitpost.2006.10.006
23. Muller, C., Perisse, J., Blanc, F., Kiesmann, M., Astier, C., Vogel, T.: Corrélation des troubles de la marche au profil neuropsychologique chez les patients atteints

de maladie áalzheimer et maladie à corps de lewy. Revue Neurologique **174**, S2–S3 (2018)

24. Pavllo, D., Grangier, D., Auli, M.: QuaterNet: a quaternion-based recurrent model for human motion. In: Proceedings of the British Machine Vision Conference (BMVC) (2018)

25. Sabo, A., Mehdizadeh, S., Iaboni, A., Taati, B.: Estimating parkinsonism severity in natural gait videos of older adults with dementia. IEEE J. Biomed. Health Inform. **26**(5), 2288–2298 (2022)

26. Shahroudy, A., Liu, J., Ng, T.T., Wang, G.: NTU RGB+D: a large scale dataset for 3D human activity analysis. In: Proceedings of the IEEE Conference on Computer Vision and Pattern Recognition, pp. 1010–1019 (2016)

27. Teufl, W., et al.: Towards an inertial sensor-based wearable feedback system for patients after total hip arthroplasty: validity and applicability for gait classification with gait kinematics-based features. Sensors **19**(22), 5006 (2019)

28. Vaswani, A., et al.: Attention is all you need. In: Advances in Neural Information Processing Systems 30 (2017)

29. Von Winterfeldt, D., Edwards, W.: Decision Analysis and Behavioral Research. Cambridge University Press, Cambridge (1986)

30. Wan, Z., Li, Z., Tian, M., Liu, J., Yi, S., Li, H.: Encoder-decoder with multi-level attention for 3D human shape and pose estimation. In: Proceedings of the IEEE/CVF International Conference on Computer Vision, pp. 13033–13042 (2021)

31. Zhou, Y., Barnes, C., Lu, J., Yang, J., Li, H.: On the continuity of rotation representations in neural networks. In: Proceedings of the IEEE/CVF Conference on Computer Vision and Pattern Recognition, pp. 5745–5753 (2019)

# Enhancing Clinical Support for Breast Cancer with Deep Learning Models Using Synthetic Correlated Diffusion Imaging

Chi-en Amy Tai[1]([✉])[ID], Hayden Gunraj[1][ID], Nedim Hodzic[1], Nic Flanagan[1],
Ali Sabri[2,3][ID], and Alexander Wong[1,4,5][ID]

[1] Department of Systems Design Engineering, University of Waterloo, Waterloo, ON,
Canada
amy.tai@uwaterloo.ca
[2] Department of Radiology, McMaster University, Hamilton, ON, Canada
[3] Niagara Health System, St. Catharines, ON, Canada
[4] Waterloo AI Institute, University of Waterloo, Waterloo, ON, Canada
[5] DarwinAI Corp., Waterloo, ON, Canada

**Abstract.** Breast cancer is the second most common type of cancer in women in Canada and the United States, representing over 25% of all new female cancer cases. As such, there has been immense research and progress on improving screening and clinical support for breast cancer. In this paper, we investigate enhancing clinical support for breast cancer with deep learning models using a newly introduced magnetic resonance imaging (MRI) modality called synthetic correlated diffusion imaging (CDI$^s$). More specifically, we leverage a volumetric convolutional neural network to learn volumetric deep radiomic features from a pre-treatment cohort and construct a predictor based on the learnt features for grade and post-treatment response prediction. As the first study to learn CDI$^s$-centric radiomic sequences within a deep learning perspective for clinical decision support, we evaluated the proposed approach using the ACRIN-6698 study against those learnt using gold-standard imaging modalities. We find that the proposed approach can achieve better performance for both grade and post-treatment response prediction and thus may be a useful tool to aid oncologists in improving recommendation of treatment of patients. Subsequently, the approach to leverage volumetric deep radiomic features for breast cancer can be further extended to other applications of CDI$^s$ in the cancer domain to further improve clinical support.

**Keywords:** breast cancer · deep learning · medical imaging · synthetic correlated diffusion imaging

## 1 Introduction

Breast cancer is the second most common type of cancer in women in Canada and the United States, representing over 25% of all new female cancer cases [4].

S. Wu et al. (Eds.): AMAI 2023, LNCS 14313, pp. 83–93, 2024.
https://doi.org/10.1007/978-3-031-47076-9_9

As such, there has been immense research and progress on improving screening techniques and processes to proactively detect the presence of breast cancer in individuals at risk [30]. However, it is estimated that 2,261,419 new cases of breast cancer were diagnosed across the world in 2020 [4] and predicted that 43,700 American women will die from breast cancer in 2023 [2].

However, not all breast cancer is fatal. When patients are first diagnosed with breast cancer, they are categorized into two main types: in situ and invasive breast cancer [2]. The former is a less severe form of breast cancer that is a precursor to the latter type. The latter type, invasive breast cancer, represents approximately 80% of diagnosed cases and signifies that the cancer has already or can spread into the nearby tissue areas [2,4].

Patients with invasive breast cancer also often receive a breast cancer grade that represents the similarity of the cancer cells to normal cells under the microscope. The three breast cancer grades (low, intermediate, and high) describe the speed of growth and likelihood of a good prognosis. Low grade (grade 1) cancer has the best prognosis with slow growth and spread of the cancer, while high grade (grade 3) cancer has the worst prognosis with the greatest difference between cancer and normal cells and represent cancer that is fast-growing with quick spread to other cells. As such, the stage and grade of breast cancer are vital factors used to determine the severity of breast cancer and discern the best treatment strategy as the stage and grade have been shown to relate to the success of various treatment strategies [9]. Specifically, the gold-standard Scarff-Bloom-Richardson (SBR) grade (with example CDI[s] shown in Fig. 1) has been shown to consistently indicate a patient's response to chemotherapy [1].

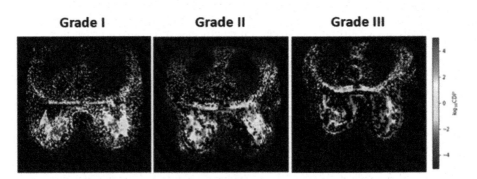

**Fig. 1.** Example breast CDI[s] images for the SBR grades.

Unfortunately, the gold-standard method of grading the breast cancer is currently determined by a pathologist looking at a tissue sample from the cancer tumour under a microscope. As such, the current method to determine the grade requires removal of some cancer cells from the patient which can lead to stress and discomfort along with high medical costs [2].

Following grading, surgery is commonly administered to prevent breast cancer from further developing and to remove cancerous tissue [2]. However, some non-metastatic breast cancer tumors are inoperable [8]. Recently, a type of treatment termed neoadjuvant chemotherapy has risen in usage as it can shrink a large tumor before surgery (so that the tumor can become operable) [8] and it may also result in a pathologic complete response (pCR) which is the absence of active cancer cells present in surgery [16]. Example breast CDI$^s$ images with and without pCR is shown in Fig. 2. However, neoadjuvant chemotherapy is expensive, time-consuming, and may expose patients to radiation as well as lead to other significant side effects such as reduced fertility [18].

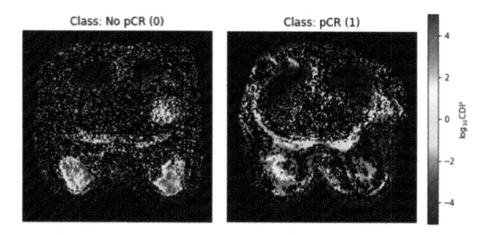

**Fig. 2.** Example breast CDI$^s$ images with and without pCR.

The current process to recommend neoadjuvant chemotherapy is based on the expert, but human judgment of the medical oncologist and/or radiation oncologist of whether the patient will live longer and benefit from the treatment [21]. With potential biases and high uncertainty in clinical judgment [27], there is potential for some erroneous recommendations leading to some patients later developing preventable detrimental advanced cancer or being exposed to unnecessary radiation.

For these clinical support tasks for breast cancer, pathologists typically consult the patient's MRI images. Current gold-standard MRI modalities include diffusion-weighted imaging (DWI), apparent diffusion coefficient (ADC), and T2-weighted (T2w). DWI is a form of MRI that measures the motion of water molecules within the tissue with the b values (0, 100, 600, 800) denoting the specific configuration of the scanner such as gradient strength with 0 indicating no diffusion sensitivity and a greater sensitivity as b increases [20]. ADC is the value obtained by taking the slope of the curve created with the different b values with lower ADC indicating regions with restricted diffusion or potentially cancerous tissue [29]. T2w is a type of contrast MRI image that enhances water signals [17]. Recently, synthetic correlated diffusion imaging (CDI$^s$) was introduced as a promising imaging modality for clinical decision support for prostate cancer [31]. CDI$^s$ introduces synthetic signals by extrapolating MRI data to introduce more data points by analyzing the direction of diffusion in the cancerous tissue.

In this paper, we investigate enhancing clinical support for breast cancer with deep learning models using a newly introduced magnetic resonance imaging (MRI) modality called synthetic correlated diffusion imaging (CDI$^s$). More specifically, we leverage a volumetric convolutional neural network to learn volumetric deep radiomic features from a pre-treatment cohort and construct a predictor based on the learnt features for breast cancer SBR grading and post-treatment response prediction to neoadjuvant chemotherapy. The dataset utilized in this study is derived from the American College of Radiology Imaging Network (ACRIN) 6698 study, which is a comprehensive multi-center study aimed at collecting patient medical images along with their treatment response to neoadjuvant breast cancer treatment [5, 24–26]. As the first study to learn CDI$^s$-centric radiomic sequences within a deep learning perspective for clinical decision support, we evaluated the proposed approach using the ACRIN-6698 study against those learnt using gold-standard imaging modalities.

## 2    Related Works

### 2.1    Breast Cancer Grading

Previous studies have examined the merit of pairing computer vision techniques for breast cancer grade prediction using radiomics [6], statistical tests [29], elasticity ratios [13], multitask learning models [11], and deep learning [7]. A comprehensive review of radiomics discussed the high potential of tumor grade prediction using radiomics on breast imaging [6] and Burnside et al. demonstrated that computer-extracted image phenotypes on magnetic resonance imaging (MRI) could accurately predict the breast cancer stage [3]. However, Surov et al. concluded that diffusion-weighted imaging used with the Mann-Whitney U test was inapt at predicting breast cancer tumour grades [29]. On the other hand, deep learning methods to identify metastatic breast cancer [30] and breast cancer grade [7] have presented high accuracies of over 80% with a review on invasive breast cancer supporting the importance of leveraging artificial intelligence on grade prediction [9].

### 2.2    Pathologic Complete Response Prediction

In the past, a variety of different modalities and methods were investigated to predict pathologic complete response with patient features such as using a nonparametric Mann-Whitney test for diffusion-weighted imaging (DWI) and MRS [28], logistic regression models on MRI images [19], hard threshold parameter values [12], AdaBoost classifier with qCT features [22], and an assortment of machine learning models with qCT features [23]. Furthermore, previous studies have also examined the usage of deep learning and volumetric data with breast cancer. Convolutional neural network algorithms were studied to predict post-NAC axillary response with breast MRI images [14], a three-layer 3D CNN architecture was trained to detect breast cancer using a dataset of 5547 images with an AUC of 0.85 [15], and convolutional neural networks with 3D MRI images were used to predict pCR to neoadjuvant chemotherapy in breast cancer [10].

## 3    Methodology

### 3.1    Patient Cohort and Imaging Protocol

The pre-treatment (T0) patient cohort in the American College of Radiology Imaging Network (ACRIN) 6698/I-SPY2 study was used as the patient cohort in this study [5,24–26]. After removing patients that had incomplete data, 252 patient cases remained for use for the task of grading, and 253 patients for the task of pathologic complete response prediction. The ACRIN study contained MRI images across 10 different institutions for patients at four different timepoints in their treatment [5,24–26]. However, only the timepoint T0 was used as patients at this stage had not received any neoadjuvant chemotherapy and thus, the images would be most representative of the ones that pathologists would evaluate to determine SBR grade and decide if the patient should receive neoadjuvant chemotherapy. To compare the performance of CDI$^s$ with current gold-standard MRI modalities used in clinical practice, diffusion-weighted imaging (DWI) acquisitions, T2-weighted (T2w) acquisitions, and apparent diffusion coefficient (ADC) maps were also obtained. Using the DWI images, we also obtain CDI$^s$ acquisitions for each of the patient cases. Finally, the SBR grade for each breast cancer patient and the post-treatment pCR to neoadjuvant chemotherapy was also obtained after pre-treatment imaging was conducted to facilitate for learning and evaluation purposes.

### 3.2    Extracting Deep Radiomic Sequences from CDI$^s$

To facilitate for the investigation into the efficacy of volumetric deep radiomic features from CDI$^s$ for the breast cancer tasks, in this study we introduce a clinical support workflow shown in Fig. 3. More specifically, CDI$^s$ acquisitions are first performed on a given patient, which involves the acquisition of multiple native DWI signals with different b-values, passing these signals into a signal synthesizer to produce synthetic signals and then mixing the native and synthetic signals together to obtain a final signal (CDI$^s$) [31]. The CDI$^s$ acquisitions are then standardized into $224 \times 224 \times 25$ volumetric data cubes to achieve dimensionality consistency for machine learning purposes. Next, motivated by the advances in deep learning as well as the volumetric nature of CDI$^s$ data, a 34-layer volumetric residual convolutional neural network architecture was constructed and leveraged to learn volumetric deep radiomic features from the standardized volumetric data cubes. The aim with leveraging volumetric deep learning at this stage is to, rather than design hand-crafted radiomic features, directly learn volumetric deep radiomic features from patient data that characterizes the intrinsic properties of breast cancer tissue as captured by CDI$^s$ that are relevant as it relates to cancer SBR grading and patient pCR to neoadjuvant chemotherapy after pre-treatment imaging. This volumetric neural network can then be used to produce deep radiomic features for each patient based on their CDI$^s$ data cubes. Finally, a grading (or pCR) predictor comprising of a fully-connected neural network architecture is then learnt based on the extracted deep radiomic feature and SBR grading (or patient post-treatment pCR) data, and subsequently used to predict patient SBR grade (or pCR post-treatment to neoadjuvant chemotherapy).

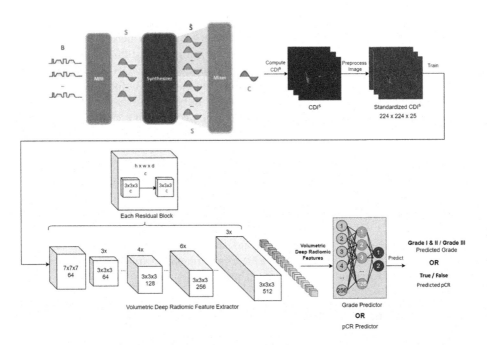

**Fig. 3.** Clinical support workflow for grade (and pCR) prediction using volumetric deep radiomic features from synthetic correlated diffusion imaging (CDI$^s$).

To evaluate the efficacy of the proposed approach, we conducted leave-one-out cross-validation (LOOCV) on the patient cohort with accuracy being the performance metric of interest. For comparison consistency, a separate volumetric deep radiomic feature extractor and grade (or pCR) predictor (with the same network architectures as for CDI$^s$ as described in the Deep Learning Method Setup section) was used to learn a set of volumetric deep radiomic features from each gold-standard MRI modality (DWI, T2w, and ADC).

As seen in Table 1, there is an uneven distribution of patients between the three grades and hence, SBR grade I and II were combined into one category.

### 3.3 pCR Prediction via Volumetric Deep Radiomic Features

Notably, we also leveraged DWI acquisitions in two different ways: 1) individual sets of features are learnt from DWI acquisitions of each b-value (b = 0, 100, 600, 800), and 2) an individual set of features are also learnt from the combined stack of DWI acquisitions (namely, the b-values are treated as another channel in the input).

**Table 1.** SBR grade distribution in the patient cohort.

| SBR Grade | Number of Patients |
|---|---|
| Grade I (Low) | 5 |
| Grade II (Intermediate) | 72 |
| Grade III (High) | 175 |

## 4 Results

### 4.1 Breast Cancer Grading (SBR Grade)

As seen in Table 2, leveraging volumetric deep radiomic features for CDI$^s$ achieves the highest grade predictive accuracy of 87.7% with both sensitivity and specificity values over 80%. Furthermore, CDI$^s$ outperforms the gold-standard imaging modalities with an improvement of over 10% on the next highest modality (T2w). With the highest gold-standard MRI modality only achieving a prediction accuracy of 76.59%, over 10% lower than CDI$^s$, the proposed approach with CDI$^s$ can increase the grade prediction performance compared to gold-standard MRI modalities. An illustrative example highlighting the visual differences between the imaging modalities of ADC, CDI$^s$, DWI (b = 800), and T2w for a patient case where grade prediction was correct for CDI$^s$ but not the other modalities is shown Fig. 4.

**Table 2.** SBR grade prediction accuracy using LOOCV for different imaging modalities.

| Modality | Accuracy | Sensitivity | Specificity |
|---|---|---|---|
| **CDIs** | **87.70%** | **90.29%** | **81.82%** |
| T2w | 76.59% | 99.43% | 24.68% |
| ADC | 69.44% | 100.00% | 0.00% |
| DWI | 69.44% | 95.43% | 10.39% |

### 4.2  pCR Prediction via Volumetric Deep Radiomic Features

As seen in Table 3, with the exception of ADC, leveraging volumetric deep radiomic features from each of the imaging modalities achieved pCR predictive accuracy over 80% with the highest accuracy obtained from the CDI$^s$ imaging modality. The volumetric deep radiomic features learnt using CDI$^s$ enabled a pCR prediction accuracy of 87.75%, which is over 3% above the next best gold-standard MRI modality (i.e., DWI (b = 800)). An illustrative example highlighting the visual differences between the imaging modalities of ADC, CDI$^s$, DWI (b = 800), and T2w for a patient case where pCR prediction was correct for CDI$^s$ and DWI (b = 800) but not the other modalities is shown Fig. 5.

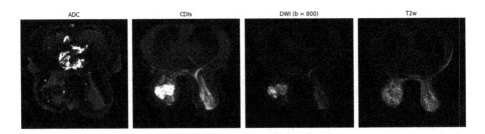

**Fig. 4.** An example slice illustrating visual differences between ADC, CDI$^s$, DWI, and T2w at pre-treatment for a patient who has SBR Grade II (Intermediate). In this patient case, grade prediction was correct for CDI$^s$ but not the other modalities.

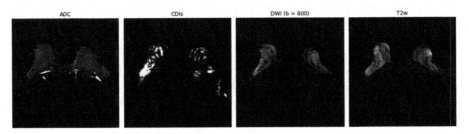

**Fig. 5.** An example slice illustrating visual differences between ADC, CDI$^s$, DWI, and T2w before neoadjuvant chemotherapy for a patient who experienced pCR. In this patient case, pCR prediction was correct for CDI$^s$ and DWI (b = 800) but not the other modalities.

**Table 3.** pCR prediction accuracy using LOOCV for different imaging modalities.

| Imaging Modality | Accuracy (%) |
|---|---|
| **CDI$^s$** | **87.75** |
| ADC | 79.84 |
| T2w | 83.79 |
| DWI (b = 0, 100, 600, 800) | 84.19 |
| DWI (b = 0) | 84.19 |
| DWI (b = 100) | 82.21 |
| DWI (b = 600) | 84.19 |
| DWI (b = 800) | 84.58 |

## 5   Conclusion

In this paper, we investigate enhancing clinical support for breast cancer with deep learning models using a newly introduced magnetic resonance imaging (MRI) modality called synthetic correlated diffusion imaging (CDI$^s$). Specifically, we leverage patients in the ACRIN-6698 study for the predictive tasks of breast cancer SBR grading and pCR prediction after neoadjuvant chemotherapy. Evaluated against current gold-standard imaging modalities, synthetic correlated diffusion imaging shows to enhance clinical support for breast cancer when paired with deep learning models, achieving a prediction accuracy of 87.70% and 87.75% for grading and pathologic complete response respectively. Given the promising results and higher performance of using CDI$^s$ over the current gold-standard MRI images, future work involves expanding the study with a larger patient cohort to further validate our findings and leveraging improved CDI$^s$ coefficient optimization to improve prediction performance.

**Prospect of Application.** The two models can be applied for the clinical tasks of breast cancer grading and pCR prediction respectively. It is envisioned that these models will be used by pathologists as an aid and to help identify patterns for more efficient breast cancer grading and effective treatment planning. These models should not be deployed standalone, rather as a tool for clinicians.

## References

1. Amat, S., et al.: Scarff-Bloom-Richardson (SBR) grading: a pleiotropic marker of chemosensitivity in invasive ductal breast carcinomas treated by neoadjuvant chemotherapy. Int. J. Oncol. **4**, 791–6 (2002). https://link.springer.com/article/10.1007/s00428-021-03141-2
2. American Cancer Society: Breast cancer (2022). https://www.cancer.org/cancer/breast-cancer. Accessed 03 Aug 2023

3. Burnside, E.S., et al.: Using computer-extracted image phenotypes from tumors on breast magnetic resonance imaging to predict breast cancer pathologic stage. ACS J. **122**(5), 748–757 (2016). https://acsjournals.onlinelibrary.wiley.com/doi/full/10.1002/cncr.29791

4. Cancer.NET: Breast cancer - statistics (2023). https://www.cancer.net/cancer-types/breast-cancer/statistics. Accessed 10 June 2023

5. Clark, K., et al.: The cancer imaging archive (TCIA): maintaining and operating a public information repository. J. Digit. Imaging **26**(6), 1045–1057 (2013)

6. Conti, A., et al.: Radiomics in breast cancer classification and prediction. Semin. Cancer Biol. **72**, 238–250 (2021). https://doi.org/10.1016/j.semcancer.2020.04.002. https://www.sciencedirect.com/science/article/pii/S1044579X20300833, precision Medicine in Breast Cancer

7. Couture, H.D., et al.: Image analysis with deep learning to predict breast cancer grade, ER status, histologic subtype, and intrinsic subtypes. NPJ Breast Cancer **4**(30) (2018). https://www.nature.com/articles/s41523-018-0079-1

8. Dimitrakakis, C., Keramopoulos, A.: Survival in primary inoperable breast cancer patients. Eur. J. Gynaecol. Oncol. **25**(3), 367–372 (2004)

9. van Dooijeweert, C., et al.: Grading of invasive breast carcinoma: the way forward. Virchows Archiv **480**, 33–43 (2022). https://link.springer.com/article/10.1007/s00428-021-03141-2

10. Duanmu, H., et al.: Prediction of pathological complete response to neoadjuvant chemotherapy in breast cancer using deep learning with integrative imaging, molecular and demographic data. In: Martel, A.L., et al. (eds.) MICCAI 2020. LNCS, vol. 12262, pp. 242–252. Springer, Cham (2020). https://doi.org/10.1007/978-3-030-59713-9_24

11. Fan, M., et al.: Joint prediction of breast cancer histological grade and KI-67 expression level based on DCE-MRI and DWI radiomics. IEEE J. Biomed. Health Inform. **24**(6), 1632–1642 (2020). https://ieeexplore.ieee.org/abstract/document/8915701

12. Fangberget, A., et al.: Neoadjuvant chemotherapy in breast cancer-response evaluation and prediction of response to treatment using dynamic contrast-enhanced and diffusion-weighted MR imaging. Eur. Radiol. **21**, 1188–1199 (2011)

13. Grajo, J.R., Barr, R.G.: Strain elastography for prediction of breast cancer tumor grades. J. Ultrasound Med. **35**(1) (2014). https://onlinelibrary.wiley.com/doi/abs/10.7863/ultra.33.1.129

14. Ha, R., et al.: Predicting post neoadjuvant axillary response using a novel convolutional neural network algorithm. Ann. Surg. Oncol. **25**, 3037–3043 (2018)

15. Haq, A.U., et al.: 3DCNN: three-layers deep convolutional neural network architecture for breast cancer detection using clinical image data. In: 17th International Computer Conference on Wavelet Active Media Technology and Information Processing (ICCWAMTIP). ICCWAMTIP, Chengdu, China. IEEE (2020)

16. DePolo, J.: Pathologic complete response to targeted therapy before surgery linked to better survival for early-stage HER2-positive breast cancer (2020). https://www.breastcancer.org/research-news/neoadjuvant-pcr-linked-to-better-survival. Accessed 02 June 2022

17. Kawahara, D., Nagata, Y.: T1-weighted and T2-weighted MRI image synthesis with convolutional generative adversarial networks. Rep. Pract. Oncol. Radiother. **26**(1), 35–42 (2021). https://doi.org/10.5603/RPOR.a2021.0005. https://journals.viamedica.pl/rpor/article/view/RPOR.a2021.0005

18. Kunst, N., et al.: Cost-effectiveness of neoadjuvant-adjuvant treatment strategies for women with ERBB2 (HER2)-positive breast cancer. JAMA Netw. Open **3**(11) (2020)

19. Li, X.B., et al.: Biomarkers predicting pathologic complete response to neoadjuvant chemotherapy in breast cancer. Am. J. Clin. Pathol. **145**(6), 871–878 (2016)

20. Martinez-Heras, E., et al.: Diffusion-weighted imaging: recent advances and applications. Seminars Ultrasound CT MRI **42**(5), 490–506 (2021). https://doi.org/10.1053/j.sult.2021.07.006.  https://www.sciencedirect.com/science/article/pii/S0887217121000846, advances in Neuroradiology I

21. Masood, S.: Neoadjuvant chemotherapy in breast cancers. Womens Health **12**(5), 480–491 (2016)

22. Moghadas-Dastjerdi, H., et al.: Machine learning-based a priori chemotherapy response prediction in breast cancer patients using textural CT biomarkers. In: 42nd Annual International Conference of the IEEE Engineering in Medicine & Biology Society (EMBC). EMBC, Montreal, QC, Canada. IEEE (2020)

23. Moghadas-Dastjerdi, H., et al.: A priori prediction of tumour response to neoadjuvant chemotherapy in breast cancer patients using quantitative CT and machine learning. Sci. Rep. **10**, 1188–1199 (2020)

24. Newitt, D.C., et al.: Test-retest repeatability and reproducibility of ADC measures by breast DWI: results from the ACRIN 6698 trial. J. Magn. Reson. Imaging **49**(6), 1617–1628 (2018)

25. Newitt, D.C., et al.: ACRIN 6698/I-SPY2 breast DWI [data set]. The Cancer Imaging Archive (2021)

26. Partridge, S.C., et al.: Diffusion-weighted MRI findings predict pathologic response in neoadjuvant treatment of breast cancer: the ACRIN 6698 multicenter trial. Radiology **289**(3), 618–627 (2018)

27. Redelmeier, D.A., et al.: Problems for clinical judgement: introducing cognitive psychology as one more basic science. Can. Med. Assoc. J. **164**(3), 358–360 (2001)

28. Shin, H.J., et al.: Prediction of pathologic response to neoadjuvant chemotherapy in patients with breast cancer using diffusion-weighted imaging and MRS. NMR Biomed. **25**(12), 1349–1359 (2012)

29. Surov, A., et al.: Can diffusion-weighted imaging predict tumor grade and expression of KI-67 in breast cancer? A multicenter analysis. Breast Cancer Res. **20**(58) (2018). https://breast-cancer-research.biomedcentral.com/articles/10.1186/s13058-018-0991-1

30. Wang, D., et al.: Deep learning for identifying metastatic breast cancer (2016). https://doi.org/10.48550/ARXIV.1606.05718. https://arxiv.org/abs/1606.05718

31. Wong, A., et al.: Synthetic correlated diffusion imaging hyperintensity delineates clinically significant prostate cancer. Sci. Rep. **12**(3376) (2022). https://doi.org/10.1038/s41598-022-06872-7

# Image-Based 3D Reconstruction of Cleft Lip and Palate Using a Learned Shape Prior

Lasse Lingens[1]([✉]), Baran Gözcü[1], Till Schnabel[1], Yoriko Lill[2], Benito K. Benitez[2,3,4], Prasad Nalabothu[2,3,4], Andreas A. Mueller[2,3,4], Markus Gross[1], and Barbara Solenthaler[1]

[1] Department of Computer Science, ETH Zurich, Zürich, Switzerland
`lasse.lingens@inf.ethz.ch`
[2] Oral and Craniomaxillofacial Surgery, University Hospital Basel and University of Basel, Basel, Switzerland
[3] Department of Clinical Research, University of Basel, Basel, Switzerland
[4] Department of Biomedical Engineering, University of Basel, Basel, Switzerland

**Abstract.** We present a novel pipeline that takes smartphone videos of the intraoral region of newborn cleft patients as input and produces a 3D mesh. The mesh can be used to facilitate the plate treatment of the cleft and support surgery planning. A retrained LoFTR-based method creates an initial sparse point cloud. Next, we utilize our collection of existing scans of previous patients to train an implicit shape model. The shape model allows for refined denoising of the initial sparse point cloud and; therefore, enhances the camera pose estimation. Finally, we complete the model with a dense reconstruction based on multi-view stereo. With Moving Least Squares and Poisson reconstruction we convert the point cloud into a mesh. This method is low-cost in hardware acquisition and supports minimal training time for a user to utilize it.

**Keywords:** Image-based 3D reconstruction · data-driven modeling · shape prior · cleft lip and palate

## 1 Introduction

Cleft lip and palate is the most common craniofacial birth defect with an estimated prevalence of 1 in 700 [13]. Presurgical orthopedic (PSO) treatment is commonly used to narrow the cleft and to enable a single-surgical repair [12]. The treatment involves the fabrication of a patient-specific plate that is inserted into the mouth and on the palate of a patient. This prevents the tongue from reaching inside the palate cleft and supports a natural narrowing of the cleft. The plate additionally eases food consumption and helps early speech development [2]. The creation of such an orthopedic plate consists of two steps. First, the practitioner acquires a 3D model of the specific intraoral region, either using an intraoral scanner or through silicon impression and subsequent fabrication of a plaster cast. Second, the digital or physical 3D model is used to design a person-specific well-fitting plate.

© The Author(s), under exclusive license to Springer Nature Switzerland AG 2024
S. Wu et al. (Eds.): AMAI 2023, LNCS 14313, pp. 94–103, 2024.
https://doi.org/10.1007/978-3-031-47076-9_10

By using an entirely digital process, and hence 3D digital models of the cleft lip and palate, the automatic computation of the plate is enabled [18]. While plaster casts can be digitized and serve as input to the digital plate computation, the mesh quality is typically lower, and more importantly, the impression is taken under airway-endangering conditions [6]. Therefore, a fully digital alternative via intraoral scanners is the preferred capture technology today. However, clinics in low- and middle-income countries (LMICs) very often do not have access to such scanning devices, due to their high costs and requirement of trained personnel.

In this work, we aim to provide an alternative solution to intraoral scanners targeted at LMICs, such that the previously developed digital plate computation [18] can be applied. Our method turns a smartphone into an intraoral scanner, which outputs a digital 3D model of the cleft lip and palate just from a set of captured photographs. We leverage state-of-the-art deep learning based methods from Computer Vision for the first step of our 3D reconstruction [21], and combine it with a cleft shape prior trained on a collected data set of cleft lip and palate scans. We show that the domain-specific prior serves as a denoiser, leading to higher-quality meshes than domain-agnostic approaches. We further present the entire digital processing pipeline - from the raw input video to the final fabricated plate - and discuss the design choices of each step. Our results highlight the enormous potential of smartphone scanners for LMICs, and our work can be seen as a first step towards achieving this goal. Our contributions can be summarized as:

- Introduction of the detector-free local feature matching using transformer networks (LoFTR) to the medical community.
- A learned shape prior for cleft lip and palate, which was trained on a dataset of patient scans and is based on deep signed distance function.
- A complete digital processing pipeline: from an RGB smartphone video as input to the final printed orthopedic plate.

## 2   Related Work

Neural approaches have led to drastic improvements of image-based 3D reconstruction quality across disciplines. In the following, we focus our discussion on photogrammetry and data-driven shape models.

*Photogrammetry:* Photogrammetry was dominated for a long time by detector-based local feature matchers. Two successful and prominent techniques are Invariant Feature Transform (SIFT) [11] and ORB [16]. These methods are hand-crafted and have been adopted in most computer vision-based tasks until recently. With the success of learning-based methods in many fields, photogrammetry progressed as well. NeRF-based methods such as NeuS [22] build a full implicit representation of the shape from the input images and camera pose estimations. Other recent notable methods include SuperPoint [8] as a feature extractor and SuperGlue [17] as a feature matcher that works in tandem with SuperPoint. The recently proposed detector-free method Detector-Free Local

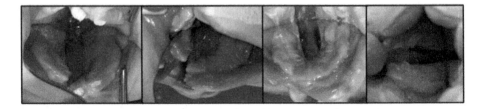

**Fig. 1.** Selected input images highlighting the challenges of the uncontrolled capture.

Feature Matching with Transformers (LoFTR) added the transformer network structure to correlate points spatially and build semi-dense correspondences between two images, offering more robust reconstructions for low feature surfaces. These properties are of great benefit for the reconstruction of the cleft region and is; therefore, featured as a central part of our proposed solution.

*Data-Driven Shape Models:* Data-Driven Shape Models find their origin in the concept of PCA-based models. They have been explored in a variety of different fields, though the main area of research focuses on faces [3,4]. The main focus of a morphable model is to learn the shape of an object class and compress that information into a compact latent. They are often used as a prior to fit observational data to and create a result within expectation of possible observations. In recent years, the statistical approach was replaced with learning-based methods. One prominent method is DeepSDF [14] and its variants [5,9]. We leverage the representative power of DeepSDF and train it on cleft data to create a domain-specific shape prior, which is particularly useful in our setting where we have noisy and incomplete point data.

## 3   Methods

The goal of our work is to compute a digital 3D model of the cleft lip and palate based on an intraoral smartphone video, which is precise enough to compute and 3D print an orthopedic plate for the pre-surgical treatment. The smartphone video is captured in an uncontrolled environment, specifically, by doctors in a clinical setting at hospitals. This comes with multiple challenges for an image-based 3D reconstruction technique, including data that is captured through a mirror, with unsteady hand motion, movement of the infant during the capturing process, varying light conditions, occlusions due to the operators' hands, small capturing angles and limited mouth opening. Moreover, the intraoral surface has low quality features, no clear edges or corners, the surface is very reflective and the object of interest might undergo movement of even non-rigid nature. Since not all mobile phones are equipped with depth sensors, our reconstruction method is solely using RGB input data. Figure 1 shows example images that serve as input to our method.

Our reconstruction pipeline consists of multiple steps. We first pre-process the video to mask out the relevant region and sub-sample the frames based on a quality score and a given interval (Sect. 3.1). Next, we create a semi-dense reconstruction with LoFTR [21] (Sect. 3.2) and refine the reconstruction with DeepSDF [14] (Sect. 3.3). These two steps represent the core of our method. The refined semi-dense reconstruction is then completed to a dense reconstruction with Multi-View Stereo (MVS) [20]. Next, we fit our shape prior to our dense reconstruction and remove points with a distance greater than 0.5 mm. We use Moving Least Squares (MLS) [1] (*radius = 2 mm, order = 3*) to smooth out the resulting point cloud. This step is manually verified and the parameters adapted, if necessary. Finally, we use Poisson Reconstruction [10] (*tree depth = 8*) to create a mesh. This resulting mesh then serves as the input to the orthopedic plate computation [18]. In Fig. 2 we show our pipeline to reconstruct the palatal area.

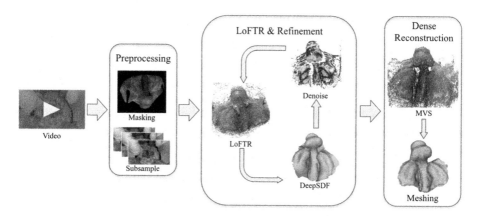

**Fig. 2.** Our pipeline uses a smartphone video as input that was captured in an uncontrolled clinical setting. After pre-processing, we compute a semi-dense reconstruction and use our DeepSDF shape prior as a denoiser, before computing the final mesh.

### 3.1  Data Pre-processing

We semi-automatically mask all the frames of the video input to only include the palate region using MiVOS [7] as masking tool. This prevents ill-posed equation systems for the camera and point positions which are caused by the mirror in the image. We then automatically sub-sample the frames based on a heuristic approach to improve the average quality of the images and further reduce the processing time of the pipeline. We sub-sample at fixed intervals while considering within a range of each interval the quality of the image depending on their blurriness. To calculate the quality score, we apply a Laplacian kernel pixel-wise to each image.

## 3.2   Semi-dense Reconstruction

For the semi-dense reconstruction, we use the state-of-the-art approach LoFTR [21], which outperforms classical feature extraction and matching methods. We verified the performance of LoFTR against a classic Structure from Motion and MVS approach with COLMAP [19,20], SuperGlue+SuperPoint [8, 17] and NeuS [22]. LoFTR was the most robust approach over all cases, while it occasionally was outperformed for a single reconstruction. LoFTR takes a number of image pairs to be matched against each other as input. We use the two matching methods NETVLAD and sequential matching for pair finding. NETVLAD calculates the best $n$ pairs based on global feature descriptions in all images. Sequential matching takes advantage that the input format is a video and matches each frame to the next $m$ sub-sampled frames. LoFTR finds matches between the resulting image pairs and we use COLMAP to extract a semi-dense reconstruction out of the resulting meshes.

## 3.3   Data-Driven Shape Prior

We use Deep Signed Distance Function (DeepSDF) [14], which has the advantage that it can be fit to point clouds, even if they are a noisy representation of a shape. The quality of the meshes produced by the model when fitted to a noisy point cloud is not sufficient for our targeted medical purpose. However, it provides a rough shape estimation for the current reconstruction. We utilize this shape estimation to denoise the point cloud that we get with the semi-dense reconstruction with LoFTR. In DeepSDF, two networks are trained in parallel. The first network is an encoder that receives sampled points of an observation and their signed distance to the mesh. The output is a latent code. The second network takes the latent code together with a single point and estimates the signed distance of that point to the mesh. We first align our point cloud with the canonical frame of reference of DeepSDF. We then sample the point cloud and create a shape estimation using our DeepSDF model. We apply the inverse transform of the initial alignment to the shape model estimation, such that it is re-projected into the reconstruction space. We calculate the distance from the point cloud to the closest point on the mesh and reject points over a threshold $d$. We track the removed points to their corresponding features and matches, and discard those as well. This in turn leads to refined camera poses, as the noisy points are no longer part of the equations system. Finally, we recompute the triangulation - now with reduced noise - to refine the result.

## 3.4   Data Collection

We collected a data set of cleft lip and palate shapes, which consists of 188 intraoral scans and 553 plaster casts of the intraoral region of 489 cleft patients. The patients at scan time have an age of mostly 1–14 months. 178 of the patients are classified with a unilateral cleft and 86 with a bilateral, while the remaining are either not clearly classifiable or classified as a different cleft type. This data set was used to train the DeepSDF model. For video acquisition we used a Google Pixel 4 and chose the 4k camera with 25 fps. We instructed the doctors to fulfill a steady slow ellipsoid movement with either a camera or a mirror to capture as many different viewing angles as possible. The duration of a video is usually between 15 and 30 seconds. Additionally, we tried to minimize occlusions, such as tubes, and non-rigid movement in the area of interest. As the object in focus are infants, sometimes awake, the videos have high variance in quality.

## 4   Results

In the following, we evaluate the quality of the 3D reconstructions (Sect. 4.1) and show the resulting pre-surgical plates (Sect. 4.2), demonstrating a proof-of-concept for the clinical use of a smartphone-based cleft and palate scanner. We further evaluate the effectiveness of the learned shape prior in Sect. 4.3.

### 4.1   3D Reconstruction

We show the reconstruction quality for two unilateral cleft and two bilateral cleft cases in Fig. 3, and compar e the reconstructed shapes (second row) to the ground truth intraoral scans (top row). We display the color-coded error maps for the entire shape (third row), with blue and red corresponding to 0 mm and 1.5 mm, respectively. As expected, higher errors can be observed near the boundary, while smaller errors can be found in the relevant region near the ridges. The latter reflects the area that is relevant for the plate, as the final, fabricated plate needs to fit tightly to these ridges. We therefore evaluate the error for the particular area of interest as visualized in the last row. For the selected patient cases, we achieve a mean error of $[0.11, 0.39, 0.37, 0.28]$mm in the relevant area.

### 4.2   Plate Evaluation

In order to evaluate if the accuracy of our smartphone based reconstruction is high enough for clinical settings, we used the digital plate computation algorithm of Schnabel et al. [18] and quantitatively assess the difference of the resulting digital plates when using an intraoral scan as input (second column) versus using our 3D reconstructed shape (third column) in Fig. 4. For the two selected patient cases, we achieve a mean error of 0.11 mm and 0.24 mm, respectively. Note that the error is again only relevant along the ridges, and hence larger errors in the area that bridges the ridge areas are acceptable. Since it is difficult to conclude from these numbers if the resulting physical plate will fit well on a patient's palate, we 3D printed four selected plates using the previously reported clinical procedure [18], and collected feedback from three healthcare professionals who assessed the fitting quality. Out of four plates, they assessed two, three and three plates, respectively, to be applicable after no or only minor subtractive adjustments.

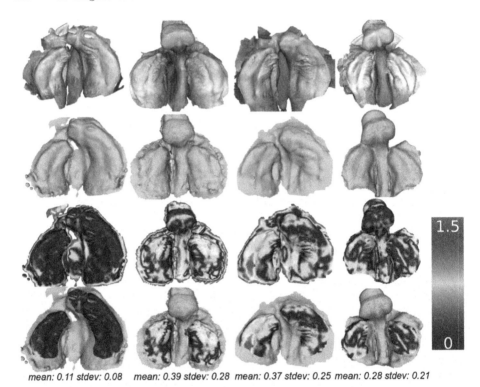

mean: 0.11 stdev: 0.08     mean: 0.39 stdev: 0.28   mean: 0.37 stdev: 0.25  mean: 0.28 stdev: 0.21

**Fig. 3.** From left to right we show four selected unilateral and bilateral patient cases. From top to bottom we show the ground truth meshes acquired with an intraoral scanner, our reconstructed meshes, and the error maps for the entire shape and partial area relevant for the pre-surgical plate. (Color figure online)

### 4.3    Learned Shape Prior

The learned shape prior is a crucial part of our pipeline, and we therefore evaluate the expressiveness of our DeepSDF model for two selected cleft shapes in Fig. 5. For the reconstruction of these two introral scans, the model achieves an average error of 0.14 mm and 0.16 mm in the area of interest, respectively. While the overall shape is approached quite accurately, it is also visible that very fine structural details are smoothed, which is a common problem of DeepSDF.

In our algorithm we use the DeepSDF shape prior as a denoiser. We have compared our method with the common denoisers Statistical Outlier Removal (SOR) and PointCleanNet (PCN) [15], and evaluated the methods based on correct identification of noise and of points that should be retained. Our data-driven shape prior noise removal outperforms the other methods (in percentages) for 1) correctly retained correct points (PCN: 45, SOR: 60, ours: 66), 2) incorrectly retained noisy points (PCN: 55, SOR: 40, ours: 34), 3) correctly removed noisy points (PCN: 81, SOR: 81, ours: 86), 4) incorrectly removed correct points

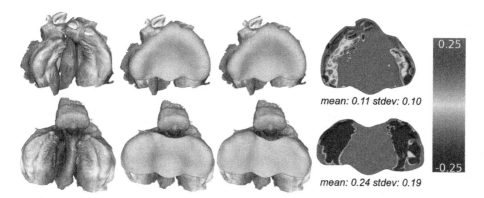

**Fig. 4.** For two selected cases we compare the resulting digital plates, once computed with an intraoral scan (second column) and our 3D reconstructed shape (third column). We visualize the plates on the original scan (left). The color-coded errors (right) are absolute distances of the region of interest around the ridges.

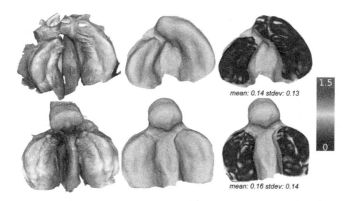

**Fig. 5.** Reconstruction of an intraoral scan (left) through our DeepSDF model (middle) and color-coded errors in the area of interest (right).

(PCN: 19, SOR: 19, ours: 14). Note that we hand-tuned the parameters for the alternative methods and applied multiple iterations to optimize their results.

## 5    Conclusion

We have presented a first smartphone-based scanning solution for the 3D reconstruction of the cleft and palatal region. All steps in our pipeline are data-driven and outperform conventional approaches when applied to input captured in uncontrolled clinical settings. We have demonstrated a proof-of-concept by computing and fabricating plates based on our reconstruction, which can then be used for the pre-surgical treatment of cleft lip and palate. The evaluation of the clinicians was overall positive, indicating great promise for using smartphone-based scanners in clinical settings. However, a larger evaluation and clinical study is needed to draw a resulting conclusion.

*Limitations.* Our current approach is heavily dependent on the quality of the input video. In some cases the video was too short, the infant moved too much or the camera was too shaky. This led to a failure of reconstruction. In addition, in some cases it proved to be difficult to capture the outside regions of the ridges as they were often occluded by the lips. Some error margin can be explained due to the global shape model and the necessary smoothing in the post-processing step, both of which reduce high frequency details in the reconstructions. Finally, there is a potential to further increase the automation level of our pipeline and eliminate the remaining manual steps such as initial mask segmentation or alignment of shape model and reconstruction.

*Prospect of Application.* Our image-based 3D reconstruction approach enables the use of the PSO in low- and middle- income countries, where intraoral scanners are often not available. Our method relies solely on RGB images, which reduces requirements related to hardware. It further supports remote check ups, as the equipment is affordable and available and the image capture process is innocuous.

# References

1. Alexa, M., Behr, J., Cohen-Or, D., Fleishman, S., Levin, D., Silva, C.: Computing and rendering point set surfaces. IEEE Trans. Visual Comput. Graphics **9**(1), 3–15 (2003). https://doi.org/10.1109/TVCG.2003.1175093
2. Alzain, I., Batwa, W., Cash, A., Murshid, Z.A.: Presurgical cleft lip and palate orthopedics: an overview. Clin. Cosmet. Investig. Dent. **9**, 53–59 (2017)
3. Blanz, V., Vetter, T.: A morphable model for the synthesis of 3d faces. In: Proceedings of the 26th Annual Conference on Computer Graphics and Interactive Techniques, SIGGRAPH 1999, pp. 187–194. ACM Press/Addison-Wesley Publishing Co., USA (1999). https://doi.org/10.1145/311535.311556
4. Booth, J., Roussos, A., Zafeiriou, S., Ponniah, A., Dunaway, D.: A 3d morphable model learnt from 10,000 faces. In: 2016 IEEE Conference on Computer Vision and Pattern Recognition (CVPR), pp. 5543–5552 (2016). https://doi.org/10.1109/CVPR.2016.598
5. Chabra, R., et al.: Deep local shapes: learning local SDF priors for detailed 3d reconstruction. CoRR abs/2003.10983 (2020). https://arxiv.org/abs/2003.10983
6. Chate, R.A.C.: A report on the hazards encountered when taking neonatal cleft palate impressions (1983–1992). Br. J. Orthod. **22**(4), 299–307 (1995). https://doi.org/10.1179/bjo.22.4.299. pMID: 8580095
7. Cheng, H.K., Tai, Y.W., Tang, C.K.: Modular interactive video object segmentation: interaction-to-mask, propagation and difference-aware fusion. In: CVPR (2021)
8. DeTone, D., Malisiewicz, T., Rabinovich, A.: Superpoint: self-supervised interest point detection and description. CoRR abs/1712.07629 (2017). https://arxiv.org/abs/1712.07629

9. Genova, K., Cole, F., Sud, A., Sarna, A., Funkhouser, T.A.: Deep structured implicit functions. CoRR abs/1912.06126 (2019). https://arxiv.org/abs/1912.06126

10. Kazhdan, M., Bolitho, M., Hoppe, H.: Poisson surface reconstruction. In: Proceedings of the Fourth Eurographics Symposium on Geometry Processing, SGP 2006, pp. 61–70. Eurographics Association, Goslar, DEU (2006)

11. Lowe, D.G.: Distinctive image features from scale-invariant keypoints. Int. J. Comput. Vis. **60**(2), 91–110 (2004). https://doi.org/10.1023/B:VISI.0000029664.99615.94

12. Mishra, B., Singh, A.K., Zaidi, J., Singh, G.K., Agrawal, R., Kumar, V.: Presurgical nasoalveolar molding for correction of cleft lip nasal deformity: experience from northern India. Eplasty **10** (2010)

13. Mossey, P., Modell, B.: Epidemiology of oral clefts 2012: an international perspective. In: Cleft Lip and Palate: Epidemiology, Aetiology and Treatment. S. Karger AG (2012). https://doi.org/10.1159/000337464

14. Park, J.J., Florence, P.R., Straub, J., Newcombe, R.A., Lovegrove, S.: DeepSDF: learning continuous signed distance functions for shape representation. CoRR abs/1901.05103 (2019). https://arxiv.org/abs/1901.05103

15. Rakotosaona, M., Barbera, V.L., Guerrero, P., Mitra, N.J., Ovsjanikov, M.: POINTCLEANNET: learning to denoise and remove outliers from dense point clouds. CoRR abs/1901.01060 (2019). https://arxiv.org/abs/1901.01060

16. Rublee, E., Rabaud, V., Konolige, K., Bradski, G.: ORB: an efficient alternative to sift or surf. In: 2011 International Conference on Computer Vision, pp. 2564–2571 (2011). https://doi.org/10.1109/ICCV.2011.6126544

17. Sarlin, P.E., DeTone, D., Malisiewicz, T., Rabinovich, A.: SuperGlue: learning feature matching with graph neural networks. In: CVPR (2020)

18. Schnabel, T.N., et al.: Automated and data-driven plate computation for presurgical cleft lip and palate treatment. Int. J. Comput. Assist. Radiol. Surg. (2023). https://doi.org/10.1007/s11548-023-02858-6

19. Schönberger, J.L., Frahm, J.M.: Structure-from-motion revisited. In: Conference on Computer Vision and Pattern Recognition (CVPR) (2016)

20. Schönberger, J.L., Zheng, E., Frahm, J.-M., Pollefeys, M.: Pixelwise view selection for unstructured multi-view stereo. In: Leibe, B., Matas, J., Sebe, N., Welling, M. (eds.) ECCV 2016. LNCS, vol. 9907, pp. 501–518. Springer, Cham (2016). https://doi.org/10.1007/978-3-319-46487-9_31

21. Sun, J., Shen, Z., Wang, Y., Bao, H., Zhou, X.: LoFTR: detector-free local feature matching with transformers. In: CVPR (2021)

22. Wang, P., Liu, L., Liu, Y., Theobalt, C., Komura, T., Wang, W.: NeuS: learning neural implicit surfaces by volume rendering for multi-view reconstruction. CoRR abs/2106.10689 (2021). https://arxiv.org/abs/2106.10689

# Breaking down the Hierarchy: A New Approach to Leukemia Classification

Ibraheem Hamdi[1(✉)], Hosam El-Gendy[1], Ahmed Sharshar[1], Mohamed Saeed[1], Muhammad Ridzuan[1], Shahrukh K. Hashmi[2], Naveed Syed[2], Imran Mirza[2], Shakir Hussain[2], Amira Mahmoud Abdalla[2], and Mohammad Yaqub[1]

[1] Mohamed Bin Zayed University of Artificial Intelligence, Abu Dhabi, UAE
{ibraheem.hamdi,hosam.elgendy,ahmed.sharshar,mohamed.saeed,
muhammad.ridzuan,mohammad.yaqub}@mbzuai.ac.ae
[2] Sheikh Shakhbout Medical City, Abu Dhabi, UAE
{shhashmi,nasyed,immirza,shahussain,amirabdalla}@ssmc.ae

**Abstract.** The complexities inherent to leukemia, multifaceted cancer affecting white blood cells, pose considerable diagnostic and treatment challenges, primarily due to reliance on laborious morphological analyses and expert judgment that are susceptible to errors. Addressing these challenges, this study presents a refined, comprehensive strategy leveraging advanced deep-learning techniques for the classification of leukemia subtypes. We commence by developing a hierarchical label taxonomy, paving the way for differentiating between various subtypes of leukemia. The research further introduces a novel hierarchical approach inspired by clinical procedures capable of accurately classifying diverse types of leukemia alongside reactive and healthy cells. An integral part of this study involves a meticulous examination of the performance of Convolutional Neural Networks (CNNs) and Vision Transformers (ViTs) as classifiers. The proposed method exhibits an impressive success rate, achieving approximately 90% accuracy across all leukemia subtypes, as substantiated by our experimental results. A visual representation of the experimental findings is provided to enhance the model's explainability and aid in understanding the classification process.

**Keywords:** Leukemia · Hierarchical · Classification · Histology

## 1 Introduction

Leukemia is a type of cancer that starts in the bone marrow and spreads to the blood. Patients commonly exhibit symptoms such as fatigue, weakness, frequent infections and more [1]. Leukemia ranks among the ten most common cancers, with hundreds of thousands of new cases and deaths every year [2].

There are two main leukemia categories based on the speed of progression: acute, which develops quickly and exhibits symptoms within weeks of forming, and chronic, which develops more slowly and may not show noticeable symptoms for years. Based on the type of blood cell affected, these can be further

S. Wu et al. (Eds.): AMAI 2023, LNCS 14313, pp. 104–113, 2024.
https://doi.org/10.1007/978-3-031-47076-9_11

divided into two subcategories: myeloid and lymphocytic [1]. Therefore, leukemia can generally be divided into four main types: acute lymphocytic leukemia (ALL), acute myeloid leukemia (AML), chronic lymphocytic leukemia (CLL), and chronic myeloid leukemia (CML).

The diagnosis of leukemia typically involves physical examinations, medical history evaluations, and laboratory tests. Blood sample analysis and bone marrow biopsies are common methods for leukemia diagnosis. Bone marrow biopsies are invasive and uncomfortable for patients [3]. In contrast, blood smears are non-invasive but provide less information and require skilled pathologists, who are in short supply [4]. Moreover, diagnosing leukemia from slides is a manual process, subject to bias and operator errors [5].

This paper investigates the potential of using computer vision algorithms to classify leukemia and its subtypes from blood smear images and proposes a novel hierarchical solution. This task is largely unexplored in the literature at the moment, therefore, an effective solution is needed to enhance accuracy, reduce costs of further testing, and reduces the use of invasive methods. The principal contributions of this work are as follows:

- Development of a hierarchical deep learning method to accurately classify different types of leukemia.
- To our knowledge, we are the first to investigate the classification of a wide range of leukemia types alongside reactive and healthy cells.
- In-depth analysis of the performance of CNNs and ViTs on the classification of leukemia.

## 2   Related Work

Previous work focused on detecting and segmenting leukemia cells from microscopic blood smear images [6–9], while some worked on classifying a specific type of leukemia against healthy cells [10–13]. However, at the time of writing, the authors are only aware of two papers that work on classifying multiple types against healthy cells, and both target the ALL, AML, CLL, and CML subtypes.

The authors in [14] propose using a small custom CNN, using the ALL-IDB [15] dataset as well as some images from the American Society of Hematology (ASH) Image Bank [16]. The authors obtained 903 images and implemented several augmentations to reduce overfitting. Despite this, their results show a large difference between the training and validation accuracies, indicating that their model is greatly overfitting. This can be attributed to the small dataset and overly simplified model. In the most recent paper [17], the authors propose using a pre-trained GoogleNet model, which is fine-tuned on 1,200 images from the ASH Image Bank. The authors do not provide detailed information on the hyperparameters used, making it difficult to study their impact on the model.

In summary, both papers lacked sufficient detail regarding the techniques used to attain their results. CNNs utilized were either small or obsolete, having been surpassed in performance by newer models such as ConvNeXt [18] or Vision Transformers (ViTs) [19].

## 3    Dataset

The dataset consists of slices from 84 slides, each representing a patient. It was collected by a local hospital using 1000× zoom on each slide. The slides were divided into patches which were annotated by a senior pathologist to obtain ground-truth labels.

The dataset, which includes four main leukemia types, normal cells, acute promyelocytic leukemia (APML), and reactive cells, is unique and represents the Middle East, making it the first of its kind for the region. APML is an aggressive, rare subtype of AML, requiring a specific treatment approach [20]. Reactive cells are non-cancerous cells that appear similar to leukemia cells [21].

### 3.1    Pre-processing

Many steps were taken to refine and clean the data in preparation for training. Specifically, scans with less than four images were excluded, and duplicates were removed. Furthermore, most images had a resolution of 1200 × 1600; therefore, images with significantly lower resolution were excluded, producing 3710 images. These images have been resized to 384 × 384. Training and validation sets were created by splitting the data per slide to prevent any leakage and prevent the model from under-performing on unseen data.

## 4    Methodology Overview

### 4.1    Flat/Leaf Classification (Baseline)

This approach is referred to as Flat/Leaf Classification, as it focuses on all 7 "leaf" classes seen in Fig. 1. The approach is simple and ignores the hierarchy of the classes, which may lead to a loss of information and a potential reduction in performance. In addition, it does not provide classification probabilities for broader classes, such as acute vs chronic which is clinically vital in cases where doctors struggle to decide on the exact leukemia types.

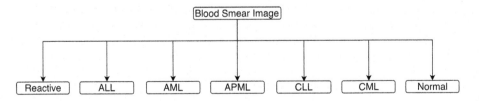

**Fig. 1.** Flat/Leaf Classification Structure.

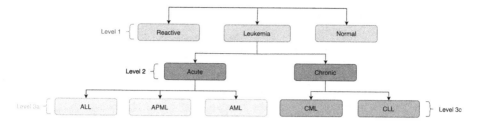

**Fig. 2.** Hierarchical structure of leukemia subtypes, showcasing different levels.

## 4.2   Hierarchical Multi-label Classification

Another way of presenting the dataset is shown in Fig. 2, providing a more intuitive structure in a tree-like diagram. This inspired the authors to develop a method that performs classification following this hierarchy. Since the chance of having multiple types of leukemia is unlikely [22], the authors assume non-overlapping subgroups in the data and produce a solution based on that. We proposed two different methods to apply the hierarchical architecture:

- **Base Hierarchical Model:** Four separate models were trained; each on an individual level of the tree shown in Fig. 2. They were then merged during inference to produce the final model. APML was included as a separate class in our study. This is because APML is unique among leukemia types in its excellent response to treatment, requiring immediate attention and intervention.
- **Proposed Multi-label Hierarchical Model:** We've developed a hierarchical deep learning model for image classification, operating sequentially and tiered. The model first differentiates among normal, reactive, and leukemia cases(level 1). If leukemia is detected, it further classifies it as acute or chronic (level 2) and subsequently refines these into subtypes(level 3). These levels are shown in Fig. 2. We employ a unique loss control strategy to ensure that the loss at each level is self-contained, preventing cross-layer interference. In essence, each stage of the hierarchy is affected only by its respective loss, promoting precise classifications throughout the model.

## 5   Experimental Setup

### 5.1   Model Selection

We utilize ConvNeXt-Tiny and ViT-Small models as they performed best, as shown in Table 1. Note that these results validate our choice of these models, which were later tweaked to match the proposed model hyper-parameters. For the baseline, the chosen configurations included the Adam optimizer [23], Focal Loss [24], and weighted-cross entropy with a learning rate of $10^{-6}$.

**Table 1.** Performance of different baselines on multi-class classification task

| Model | Macro-Averaged F1 |
|---|---|
| ResNet-18 | 62.18 |
| ResNet-50 | 58.32 |
| GoogleNet | 69.3 |
| DenseNet-121 | 70.5 |
| **ConvNeXt-Tiny** | **78.56** |
| **ViT-Small** | **79.93** |

## 5.2   Simulating Pathological Evaluation

The holistic examination process taken by pathologists was taken into consideration. Hence, this study introduces a post-processing methodology that aggregates the mode of all predictions per slide (patient) at the end of the validation or testing phases. This approach mirrors the pathologists' diagnostic process and mitigates the impact of minor misclassifications by the models. Consequently, the models yield a singular dominant label per slide, eliminating the occurrence of edge cases that each slide has only one label.

## 5.3   Experimental Procedures

We further modified the baseline configurations. Using Focal Loss function instead of weighted-cross entropy enhanced the model's performance. The Adam optimizer was replaced with AdamW with a learning rate of $1 \times 10^{-6}$, and each experimental run was limited to 80 epochs for the sake of time, and this was enough for the model to saturate.

## 5.4   Evaluation Metrics

Experiments were evaluated using accuracy and F1 score metrics. For hierarchical classification, the hierarchical precision (hP), recall (hR), and F1-score (hF) were computed using Eq. 1.

$$hP = \frac{\sum_i \left| \hat{P}_i \cap \hat{T}_i \right|}{\sum_i \left| \hat{P}_i \right|} \quad hR = \frac{\sum_i \left| \hat{P}_i \cap \hat{T}_i \right|}{\sum_i \left| \hat{T}_i \right|} \quad hF = \frac{2 * hP * hR}{hP + hR} \tag{1}$$

The set $\hat{P}i$ contains the most specific class or classes that are predicted for a given test example $i$ and all of its ancestor classes. Likewise, $\hat{T}i$ is the set that includes the true most specific class or classes for that test example $i$ and all of its ancestor classes. These sets are used to compute summations over all test examples, and it is important to note that the measures being used are extended versions of the commonly used precision metrics [25].

# 6    Results and Discussion

## 6.1    Flat/Leaf Classification

The classification outcomes of all seven leaf classes within a flat structure are concisely delineated in Table 2. A performance comparison revealed the ViT-Small model's superior efficacy and accelerated convergence pace compared to the ConvNext-Tiny model.

Analyzing confusion matrices revealed challenges in classifying reactive cells, known to pathologists for their ambiguous state between "Normal" and "Leukemia". Experiments excluding these cells improved performance.

Table 2 shows performance variations in 5-fold cross-validation due to dataset slides and labeling discrepancies. The lower standard deviation for ViTs, compared to CNNs, in six and seven-class classifications support adopting ViTs.

## 6.2    Base vs Proposed Hierarchical Classification

Table 3 presents the comparative analysis of Base and Proposed hierarchical models in ConvNext and ViT architectures. Each level underwent an intermediate evaluation. While the Base model excels in intermediate binary classification due to dedicated tuning, the Proposed model marginally surpasses in seven-class classification due to its automated learning and scalability without the additional overhead of training multiple models separately.

Interestingly, ConvNeXt outperforms ViT in internal levels, likely due to smaller training data sizes as ViT needs much more data for training; therefore, smaller models fit better. Nonetheless, the highest performance of 90.97% was achieved with the ViT architecture in the Proposed model for all seven classes.

Moreover, although the ViT yields high flat/leaf multi-class classification results, the ConvNext-Tiny outperforms the ViT in most binary experiments. This can be due to the reduction of samples for the ViT. ViTs require large quantities of data to obtain reasonable representations [26].

**Table 2.** Comparison of performance using CNN and ViT on multi-class.

| All Classes | | | | | | Without Reactive | | | | | |
|---|---|---|---|---|---|---|---|---|---|---|---|
| ConvNeXt | | | ViT | | | ConvNeXt | | | ViT | | |
| Fold | ACC | F1 | AUROC | ACC | F1 | AUROC | ACC | F1 | AUROC | ACC | F1 | AUROC |
| 1 | 61.58 | 62.26 | 91.17 | 67.73 | 67.08 | 92.05 | 70.30 | 71.62 | 92.60 | 80.78 | 74.15 | 93.21 |
| 2 | 77.02 | 72.31 | 92.18 | 74.12 | 75.37 | 94.11 | 77.07 | 72.01 | 92.20 | 84.11 | 84.96 | 94.85 |
| 3 | 81.76 | 81.82 | 90.59 | 87.89 | 86.79 | 95.56 | 87.07 | 87.21 | 98.61 | 90.82 | 90.23 | 97.69 |
| 4 | 79.27 | 79.93 | 96.34 | 77.45 | 75.21 | 97.08 | 82.34 | 82.98 | 97.45 | 85.55 | 85.54 | 98.16 |
| 5 | 79.04 | 77.29 | 95.83 | 79.93 | 77.01 | 93.50 | 83.27 | 80.19 | 92.83 | 83.74 | 81.82 | 94.35 |
| Avg | 75.73 | 74.72 | 93.22 | **77.42** | **76.29** | **94.46** | 80.01 | 78.80 | 94.73 | **85.00** | **83.34** | **95.65** |
| Std | 8.09 | 7.83 | 2.68 | 7.43 | 7.03 | 1.93 | 6.50 | 6.85 | 3.04 | 3.69 | 5.95 | 2.16 |

**Table 3.** Accuracy of Hierarchical models at different stages

| Subtask | ConvNeXt | ViT | ConvNeXt | ViT |
|---|---|---|---|---|
| | Base | | Proposed | |
| Normal vs Reactive vs Leukemia | **95.41** | 94.23 | 93.58 | 92.04 |
| Acute vs Chronic | **94.75** | 93.21 | 91.16 | 92.80 |
| ALL vs AML vs APML | 81.65 | **83.47** | 79.96 | 82.59 |
| CLL vs CML | **97.02** | 96.74 | 95.08 | 94.47 |
| All 7 Classes | 89.34 | 90.01 | 90.48 | **90.97** |

## 6.3 Flat vs Proposed Hierarchical Classification

The comparison between the Flat and Proposed Hierarchical models can be shown in Table 4. These results show that our hierarchical structure is boosting the model performance in terms of precision and recall compared to the flat structure. This is more evident in the "visually confusing" classes, such as ALL and Reactive classes, where the flat structure model struggles to differentiate these classes from other classes. However, when placed in a hierarchical structure, it becomes easier for the model to differentiate between these classes.

**Table 4.** Hierarchical and flat evaluation metric comparisons on the ViT-Small model

| Class | Flat/Leaf | | | Hierarchical | | |
|---|---|---|---|---|---|---|
| | Precision | Recall | F1 | Precision | Recall | F1 |
| ALL | 0.66 | 0.42 | 0.52 | 0.98 | 0.88 | **0.93** |
| AML + APML | 0.75 | 0.91 | 0.82 | 0.93 | 0.95 | **0.94** |
| CLL | 0.86 | 0.63 | 0.73 | 0.98 | 0.95 | **0.97** |
| CML | 0.93 | 0.93 | 0.93 | 0.97 | 0.96 | **0.96** |
| Reactive | 0.58 | 0.79 | 0.67 | 0.85 | 0.95 | **0.89** |

## 6.4 Visual Experimental Results

To verify performance, Grad-CAM was used to visualize the ViT's localization of features by targeting the final stage of the model and generating a heatmap. In Fig. 3, three sample input images (top row) are selected for testing with Grad-CAM.

It is expected that the model should perform well in identifying white blood cells (WBCs) from the images. Figure 3 shows the leaf classification model (middle row) identifying WBCs, but does not distinctively pick-out WBCs from the red blood cells (RBCs). However, the hierarchical model (bottom row) excels at pinpointing WBCs in every sample, signifying its higher effectiveness over the flat model. Yet, the hierarchical model displays certain limitations when interpreting Grad-CAM results. The heatmap spots appear wider in initial levels, becoming most precise at the lowest level of the hierarchy.

The authors believe this might be due to the model's multi-level hierarchical training, which necessitates a broader image area for decision-making. Additionally, it is observed that instances of lower model performance match with poorer localization in the heatmap. This is possibly due to visual similarities between classes, leading to the model's underperformance in these instances.

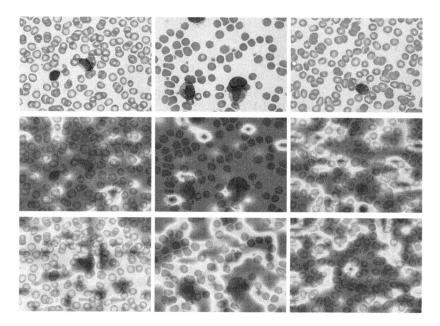

**Fig. 3.** Qualitative analysis of the ViT results using Grad-CAM. From left to right: CLL, CML, and Normal samples. From top to bottom: Input image, leaf classification output, and hierarchical classification output. The leaf model output has less discriminative distinction between WBCs and RBCs.

## 7   Conclusion

Our work demonstrates that multi-label hierarchical classification using ConvNext-Tiny and ViT-Small, holds great promise for leukemia subtype classification. Qualitative results further authenticated the model's reliability by showcasing its localization capabilities.

Naturally, this work is not without limitations. Early-stage leukemia may not be detectable via blood smear images. Other limitations to consider include the assumption of non-overlapping subgroups in the data.

For future research, we recommend gathering more data to enhance model performance. Moreover, studying inter and intra-observer variability could offer comparative insights against real pathologists. Furthermore, implementing newer algorithms and pre-training models on histology data are additional measures to consider for refining the classification process.

**Prospect of Application:** Leukemia is a curable disease; however, only if diagnosed properly. This work can be deployed to hospitals to reduce pathologists' errors, bias, and fatigue. It can also speed up the detection of leukemia subtypes and potentially save the lives of patients and the costs associated with cancer detection through a non-invasive technique.

# References

1. Mayo Clinic Staff. Leukemia - Symptoms and Causes (2021)
2. Huang, J., et al.: Disease burden, risk factors, and trends of leukaemia: a global analysis. Front. Oncology **12**, 904292 (2022)
3. Bone Marrow Biopsy—Johns Hopkins Medicine (2021)
4. Bychkov, A., Schubert, M.: Constant demand, patchy supply (2023)
5. Mohapatra, S., Patra, D., Satpathi, S.: Image analysis of blood microscopic images for acute leukemia detection. In: 2010 International Conference on Industrial Electronics, Control and Robotics, pp. 215–219. IEEE (2010)
6. Dhal, K.G., Gálvez, J., Ray, S., Das, A., Das, S.: Acute lymphoblastic leukemia image segmentation driven by stochastic fractal search. Multimedia Tools Appl. **79**(17), 12227–12255 (2020)
7. Genovese, A., Hosseini, M.S., Piuri, V., Plataniotis, K.N., Scotti, F.: Acute lymphoblastic leukemia detection based on adaptive unsharpening and deep learning. In: ICASSP 2021–2021 IEEE International Conference on Acoustics, Speech and Signal Processing (ICASSP), pp. 1205–1209. IEEE (2021)
8. Das, P.K., Meher, S.: Transfer learning-based automatic detection of acute lymphocytic leukemia. In: 2021 National Conference on Communications (NCC), pp. 1–6. IEEE (2021)
9. Mohapatra, S., Patra, D., Kumar, S., Satpathy, S.: Lymphocyte image segmentation using functional link neural architecture for acute leukemia detection. Biomed. Eng. Lett. **2**(2), 100–110 (2012)
10. Jothi, G., Inbarani, H.H., Azar, A.T., Devi, K.R.: Rough set theory with jaya optimization for acute lymphoblastic leukemia classification. Neural Comput. Appl. **31**(9), 5175–5194 (2019)
11. Shah, S., Nawaz, W., Jalil, B., Khan, H.A.: Classification of normal and leukemic blast cells in B-ALL cancer using a combination of convolutional and recurrent neural networks. In: Gupta, A., Gupta, R. (eds.) ISBI 2019 C-NMC Challenge: Classification in Cancer Cell Imaging. LNB, pp. 23–31. Springer, Singapore (2019). https://doi.org/10.1007/978-981-15-0798-4_3
12. Negm, A.S., Hassan, O.A., Kandil, A.H.: A decision support system for acute leukaemia classification based on digital microscopic images. Alexandria Eng. J. **57**(4), 2319–2332 (2018)
13. Rawat, J., Singh, A., Bhadauria, H.S., Virmani, J., Devgun, J.S.: Computer assisted classification framework for prediction of acute lymphoblastic and acute myeloblastic leukemia. Biocybern. Biomed. Eng. **37**(4), 637–654 (2017)

14. Ahmed, N., Yigit, A., Isik, Z., Alpkocak, A.: Identification of leukemia subtypes from microscopic images using convolutional neural network. Diagnostics **9**(3), 104 (2019)
15. Labati, R.D., Piuri, V., Scotti, F.: All-idb: the acute lymphoblastic leukemia image database for image processing. In: 2011 18th IEEE International Conference on Image Processing, pp. 2045–2048 (2011)
16. Imagebank—home—regular bank (2015)
17. Aftab, M.O., Awan, M.J., Khalid, S., Javed, R., Shabir, H.: Executing spark bigdl for leukemia detection from microscopic images using transfer learning. In: 2021 1st International Conference on Artificial Intelligence and Data Analytics (CAIDA), pp. 216–220 (2021)
18. Liu, Z., Mao, H., Wu, C.Y., Feichtenhofer, C., Darrell, T., Xie, S.: A convnet for the 2020s. In: Proceedings of the IEEE/CVF Conference on Computer Vision and Pattern Recognition, pp. 11976–11986 (2022)
19. Dosovitskiy, A., et al.: An image is worth 16×16 words: transformers for image recognition at scale. arXiv preprint arXiv:2010.11929 (2020)
20. Acute Promyelocytic Leukaemia Treatment. Leukemia Foundation (2019)
21. Hamad, H., Mangla, A.: Lymphocytosis. StatPearls Publishing, Treasure Island (2019)
22. George, B.S., Yohannan, B., Gonzalez, A., Rios, A.: Mixed-phenotype acute leukemia: clinical diagnosis and therapeutic strategies. Biomedicines **10**(8), 1974 (2022)
23. Kingma, D.P., Ba, J.: Adam: a method for stochastic optimization. arXiv preprint arXiv:1412.6980 (2014)
24. Lin, T.Y., Goyal, P., Girshick, R., He, K., Dollár, P.: Focal loss for dense object detection. In: Proceedings of the IEEE International Conference on Computer Vision, pp. 2980–2988 (2017)
25. Silla, C.N., Freitas, A.A.: A survey of hierarchical classification across different application domains. Data Mining Knowl. Disc. **22**, 31–72 (2011)
26. Lee, S.H., Lee, S., Song, B.C.: Vision transformer for small-size datasets. arXiv preprint arXiv:2112.13492 (2021)

# Single-Cell Spatial Analysis of Histopathology Images for Survival Prediction via Graph Attention Network

Zhe Li[1,2,3], Yuming Jiang[3], Leon Liu[4], Yong Xia[1,2(✉)], and Ruijiang Li[3]

[1] National Engineering Laboratory for Integrated Aero-Space-Ground-Ocean Big Data Application Technology, School of Computer Science and Engineering, Northwestern Polytechnical University, Xi'an 710072, China
yxia@nwpu.edu.cn
[2] Ningbo Institute of Northwestern Polytechnical University, Ningbo 315048, China
[3] Department of Radiation Oncology, Stanford University School of Medicine, Stanford, CA 94304, USA
[4] University of Chicago Laboratory Schools, Chicago, IL 60637, USA

**Abstract.** The tumor microenvironment is a complex ecosystem consisting of various immune and stromal cells in addition to neoplastic cells. The spatial interaction and organization of these cells play a critical role in tumor progression. Single-cell analysis of histopathology images offers an intrinsic advantage over traditional patch-based approach by providing fine-grained cellular information. However, existing studies do not perform explicit cell classification, and therefore still suffer from limited interpretability and lack biological relevance, which may negatively affect the performance for clinical outcome prediction. To address these challenges, we propose a cell-level contextual learning approach to explicitly capture the major cell types and their spatial interaction in the tumor microenvironment. To do this, we first segmented and classified each cell into tumor cells, lymphocytes, fibroblasts, macrophages, neutrophils, and other nonmalignant cells on histopathology images. Given this single-cell map, we constructed a graph and trained a graph attention network to learn the cell-level contextual features for survival prediction. Extensive experiments demonstrate that our model consistently outperform existing patch-based and cell graph-based approaches in two independent datasets. Further, we used the feature attribution method to discover distinct spatial patterns that are associated with prognosis, leading to biologically meaningful and interpretable results.

**Keywords:** Gastric cancer · Survival analysis · Graph neural network · Spatial pattern analysis · Cell type identification

## 1 Introduction

The tumor microenvironment (TME) is a complex milieu of cells that includes not only tumor cells but also various immune and stromal cells. It has been well established that TME plays a critical role in tumor control and progression. Therefore, it is important to

S. Wu et al. (Eds.): AMAI 2023, LNCS 14313, pp. 114–124, 2024.
https://doi.org/10.1007/978-3-031-47076-9_12

investigate the spatial interactions among various immune/stromal cell subpopulations. Histopathology hematoxylin-eosin (H&E)-stained images are routinely used in clinical practice for disease diagnosis and contain a rich amount of information about the TME [1].

Spurred by the recent innovations in digital pathology (DP) imaging, many prognostic models have been proposed [2]. Most common techniques focus on establishing patch-based histopathologic biomarkers in a top-down manner [3–5]. Researchers used either conventional hand-crafted features (*e.g.*, the morphology and textural in TME) or deep convolutional neural networks (CNNs) to analyze histopathology images.

Though these techniques have achieved promising performance [6], they ignore the complex connections among cells and lack a fine-grained understanding of how the spatial organization of different cells in TME contributes towards survival risks [7]. To overcome this, researchers used the graph theory approach [8] or the graph neural network (GNN) [9] to profile different cellular architectures in histopathology images. In contrast to the graph theory approach using hand-crafted features, GNN aims to automatically learn cell-level graph representations from histopathology images and shows great potential in modeling the notion and interaction of cells for cancer prognosis [10, 11]. For example, Chen et al. [12] used GNN to learn cell graph features in histopathology tissue, which serves as a complementary method to CNNs for fine-grained feature extraction. However, after cell segmentation, most cell-level GNN approaches use either hand-crafted features (*e.g.*, the nuclear morphology and texture), unsupervised clustering features, or deep features extracted by pre-trained CNNs as node/cell features, thereby limiting the ability of GNN to distinguish between different cellular classes and decreasing its accuracy and interpretability. Furthermore, survival prediction is a challenging regression task in histopathology images, which aims to analyze the expected duration of time until events happen and is very dependent on the complex interactions of different cellular classes. For example, tumor-infiltrating lymphocytes (TILs) are demonstrated to have significant associations with the prognosis in gastric cancer (GC) [13]. There is no study exploring the use of GNN to model such cell-level interactions for survival prediction of GC on routine histopathology images.

To tackle these challenges, we propose a Cell-level Contextual Learning approach using the Graph Attention Network (CCL-GAT). We first use deep learning to segment and classify cells into six types including tumor cells, lymphocytes, fibroblasts, macrophages, neutrophils, and other nonmalignant cells, which play important roles in survival prediction. Then we use the K-Nearest Neighbors (KNN) algorithm to construct the cell graph and extract the class-related cell features and geometric features as node and edge features, respectively, which can enrich relevant biological information in the cell graph. Finally, we choose an improved graph attention network (GAT) that utilizes the attention mechanism within GNN to learn the cell-level contextual information and predict patient survival. Through cell-level contextual learning, the proposed CCL-GAT explicitly captures different cells and their spatial organization patterns.

The main contributions of this work are four-fold. **First**, we curated a large dataset of 54,269 nuclear images with expert annotation and labeled them into six classes including tumor cells, lymphocytes, fibroblasts, macrophages, neutrophils, and other nonmalignant cells. We employed these cells to train a CNN, which can then be used to extract important class-related node features for the cell graph. **Second**, equipped with class-related node features and geometric edge features, our CCL-GAT effectively learns the relevant cell-level contextual information in histopathology images. **Third**, we evaluated our model on two independent cohorts of 513 patients with GC, which is one of the most common malignancies and a leading cause of cancer-related deaths [14]. Our experimental results show that CCL-GAT model outperforms existing patch-based and cell graph-based approaches. **Fourth**, we used the feature attribution method to discover distinct spatial patterns that are associated with prognosis, leading to biologically meaningful and interpretable results.

## 2   Method

Figure 1 shows a schematic diagram of the proposed CCL-GAT. It first segments nuclei in histopathology images using a nuclei segmentation network. Then a trained classification network is used to identify nucleus types and subsequently extract class-related cell features. The KNN algorithm is adopted to construct the cell graph, into which class-related cell features and geometric features are incorporated. Next, a GAT aggregates the neighborhood features of the target cell with an attention mechanism and updates its cell features to include the cell-level contextual information. Finally, the contextual features extracted by GAT are fed to the Cox proportional hazards model for survival prediction. We now delve into the details of our CCL-GAT.

### 2.1   Nuclei Classification

For nuclei segmentation in histopathology images, many excellent segmentation models and tools have been proposed, such as Cellpose [15], HoverNet [16], and Mesmer [17]. For this study, we choose the HoverNet pre-trained on the multi-organ dataset [18] for nuclei segmentation, since it shows high accuracy at a low inference time cost.

To classify nuclei accurately in the histopathology images of GC, we manually collected and annotated nuclear images into six classes including tumor cells, lymphocytes, fibroblasts, macrophages, neutrophils, and other nonmalignant cells, which are important for survival prediction of GC (details are provided in Sect. 3.1). Then we train a ResNet18 with the annotated images and use it to classify cells segmented by HoverNet in histological images.

### 2.2   Cell Graph Construction

After getting the segmentation and classification results of cells, we construct the cell graph to describe their spatial correlation. Let $G = (V, E)$ denote a graph with nodes $V$ and edges $E$. All cells in a histopathology image are defined as our set of nodes $V$. We use the KNN algorithm from the Fast Library for Approximate Nearest Neighbors (FLANN) [19] to find the connections between $K$ adjacent cells to define our set of edges $E$. For this study, we empirically set $K = 5$ to model cell interactions [12].

For each cell, we use the trained ResNet18 (Sect. 2.1) to extract 512 deep features and also extract the hand-crafted features used in [12] to represent the shape and texture of each cell. Eight shape features include the major axis length, minor axis length, angular orientation, eccentricity, roundness, area, perimeter, and solidity. Four texture features include the dissimilarity, homogeneity, angular second moment, and energy from gray-level co-occurrence matrices. Then, we concatenate these features with the probability of the cell belonging to each of six cell types, resulting in a 530-dimensional class-related cell feature that provides rich prognostic information to the cell graph.

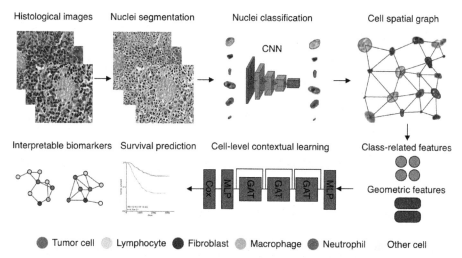

**Fig. 1.** Framework of proposed CCL-GAT. Nuclei are segmented and classified by HoverNet and ResNet18, respectively. Cell spatial graph is constructed with class-related node features and geometric edge features. GAT is used to learn contextual features for survival prediction.

To include the geometric information from edges in the graph, we first calculate the polar coordinates of linked cells, then quantize the patient-wise normalized spatial distance and angle between two cells into 0–10 numbers and construct look-up tables, resulting in learnable features for the distance and angle [20]. We embed the distance and angle as edge features during graph construction.

### 2.3 Graph Attention Network

We employ GAT to learn cell-level contextual features from heterogeneous TME, as it uses the attention mechanism to differentiate the weight of each node when aggregating the neighborhood node features. Let $h = \{h_1, h_2, \ldots h_M\} \in \mathbb{R}^{M*v}$ denote a set of class-related node features, $d = \{d_{11}, d_{12}, \ldots d_{MM-1}, d_{MM}\} \in \mathbb{R}^{M*e}$ be the embedded distance, and $a = \{a_{11}, a_{12}, \ldots a_{MM-1}, a_{MM}\} \in \mathbb{R}^{M*e}$ be the embedded angle, where $M$, $v$, and $e$ are the number of cells, node features, and edge features, respectively.

To better reflect the complex cell-level contextual information in TME, we adopt the improved attention coefficient $e_{ij}$ between two adjacent cells to include the embedded distance and angle features [20].

$$e_{ij} = LeakyReLu\left(\beta_s^T W_s h_i + \beta_t^T W_t h_j + \beta_d^T W_d d_{ij} + \beta_a^T W_a a_{ij}\right) \tag{1}$$

where $W_s$, $W_t$, $W_d$, and $W_a$ are the initial linear transformations of the source node, target node, distance, and angle features, respectively, $\beta_s$, $\beta_t$, $\beta_d$, and $\beta_a$ represent the single-layer feedforward neural networks of the source node, target node, distance, and angle features, respectively. Then a SoftMax function across all the neighborhood cells $j \in N_i$ is used to normalize $e_{ij}$. This process can be expressed as:

$$\alpha_{ij} = \frac{exp(e_{ij})}{\sum_{j \in N_i} exp(e_{ij})} \qquad (2)$$

Once obtained, the normalized attention scores are used to compute the weighted summation over all neighborhood features, to serve as the final contextual features $\bar{h}_i$.

$$\bar{h}_i = \sigma\left(\sum_{j \in N_i} \alpha_{ij} W h_i\right) \qquad (3)$$

where $\sigma$ represents a non-linearity function.

For survival prediction, we adopt the negative logarithm of Cox partial likelihood [21] as the loss function to adapt the survival prediction into GAT.

$$L\left(\gamma^T, X\right) = -\sum_{i \in U}\left(\gamma^T X_i - \log \sum_{j \in R_i} exp\left(\gamma^T X_i\right)\right) \qquad (4)$$

where $U$ is the set of uncensored patients, $R_i$ represents a set of patients living longer than the $i$-th patient, $\gamma$ is the weight of the last fully connected layer whose input is $X$.

### 2.4  Model Interpretability

We use the integrated gradients (IG) to assess cell attributes. IG is a gradient-based feature attribution method that attributes the prediction of model to their inputs. For this study, the features with positive attribution favor an increase in the output value (high risk), whereas negative attribution contributes to decreasing the output value (low risk). To better show the interpretability of our CCL-GAT, we use attention scores in Sect. 2.3 to indicate the importance of each connection between different cells.

## 3  Experimental and Results

### 3.1  Dataset

**Nuclei Classification.** We collected 54,269 nuclear images (at 40x) from diagnostic whole slide images (WSI) in two GC datasets, i.e., TCGA-STAD [22] and an in-house dataset [1]. Then an experienced pathologist manually annotated them into six classes, yielding 12626 tumor cells, 13230 lymphocytes, 12223 fibroblasts, 3272 macrophages, 7206 neutrophils, and 5712 other nonmalignant cells. We randomly divided them into a training set (80%) and a test set (20%).

**Patients.** We also used TCGA-STAD and the same in-house GC dataset for survival prediction. We collected 359 diagnostic H&E WSIs of 309 patients with age, gender, grade, and survival information from TCGA-STAD. An experienced pathologist manually annotated the region of interest (ROI) and extracted three $512 \times 512$ 40x image patches per WSI, yielding 1077 patches in total. The in-house dataset contains 612 512 $\times$ 512 40x image patches acquired from 204 diagnostic H&E WSIs of 204 patients. All patients have age, gender, grade, and survival information. For each dataset, we use five-fold cross validation at patient level. When training, each image was treated as a single data point in cross-validation. During validation, we compute the mean of predicted risks from all ROIs for each patient.

### 3.2 Implementation Details

The proposed method was built with PyTorch 1.9.1 and PyTorch Geometric 1.7.1. The ResNet18 was initialized using pretrained weights from ImageNet and subsequently finetuned using the cross-entropy loss, Adam optimizer, a learning rate of $1e^{-5}$, and a batch size of 32. Random vertical and horizontal flips, color jittering, and random rotation were performed for the augmentation of nuclear images. Our CCL-GAT used a two-layer MLP (200 and 100 neurons) for node feature preprocessing, a three-layer GAT with two attention heads for graph input, and another two-layer MLP (100 and 50 neurons) for post-processing. We optimized CCL-GAT using the Adam optimizer, a learning rate of $5e^{-5}$, and a batch size of 24. We used the cross-validated concordance index (C-index) to measure the performance of all prognostic models. We also used the Kaplan–Meier (KM) analysis to visualize how models were stratifying patients.

### 3.3 Comparison with State-of-the-Art Methods

**Nuclei Classification.** The ResNet18 trained on annotated nuclear images achieved a high accuracy of nuclei classification on the test set. The area under the curves (AUC) for tumor cells, lymphocytes, fibroblasts, macrophages, neutrophils, and other nonmalignant cells are 0.996, 0.995, 0.991, 0.988, 0.994, and 0.994, respectively, with a one-versus-rest macro-averaged AUC of 0.993

**Survival Prediction.** We evaluated our CCL-GAT against two CNN-based models (i.e., VGG19 [23] and ResNet50 [24]) which were pretrained on the ImageNet dataset, a instance-based Vision Transformer (I-ViT) [25], and three GNN-based models (i.e., Graph Pathomic Network (GPN) [12], CGC-Net [11], and spatial-hierarchical GNN (SHGNN) [26]). In contrast of CCL-GAT, I-ViT uses segmented nuclei as instance patches for Transformer, GPN uses contrastive predictive coding (CPC) features as node features, CGC-Net incorporates multi-level features into GNN, and SHGNN uses dynamic structure learning for GNN. For each method, we performed the same fivefold cross-validation on two GC datasets

Table 1 shows the results of all methods on two datasets. Our CCL-GAT outperforms all CNN-based, Transformed-based, and GNN-based competing algorithms. Comparing to the second best method-VGG19, CCL-GAT obtains 4.2% and 6.2% performance gains on TCGA-STAD and the in-house dataset, respectively. To further improve prognostication, we combined the risk scores of CCL-GAT with age, gender, and grade by training a Cox proportional hazard model within each cross validation. Table 1 also shows that the combination further improves the C-index for survival prediction, suggesting that CCL-GAT provides additional prognostic information that the other clinical data cannot represent.

**Table 1.** Performance comparison using C-index on TCGA-STAD and in-house dataset.

| Methods | In-house | TCGA-STAD | Overall |
|---|---|---|---|
| Cox (Age + Gender) | 0.562 ± 0.014 | 0.589 ± 0.036 | 0.576 |
| Cox (Grade) | 0.544 ± 0.056 | 0.537 ± 0.052 | 0.541 |
| VGG19 | 0.594 ± 0.055 | 0.600 ± 0.065 | 0.597 |
| ResNet50 | 0.576 ± 0.069 | 0.586 ± 0.073 | 0.581 |
| GPN | 0.586 ± 0.057 | 0.595 ± 0.072 | 0.591 |
| CGC-Net | 0.583 ± 0.038 | 0.580 ± 0.029 | 0.582 |
| SHGNN | 0.568 ± 0.062 | 0.562 ± 0.041 | 0.565 |
| I-ViT | 0.579 ± 0.077 | 0.585 ± 0.073 | 0.582 |
| CCL-GAT | **0.631 ± 0.027** | **0.625 ± 0.035** | **0.628** |
| CCL-GAT + Age + Gender + Grade | **0.657 ± 0.039** | **0.686 ± 0.050** | **0.672** |

To further investigate the ability of our CCL-GAT on patient stratification, we plotted the KM curves of CCL-GAT against VGG19 (the best CNN-based model), GPN (the best GNN-based model), and I-ViT in Fig. 2. The Log rank test was used for statistical significance test in survival curves between low and high-risk patients. It shows that our CCL-GAT achieves the best discrimination of two risk groups of GC patients (50–100 percentile) with consistently lowest p-values than competing methods.

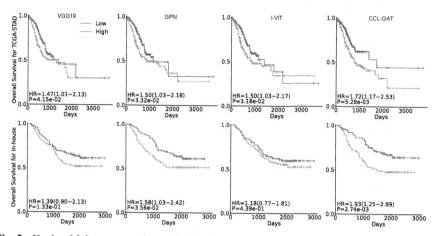

**Fig. 2.** Kaplan-Meier comparative analysis of using VGG19, GPN, I-ViT, and our CCL-GAT in patient stratification. HR means the hazard ratio. P values were determined by two-sided log-rank test.

**Table 2.** Ablation study on different variations of CCL-GAT.

| CPC | Deep | Hand-crafted | Probability | Geometric | In-house | TCGA-STAD |
|-----|------|--------------|-------------|-----------|----------|-----------|
| ✓ | | | | | 0.591 ± 0.059 | 0.597 ± 0.062 |
| ✓ | | | | ✓ | 0.603 ± 0.054 | 0.605 ± 0.067 |
| | ✓ | | | ✓ | 0.621 ± 0.036 | 0.614 ± 0.041 |
| | ✓ | ✓ | | ✓ | 0.624 ± 0.033 | 0.618 ± 0.042 |
| | ✓ | ✓ | ✓ | | 0.619 ± 0.041 | 0.610 ± 0.039 |
| | ✓ | ✓ | ✓ | ✓ | **0.631 ± 0.027** | **0.625 ± 0.035** |

We evaluated different variations of CCL-GAT to investigate the effectiveness of its components. Table 2 shows the C-index of CCL-GAT variants, including (1) using CPC features, (2) using CPC features and geometric edge features, (3) excluding nuclei classification probability and hand-craft features, (4) excluding nuclei classification probability, (5) excluding geometric edge features. Overall, it reveals that both class-related cell features and geometric features contribute to better performance of CCL-GAT.

**Interpretability of CCL-GAT.** Our CCL-GAT is also highly interpretable, in which we learn how each cell and edge affect predicted risks and investigate cell-level heterogeneous contextual features of tumors. Some examples in Fig. 3 show that our CCL-GAT can distinguish different cell contexts, such as the invasive margin of tumor, lymphocyte cluster, and tumor core, and reflect the impact of the context on risk prediction via IG values and attention scores. Thus, doctors may use the cell-level contextual learning of CCL-GAT to explore biologically meaningful prognostic biomarkers

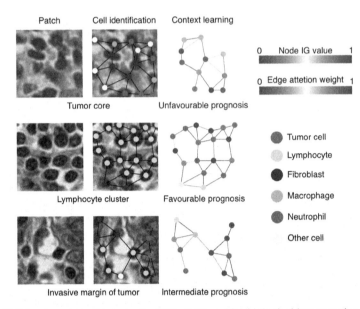

**Fig. 3.** Cell-level contextual learning by CCL-GAT enables biological interpretation of results.

## 4    Conclusion

In this paper, we propose the CCL-GAT model for the survival prediction of GC using histopathology images. We first use a CNN trained by annotated nuclear images to classify each nucleus in ROIs into six types. Then we incorporate class-related features and geometric features into cell graph construction. A modified GAT is finally used to analyze complex cell-level contextual features for survival prediction. Our results indicate that the proposed CCL-GAT is highly interpretable and outperforms all CNN-based, Transformed-based, and GNN-based competing algorithms on TCGA-STAD and the in-house dataset.

**Prospect of Application**: We propose a novel graph attention network approach for single-cell spatial analysis of routine histopathology images. Our method discovers distinct spatial patterns that are associated with prognosis, leading to biologically meaningful and interpretable model for survival prediction. This model may be combined with established clinicopathologic factors to improve risk stratification and guide personalized therapy of cancer patients.

**Acknowledgements.** This work was supported in part by the National Key R&D Program of China under Grant 2022YFC2009903 / 2022YFC2009900, in part by the National Natural Science Foundation of China under Grants 62171377, in part by the Ningbo Clinical Research Center for Medical Imaging under Grant 2021L003 (Open Project 2022LYKFZD06), and in part by the Natural Science Foundation of Ningbo City, China, under Grant 2021J052.

# References

1. Li, Z., et al.: Development and validation of a machine learning model for detection and classification of tertiary lymphoid structures in gastrointestinal cancers. JAMA Netw. Open **6**, e2252553–e2252553 (2023)
2. Javed, S., et al.: Cellular community detection for tissue phenotyping in colorectal cancer histology images. Med. Image Anal. **63**, 101696 (2020)
3. Chang, J.-R., Lee, C.-Y., Chen, C.-C., Reischl, J., Qaiser, T., Yeh, C.-Y.: Hybrid aggregation network for survival analysis from whole slide histopathological images. In: de Bruijne, M., Cattin, P.C., Cotin, S., Padoy, N., Speidel, S., Zheng, Y., Essert, C. (eds.) MICCAI 2021. LNCS, vol. 12905, pp. 731–740. Springer, Cham (2021). https://doi.org/10.1007/978-3-030-87240-3_70
4. Agarwal, S., Eltigani Osman Abaker, M., Daescu, O.: Survival prediction based on histopathology imaging and clinical data: A novel, whole slide cnn approach. In: de Bruijne, M., Cattin, P.C., Cotin, S., Padoy, N., Speidel, S., Zheng, Y., Essert, C. (eds.) MICCAI 2021. LNCS, vol. 12905, pp. 762–771. Springer, Cham (2021). https://doi.org/10.1007/978-3-030-87240-3_73
5. Braman, N., Gordon, J.W.H., Goossens, E.T., Willis, C., Stumpe, M.C., Venkataraman, J.: Deep orthogonal fusion: multimodal prognostic biomarker discovery integrating radiology, pathology, genomic, and clinical data. In: de Bruijne, M., Cattin, P.C., Cotin, S., Padoy, N., Speidel, S., Zheng, Y., Essert, C. (eds.) MICCAI 2021. LNCS, vol. 12905, pp. 667–677. Springer, Cham (2021). https://doi.org/10.1007/978-3-030-87240-3_64
6. Li, H., et al.: DT-MIL: Deformable Transformer for Multi-instance Learning on Histopathological Image. In: de Bruijne, M., Cattin, P.C., Cotin, S., Padoy, N., Speidel, S., Zheng, Y., Essert, C. (eds.) MICCAI 2021. LNCS, vol. 12908, pp. 206–216. Springer, Cham (2021). https://doi.org/10.1007/978-3-030-87237-3_20
7. Chen, R.J., et al.: Pan-cancer integrative histology-genomic analysis via multimodal deep learning. Cancer Cell **40**, 865–878. e866 (2022)
8. Bag, S., et al.: Computational analysis of p63+ nuclei distribution pattern by graph theoretic approach in an oral pre-cancer (sub-mucous fibrosis). J. Pathol. Inform. **4**, 35 (2013)
9. Chen, R.J., et al.: Whole slide images are 2d point clouds: Context-aware survival prediction using patch-based graph convolutional networks. In: de Bruijne, M., Cattin, P.C., Cotin, S., Padoy, N., Speidel, S., Zheng, Y., Essert, C. (eds.) MICCAI 2021. LNCS, vol. 12908, pp. 339–349. Springer, Cham (2021). https://doi.org/10.1007/978-3-030-87237-3_33
10. Pati, P., et al.: Hact-net: A hierarchical cell-to-tissue graph neural network for histopathological image classification. In: Sudre, C.H., Fehri, H., Arbel, T., Baumgartner, C.F., Dalca, A., Tanno, R., Van Leemput, K., Wells, W.M., Sotiras, A., Papiez, B., Ferrante, E., Parisot, S. (eds.) UNSURE/GRAIL -2020. LNCS, vol. 12443, pp. 208–219. Springer, Cham (2020). https://doi.org/10.1007/978-3-030-60365-6_20
11. Zhou, Y., et al.: CGC-Net: cell graph convolutional network for grading of colorectal cancer histology images. In: Proceedings of the IEEE/CVF International Conference on Computer Vision Workshops (2019)
12. Chen, R.J., et al.: Pathomic fusion: an integrated framework for fusing histopathology and genomic features for cancer diagnosis and prognosis. IEEE Trans. Med. Imaging (2020)
13. Kang, B., et al.: Prognostic value of tumor-infiltrating lymphocytes in Epstein-Barr virus-associated gastric cancer. Ann. Oncol. **27**, 494–501 (2016)
14. Jiang, Y., et al.: Predicting peritoneal recurrence and disease-free survival from CT images in gastric cancer with multitask deep learning: a retrospective study. The Lancet Digit. Health **4**, e340–e350 (2022)

15. Stringer, C., Wang, T., Michaelos, M., Pachitariu, M.: Cellpose: a generalist algorithm for cellular segmentation. Nat. Methods **18**, 100–106 (2021)
16. Graham, S., et al.: Hover-net: Simultaneous segmentation and classification of nuclei in multi-tissue histology images. Med. Image Anal. **58**, 101563 (2019)
17. Greenwald, N.F., et al.: Whole-cell segmentation of tissue images with human-level performance using large-scale data annotation and deep learning. Nat. Biotechnol. **40**, 555–565 (2022)
18. Gamper, J., et al.: Pannuke dataset extension, insights and baselines. arXiv preprint arXiv:2003.10778 (2020)
19. Muja, M., Lowe, D.G.: Fast approximate nearest neighbors with automatic algorithm configuration. In: VISAPP 2009 - Proceedings of the Fourth International Conference on Computer Vision Theory and Applications (1) 2, 2 (2009)
20. Lee, Y., et al.: Derivation of prognostic contextual histopathological features from whole-slide images of tumours via graph deep learning. Nat. Biomed. Eng., 1–15 (2022)
21. Lin, D.Y., Wei, L.-J., Ying, Z.: Checking the Cox model with cumulative sums of martingale-based residuals. Biometrika **80**, 557–572 (1993)
22. Liu, J., et al.: An integrated TCGA pan-cancer clinical data resource to drive high-quality survival outcome analytics. Cell **173**, 400–416. e411 (2018)
23. Simonyan, K., Zisserman, A.: Very deep convolutional networks for large-scale image recognition. arXiv preprint arXiv:1409.1556 (2014)
24. He, K., Zhang, X., Ren, S., Sun, J.: Deep residual learning for image recognition. In: Proceedings of the IEEE Conference on Computer Vision and Pattern Recognition, pp. 770–778 (2016)
25. Gao, Z., et al.: Instance-based vision transformer for subtyping of papillary renal cell carcinoma in histopathological image. In: de Bruijne, M., Cattin, P.C., Cotin, S., Padoy, N., Speidel, S., Zheng, Y., Essert, C. (eds.) MICCAI 2021. LNCS, vol. 12908, pp. 299–308. Springer, Cham (2021). https://doi.org/10.1007/978-3-030-87237-3_29
26. Hou, W., Huang, H., Peng, Q., Yu, R., Yu, L., Wang, L.: Spatial-hierarchical graph neural network with dynamic structure learning for histological image classification. In: Medical Image Computing and Computer Assisted Intervention–MICCAI 2022: 25th International Conference, Singapore, September 18–22, 2022, Proceedings, Part II, pp. 181–191. Springer, Cham (2022). https://doi.org/10.1007/978-3-031-16434-7_18

# Ultrafast Labeling for Multiplexed Immunobiomarkers from Label-free Fluorescent Images

Zixia Zhou, Yuming Jiang, Ruijiang Li, and Lei Xing[✉]

Department of Radiation Oncology, Stanford University, Stanford, CA 94305, USA
lei@stanford.com

**Abstract.** Labeling pathological images based on different immunobiomarker holds immense clinical significance, serving as an instrumental tool in various fields such as disease diagnostics and biomedical research. However, the existing predominant techniques harnessed for immunobiomarker labeling, such as immunofluorescence (IF) and immunohistochemistry (IHC), are marred by shortcomings such as inconsistent specificity, cost/time-intensive staining procedures, and potential cellular damage incurred during labeling. In response to these impediments, deep-learning-powered generative models have emerged as a promising avenue for immunolabeling prediction, owing to their adeptness in image-to-image translation. To realize automatic immunolabeling prediction, we devised an auto-immunolabeling (Auto-iL) network capable of simultaneous labeling various immunobiomarkers by generating the corresponding immunofluorescence-stained images from dual-modal label-free inputs. To enhance the feature extraction potential of the Auto-iL network, we utilize random masked autoencoders on dual-modal. Subsequently, a self-attention block adeptly merges the dual features, which empowers a robust predictive capacity. In the experiments, immunolabeling performance of four biomarkers for gastric cancer patients was validated. Moreover, pathologists carried out clinical observation assessments on the immunolabeled results to ensure the reliability at the cellular level.

**Keywords:** Pathological Image · Immunobiomarker labeling · Immunofluorescence Staining · Deep Learning

## 1 Introduction

Immunobiomarker labeling is of pronounced clinical value, which is used to identify and diagnose various diseases [1–3]. The visualization of specific biomolecules within tissue samples allows pathologists to uncover significant insights about the underlying pathology, thereby guiding the treatment decisions. Immunohistochemistry (IHC) and immunofluorescence (IF) are frequently employed staining methods used for the identification and localization of a range of biomarkers within different tissues. Nonetheless, these techniques come with certain downsides such as inconsistencies in staining, along with considerable demands on time and resources. [4, 5]. Specifically, IHC staining is of

S. Wu et al. (Eds.): AMAI 2023, LNCS 14313, pp. 125–134, 2024.
https://doi.org/10.1007/978-3-031-47076-9_13

lower quality compared to IF and is limited in the number of antigens that can be labeled simultaneously, thus limiting the information obtained from a single experiment [6]. In contrast, although IF yields superior staining quality and is typically favored for multiplexing, while IF delivers high-quality staining and is often preferred for multiplexing, it can be expensive and associated with issues like photobleaching and phototoxicity [7].

Recent advancements in deep learning techniques have shown promise in image-to-image translation [8–10]. Researchers have leveraged the capabilities of deep neural networks (DNNs) and developed various regression-based models to learn the mapping rules between different pathological modalities. For example, Cao et al. [11] utilized a CycleGAN-based deep learning method to perform virtual hematoxylin and eosin (H&E) staining on grayscale ultraviolet-photoacoustic-microscopy images, enabling rapid diagnoses of bone-tissue pathologies. Rivenson et al. [12] adopted a generative adversarial network to transform wide-field autofluorescence images of unlabeled tissue sections into corresponding H&E-stained bright-field images. In the domain of pathological functional image generation, pertinent research can be bifurcated into two broad categories. The first category involves generating high-quality functional stained images from low-quality counterparts to optimize time and cost efficiency. For instance, a recent study introduced a multitask DNN to translate IHC-stained images into corresponding IF-stained images [13], considering the higher cost and informativeness of IF compared to IHC. Although this approach offers cost-saving benefits, acquiring low-quality functional stained input images still requires relatively complex procedures. The second category focuses on automatically predicting labeled immunostaining images with DNNs from unlabeled slides. For example, He et al. [14] developed deep learning algorithms to computationally generate in silico IHC staining from H&E stained tissue images. Christiansen et al. [15] created a DNN to directly predict fluorescent labels in unlabeled transmitted-light z stacks. However, these approaches are limited in their widespread usage due to their input modality selection. Specifically, H&E staining is known to be time-consuming, which hinders its efficiency in clinical settings [16]. Similarly, the collection of transmitted-light z stacks requires specialized equipment, posing challenges in terms of accessibility and practicality [17].

The aforementioned studies underscore that non-labeled images contain useful yet undiscovered information pertinent to immunolabeling. Despite numerous explorations in the field, the quest for a potent and effective deep learning model capable of reduce time and cost consumption and mitigate the negative influence of staining protocols remains a trending topic. Furthermore, there is a conspicuous lack of research investigating the authenticity and applicability of the generated stained slides, aspects crucial for their practical use in a clinical setting.

To address the issues mentioned above, in this paper, we developed an automatic immunobiomarker labeling network, called auto-immunolabeling (Auto-iL) network, which can achieve multiplexed immunofluorescence staining for the labeling of different biomarkers with stable performance and highly cost-effective. In the experiments, we validated the staining performance for both cancer and noncancer tissues by predicting four different immunobiomarkers. Moreover, multiple pathologists examine the predicted results and assess them from a clinical perspective.

The main contribution includes: 1) establishing a generative AI model called Auto-iL network, to automatically perform multiplex IF staining in a time-saving and cost-effective manner, 2) improving the feature extraction ability of Auto-iL network with a pretrained masked auto-encoder (MAE), 3) validating the usability of the Auto-iL network through the analysis and statistics conducted by pathologists, who evaluate it from a clinical viewpoint at the individual cell level.

## 2 Method

### 2.1 Framework Overview

To construct a versatile DNN model capable of automatically and reliably producing multiplexed IF-stained images for various immunobiomarkers, we developed the Auto-iL network as depicted in Fig. 1. This end-to-end model utilizes dual-modal label-free inputs, including autofluorescence and DAPI images, to generate multiplexed IF-stained images and realize ultrafast immunolabeling. The training of the Auto-iL network unfolds in two stages. First, we pre-trained two random MAE embedding networks separately to capture complementary and informative features from autofluorescence and DAPI images. Second, we employed a dual feature extractor, which combines the dual-modal features extracted from the pre-trained MAEs, alongside parallel decoders and residual finetune blocks to generate small patches of the whole slides. During training, the Auto-iL network is optimized in a supervised manner by minimizing a composite loss function. After the network reaches convergence, it can execute end-to-end prediction for whole slide images.

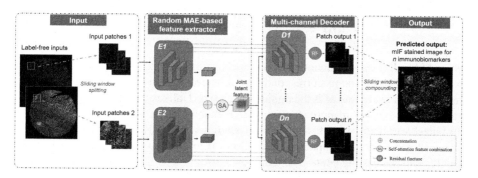

**Fig. 1.** Overview of the proposed Auto-iL network.

### 2.2 Random MAE Feature Extractor

Within the Auto-iL network, we introduced random masked mechanisms to bolster the feature extraction. Each MAE is trained using patches of size $256 \times 256$ selected from all whole slide images in the training set. A random masked mechanism is employed, where a mask of random size ($<64 \times 64$) is applied to each patch at a random location during MAE training in each epoch. In the next epoch, a new random mask is generated. The outputs from the encoders of the two MAEs are combined using a concatenation layer, as illustrated in Fig. 1. The detailed structure of the MAE with random masked mechanism is demonstrated in Fig. 2.

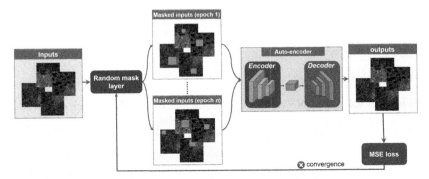

**Fig. 2.** Detailed structure of the MAE with random masked mechanism.

The two MAE models, termed MAE-AF and MAE-DAPI, share identical architectures and utilize Mean Square Error (MSE) as their loss metric, concurrently deploying masks of arbitrary dimensions and positions to the training patches within each epoch. This network's chief objective is to generate unmasked patches that correspond to the input patches after processing via an encoder-decoder architecture composed of numerous convolutional layers. Here's the definition for the applied loss function:

$$l_{MAE} = \frac{1}{M} \sum_{i=1}^{M} \|I_i^{ref} - \text{MAE}\left(I_i^{in}\right)\|_2^2 \tag{1}$$

where $\text{MAE}\left(I_i^{in}\right)$ and $I_i^{ref}$ denote the predicted results generated by the Auto-iL network in the training batch and its corresponding referenced manual-stained images of the $i$-th sample, respectively, and $M$ is the training batch size. Unlike conventional auto-encoder-based feature extraction approaches, the MAE enables the network to anticipate hidden attributes by utilizing the data from the surrounding context. This endows the MAE with enhanced generalization capacities and allows it to excel at both discerning inherent features and forecasting contextual data.

### 2.3  Dual-Modal Feature Combination With Self-Attention Mechanism

Following the pretraining phase of the two MAE models, their encoder components were repurposed, utilizing the pretrained weights. Subsequently, a concatenation layer was employed to merge the dual latent features. A self-attention module was then integrated to selectively harness valuable features from the concatenated feature, giving precedence to relevant and information-rich regions. The methodology for computing self-attention is aligned with the research presented in [18]. Assuming that the input to a module $H$ is $x$, the output of the trunk branch is $T(x)$, and the output of the mask branch is $M(x)$, then the output of module $H$ is $H_{i,c}(x) = \left(1 + M_{i,c}(x)\right) * T_{i,c}(x)$, where $i$ represents the pixel position and $c$ represents the corresponding channel position.

By integrating autofluorescence and DAPI inputs in parallel, the network can fully exploit the synergistic information provided by multiple channels. Autofluorescence input effectively captures a range of complex signal origins, including various intrinsically fluorescent tissue components. Despite its potential, autofluorescence data can often be undermined by instability and noise. On the other hand, DAPI input offers detailed and stable nuclear information, allowing precise localization of individual cell nuclei, thereby aiding in the generation of more sophisticated staining effects.

### 2.4 Multitasked Composite Loss Function

Next, to maintain the distinctness of predictions for each immunobiomarker, while taking advantage of their mutual information, we utilized a shared structure within the encoder and feature combination elements. This was followed by separate decoders for generating diverse labeling predictions. The Auto-iL network's loss function comprises two parts: restrictions on the outputs of the decoders and the residual finetune blocks. Our aim is to minimize the MSE between the predicted labeling results and the corresponding manual-stained results, with the intention to diminish the disparities between them. The final loss can be represented as follows:

$$l_{MAS} = \sum_{n=1}^{N} l_{MAS}^{n} \tag{2}$$

$$l_{MAS}^{n} = \frac{1}{M}\left[\sum_{i=1}^{M} I_i^{r1} - D\left(I_i^{AU}, I_i^{DA}\right)_2^2 + \sum_{i=1}^{M} I_i^{r2} - RF\left(D\left(I_i^{AU}, I_i^{DA}\right)\right)_2^2\right] \tag{3}$$

where $M$ is the training batch size, $N$ is the number of output channels, $l_{MAS}^{n}$ represents the sub-loss for $n$-th prediction. $D(\cdot)$ and $RF(\cdot)$ are the calculations of decoders and residual finetune blocks, respectively. $I_i^{AU}$, $I_i^{DA}$, $I_i^{r1}$ and $I_i^{r2}$ represent the autofluorescence input, DAPI input, referenced labeled image covered on DAPI image and the referenced labeled stained image, respectively.

## 3   Experiments

### 3.1   Data Preparation

In the data preparation stage, we captured autofluorescence images of unstained, label-free tissues utilizing a standard fluorescence microscope (IX83, Olympus) outfitted with a motorized stage. mIF staining was carried out by the Shanghai Outdo Biotech Company. Biomarkers including CD3, PD1, CD20, and FOXP3 were sequentially detected. All slides were counterstained with DAPI for five minutes. Afterwards, we synchronized an autofluorescence image of unstained tissue with mIF images of the same tissue sample post histological staining. Tissue microarrays of gastric cancer subjected to mIF staining for each fluorophore were imaged using the Vectra Multi-spectral Imaging System version 2 (Perkin Elmer, USA). This step was undertaken using appropriate fluorescent filters to construct the spectral library crucial for multispectral analysis. A whole-slide scan of the multiplex tissue sections resulted in multispectral fluorescent images, which were visualized in Phenochart (Perkin Elmer, USA) and imaged at 20x magnification for subsequent analysis. Finally, inForm image analysis software (Perkin Elmer, USA) was used to analyze the multispectral images.

We gathered data from 94 gastric cancer patients, including pathological slides from both cancerous and noncancerous tissues. To procure aligned training pairs, we initially produced DAPI and autofluorescence images for each tissue slice and then simultaneously stained them with CD3, CD20, FOXP3, and PD1 markers. After these steps, we secured 180 paired, aligned images. For the network's training phase, we utilized data from 80 patients as the training dataset, while data from the remaining 14 patients constituted a separate test set. Furthermore, all images within the patches were resized to a $256 \times 256$ resolution, normalized to a range of 0 to 1, and underwent augmentation procedures, including random shifting, rotation, shearing, zooming, and flipping.

### 3.2 Assessment Scores

To assess the effectiveness of different methods, we incorporated a combination of similarity-based evaluation and clinical observation assessment.

**Similarity-Based Evaluation**

In the assessment, we utilized similarity-based metrics such as the Peak Signal-to-Noise Ratio (PSNR) and the Structural Similarity Index Measure (SSIM) [19]. These metrics offer measures of pixel-level and perception-based similarities between the predicted result and the referenced labeled image, respectively. The calculation for PSNR is carried out using the following equation:

$$\text{PSNR} = 10 \times \log_{10} \frac{255^2}{(y_{\text{PL}}^{(i)} - \hat{y}_{\text{RL}}^{(i)})^2}, \tag{4}$$

where $y_{\text{PL}}^{(i)}$ and $\hat{y}_{\text{RL}}^{(i)}$ denote the $i$-th predicted result in the testing dataset and its corresponding referenced labeled image, respectively. The SSIM is defined as:

$$\text{SSIM} = \frac{(2\mu_M \mu_A + C_1)(2\sigma_{A,M} + C_2)}{(\mu_M^2 + \mu_A^2 + C_1)(\sigma_M^2 + \sigma_A^2 + C_2)}, \tag{5}$$

where $\mu_R$, $\mu_P$, $\sigma_R$, $\sigma_P$ and $\sigma_{R,P}$ denote the means, standard deviations and covariance of the predicted result and the referenced labeled image, respectively. $C1$ and $C2$ are defined values used to stabilize the calculation.

**Clinical Observation Assessment**

To quantify the density of stained cells after immunolabeling, we calculated the count of cells with nuclear staining per core. This assessment was independently conducted by two pathologists specializing in gastroenterology, who were blinded to the clinical outcomes. In cases where there was a disagreement in the initial evaluations, a third pathologist was consulted to achieve a consensus. For each task of biomarker prediction, we randomly selected 40 patch sets.

### 3.3 Software and Platform

The experiments were performed in Linux operating system (Ubuntu 16.04 LTS), with Python 3.6. The training process was conducted using Keras with Tensorflow [20] as the backend. In addition, an NVIDIA Tesla V100 DGXS graphic processing unit (GPU) was adopted to increase the training speed.

## 4 Results

### 4.1 Comparison with Other Techniques

The generated predictions for multiple immunobiomarkers exhibit remarkable similarity to the referenced manual-stained images, verifying the capability of the proposed Auto-iL network to achieve accurate labeling for immune cells. Besides, compared to the time-consuming traditional manual labeling process that often requires more than 24 h, the Auto-iL network can achieve ultrafast immunolabeling in less than one second with the label-free inputs (Fig. 3).

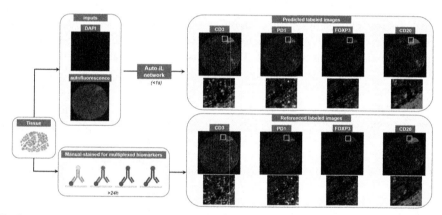

**Fig. 3.** Comparison between the predicted labeling results generated by Auto-iL network and the corresponding manual-stained images.

Additionally, we compared the performance differences between Auto-iL network and other methods. The comparative methods include the vanilla U-Net and U-Net with self-attention (U-Net + SA). The evaluation results are shown in Table 1. Overall, the proposed Auto-iL network is able to achieve the most superior predicted results, with the highest similarity to manual stained images.

### 4.2 Clinical Observation Assessment

The results of the clinical observation assessments are depicted in Fig. 4. The scatter plots reveal a robust positive correlation between the predicted labeling outcomes and the reference manual-stained images. The Pearson correlation coefficient (PCC) values

**Table 1.** Quantitative comparison of different deep learning methods in predicting CD3, CD20, FOXP3, and PD1 biomarkers.

| Biomarkers | Index | vanilla U-Net | U-Net + SA | Auto-iL |
|---|---|---|---|---|
| CD3 | PSNR | 27.053 ± 4.10 | 27.419 ± 4.15 | **28.162 ± 4.85** |
| | SSIM | 0.733 ± 0.07 | 0.724 ± 0.07 | **0.736 ± 0.07** |
| PD1 | PSNR | 27.908 ± 4.47 | 27.950 ± 4.43 | **29.983 ± 4.37** |
| | SSIM | 0.654 ± 0.13 | 0.659 ± 0.13 | **0.694 ± 0.14** |
| FOXP3 | PSNR | 31.769 ± 3.29 | 31.838 ± 3.10 | **31.855 ± 3.24** |
| | SSIM | 0.613 ± 0.11 | 0.618 ± 0.11 | **0.619 ± 0.11** |
| CD20 | PSNR | 28.835 ± 4.66 | **29.244 ± 4.76** | 29.241 ± 4.81 |
| | SSIM | 0.921 ± 0.058 | 0.921 ± 0.057 | **0.924 ± 0.056** |

[21] corresponding to the CD3, PD1, FOXP3, and CD20 biomarkers were measured to be 0.908, 0.983, 0.986, and 0.973, respectively. The corresponding p-values are $8.85 \times 10^{-20}$, $2.79 \times 10^{-37}$, $2.62 \times 10^{-39}$, and $3.13 \times 10^{-32}$, respectively. These results from the pathologists' clinical observation supply strong evidence that the predicted labeling outputs, generated by the Auto-iL network, showcase a high level of resemblance to the reference manual-stained images. This underscores the reliability of our proposed method.

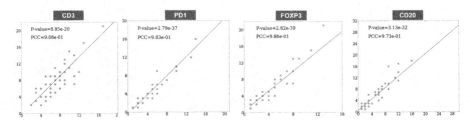

**Fig. 4.** Scatter plots of the predicted auto-stained data and referenced manual-stained data for CD3, PD1, FOXP3, and CD20 labels.

## 5 Conclusion

In this paper, we introduced an Auto-iL network for the labeling of different immuno-biomarkers. By designing an advanced feature extractor based on random MAE, the network can capture useful information from label-free images. Additionally, through the employment of a self-attention structure, dual-modal features are effectively integrated. Experimental validation demonstrated the Auto-iL network's capacity to outperform existing technologies by delivering ultrafast, efficient labeling across diverse immunobiomarkers.

# References

1. Andreou, C., Weissleder, R., Kircher, M.F.: Multiplexed imaging in oncology. Nat. Biomed. Eng **6**(5), 5 (2022)
2. Snyder, M.P., et al.: The human body at cellular resolution: the NIH Human Biomolecular Atlas Program. Nature **574**(7777), 7777 (2019)
3. Schürch, C.M., et al.: Coordinated cellular neighborhoods orchestrate antitumoral immunity at the colorectal cancer invasive front. Cell **182**(5), 1341-1359.e19 (2020)
4. Duraiyan, J., Govindarajan, R., Kaliyappan, K., Palanisamy, M.: Applications of immuno-histochemistry. J. Pharm. Bioallied. Sci. 4(Suppl 2), S307–S309 (2012)
5. Im, K., Mareninov, S., Diaz, M.F.P., Yong, W.H.: An introduction to performing immunofluorescence staining. Methods Mol. Biol. **1897**, 299–311 (2019)
6. Rizzardi, A.E., et al.: Quantitative comparison of immunohistochemical staining measured by digital image analysis versus pathologist visual scoring. Diagn. Pathol. **7**(1), 42 (2012)
7. Chen, H., Xue, J., Zhang, Y., Zhu, X., Gao, J., Yu, B.: Comparison of quantum dots immunofluorescence histochemistry and conventional immunohistochemistry for the detection of caveolin-1 and PCNA in the lung cancer tissue microarray. J. Mol. Histol. **40**(4), 261–268 (2009)
8. Armanious, K., et al.: MedGAN: Medical image translation using GANs. Comput. Med. Imaging Graph. **79**, 101684 (2020)
9. Isola, P., Zhu, J.-Y., Zhou, T., Efros, A.A.: Image-to-image translation with conditional adversarial networks. In: Presented at the 2017 IEEE Conference on Computer Vision and Pattern Recognition (CVPR), IEEE Computer Society, pp. 5967–5976 (2017)
10. Zhang, R., et al.: MVFStain: multiple virtual functional stain histopathology images generation based on specific domain mapping. Med. Image Anal. **80**, 102520 (2022)
11. Cao, R., et al.: Label-free intraoperative histology of bone tissue via deep-learning-assisted ultraviolet photoacoustic microscopy. Nat. Biomed. Eng. **7**(2), 2 (2023)
12. Rivenson, Y., et al.: Virtual histological staining of unlabelled tissue-autofluorescence images via deep learning. Nat. Biomed. Eng. **3**(6), 6 (2019)
13. Ghahremani, P., et al.: Deep learning-inferred multiplex immunofluorescence for immuno-histochemical image quantification. Nat. Mach. Intell. **4**(4), 4 (2022)
14. He, B., et al.: AI-enabled in silico immunohistochemical characterization for Alzheimer's disease. Cell Rep. Methods **2**(4), 100191 (2022)
15. Christiansen, E.M., et al.: In silico labeling: predicting fluorescent labels in unlabeled images. Cell **173**(3), 792-803.e19 (2018)
16. Bayramoglu, N., Kaakinen, M., Eklund, L., Heikkilä, J.: Towards Virtual H&E staining of hyperspectral lung histology images using conditional generative adversarial networks. In: 2017 IEEE International Conference on Computer Vision Workshops (ICCVW), pp. 64–71 (2017)
17. Ounkomol, C., Seshamani, S., Maleckar, M.M., Collman, F., Johnson, G.R.: Label-free prediction of three-dimensional fluorescence images from transmitted-light microscopy. Nat. Methods **15**(11), 917–920 (2018)
18. Zhang, H., Goodfellow, I., Metaxas, D., Odena, A.: Self-attention generative adversarial networks. In: Proceedings of the 36th International Conference on Machine Learning, PMLR, May 2019, pp. 7354–7363 (2023)
19. Horé, A., Ziou, D.: Image Quality Metrics: PSNR vs. SSIM. In: 2010 20th International Conference on Pattern Recognition, pp. 2366–2369 (2010)
20. Abadi, M.: TensorFlow: learning functions at scale. In: Proceedings of the 21st ACM SIGPLAN International Conference on Functional Programming, in ICFP 2016. New York, NY, USA: Association for Computing Machinery, p. 1 (2016)

21. Benesty, J., Chen, J., Huang, Y., Cohen, I.: Pearson correlation coefficient. In: I., Huang, Y., Chen, J., Benesty, J., Eds., Noise Reduction in Speech Processing, Cohen, pp. 1–4. Springer Topics in Signal Processing. Berlin, Heidelberg (2009)

# M U-Net: Intestine Segmentation Using Multi-dimensional Features for Ileus Diagnosis Assistance

Qin An[1], Hirohisa Oda[2], Yuichiro Hayashi[1], Takayuki Kitasaka[3],
Akinari Hinoki[4], Hiroo Uchida[4], Kojiro Suzuki[5], Aitaro Takimoto[4],
Masahiro Oda[1,6], and Kensaku Mori[1,7,8(✉)]

[1] Graduate School of Informatics, Nagoya University, Nagoya, Japan
`qinan@mori.m.is.nagoya-u.ac.jp, kensaku@is.nagoya-u.ac.jp`
[2] School of Management and Information, University of Shizuoka, Shizuoka, Japan
[3] School of Information Science, Aichi Institute of Technology, Toyota, Japan
[4] Graduate School of Medicine, Nagoya University, Nagoya, Japan
[5] Department of Radiology, Aichi Medical University, Toyota, Japan
[6] Strategy Office, Nagoya University, Information and Communications, Nagoya, Japan
[7] Information Technology Center, Nagoya University, Nagoya, Japan
[8] National Institute of Informatics, Research Center for Medical Bigdata, Tokyo, Japan

**Abstract.** The intestine is an essential digestive organ that can cause serious health problems once diseased. This paper proposes a method for intestine segmentation to intestine obstruction diagnosis assistance called multi-dimensional U-Net (M U-Net). We employ two encoders to extract features from two-dimensional (2D) CT slices and three-dimensional (3D) CT patches. These two encoders collaborate to enhance the segmentation accuracy of the model. Additionally, we incorporate deep supervision with the M U-Net to reduce the limitation of training with sparse label data sets. The experimental results demonstrated that the Dice of the proposed method was 73.22%, the recall was 79.89%, and the precision was 70.61%.

**Keywords:** Intestine segmentation · Ileus · Computer-aided diagnosis · Sparse label

## 1 Introduction

The intestine is a vital digestive organ, which is highly folded in the abdominal cavity and surrounded by various organs, which brings a great challenge for clinicians to diagnose intestinal diseases accurately.

---

Q. An—Contributing author.

Ileus [1] is one kind of intestine obstruction, a temporary lack of regular muscle contractions of the intestines. Finding the intestines is significant for acquiring more detailed information for giving the preoperative diagnosis. Computed Tomography (CT) has been used as a prevalent diagnostic method for intestinal diseases. However, it takes a long time for clinicians to find lesions from one patient's CT volume. Therefore, the automatic intestine segmentation method assists clinicians in diagnosing the disease accurately and quickly. Figure 1 shows an example of ileus case CT volume.

Over the past decades, deep learning has gradually emerged as a practical approach to medical image segmentation [2–5]. However, these methods focus on processing CT images from two-dimension, which overlooks crucial three-dimensional spatial features required for 3D medical images. After that, three-dimensional networks [6] appear gradually. However, 3D deep learning methods with many parameters often suffer from high computational costs, hindering their ability to extract image features effectively. Consequently, intestines still exhibit lower segmentation accuracy than larger organs with simpler spatial features, primarily due to boundary and shape variability. Researchers have proposed many methods to tackle this challenge that combine two-dimensional (2D) and three-dimensional (3D) features. For instance, 2.5D U-Net [7,8] and RIUNet [9] utilize consecutive 2D slices as input to extract 3D semantic features. However, relying only on 2D convolutional layers processing continuous 2D slices may not adequately capture the spatial features. H-DenseUNet [10] addresses this limitation by training a 2D DenseUNet and a 3D DenseUNet, which fuse intra-slice and inter-slice features for liver and tumor segmentation.

In addition, some researchers have explored segmentation methods for the intestine [11–15]. However, these methods rely on hand-crafted features, such as intensity thresholding and region growing. Besides, a few works also address intestine segmentation with deep-learning methods. In 2020, Shin et al. [16] proposed using a cylinder topological constraint within a neural network to segment the small intestine from CT. Oda et al. [17] proposed using 3D U-Net to segment intestines in the same year. However, these methods only focus on utilizing 3D features and may need to be improved in capturing other essential semantic information about the intestines from two-dimension images.

Currently, 2D methods mainly focus on extracting texture features from 2D slices, while 3D methods emphasize capturing volumetric features. The former often overlook crucial spatial features essential for accurate segmentation. The latter heavily relies on a large number of labelled data sets. To address those problems and take inspiration from previous methods, we propose a novel multi-dimensional approach to improve intestine segmentation accuracy and decrease the influence of limited labelled data sets. This method can effectively assist doctors in quickly and accurately diagnosing intestinal diseases. The contributions of this paper are summarized as follows:

1) We propose a multi-dimensional U-Net (M U-Net) framework designed to extract intra-slice and inter-slice features for intestine segmentation. The

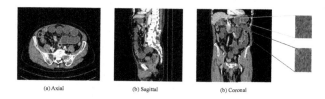

(a) Axial                (b) Sagittal                (b) Coronal

**Fig. 1.** Example of ileus case CT volume. (a), (b), and (c) are axial, sagittal, and coronal CT images, respectively. The intensities of the intestine and that of the surrounding tissues are close. The red box designates the intestinal region, whereas the green box indicates other tissues, exhibiting low contrast between the two regions. (Color figure online)

novel network architecture incorporates a 2D and a 3D encoder to utilize various features extracted from CT volumes.

2) We apply the multi-dimensional U-Net to the intestines segmentation based on a sparse label data set. Our approach achieves competitive results, effectively mitigating the impact of the limited labelled data set.

Furthermore, we incorporate deep supervision [18, 19] into our approach. This strategy allows our network to extract more comprehensive semantic information from 3D CT volumes.

## 2 Method

### 2.1 Overview

Our M U-Net is designed to tackle the challenge of inadequate intestine segmentation from CT volumes. The network employs the 3D encoder to capture crucial 3D spatial information, while the 2D encoder extracts valuable 2D contextual features. Furthermore, we amplify the network's learning capability for sparse labels by integrating deep supervision techniques.

The method takes 3D CT patches as input, cropped from entire CT volumes using a sliding window, and produces a CT volume with intestine segmentation as output. The 2D and 3D encoders are trained simultaneously, after which the features derived from different dimensions are fused using an additive operation. In the decoder part, deep supervision is employed to calculate the loss, thereby enhancing the transparency of the hidden layers during the training process. The detailed structure of the M U-Net and training using deep supervision are shown in Fig. 2.

### 2.1.1 Multi-dimensional Encoder

The multi-dimensional encoder is a critical optimization in our M U-Net. We construct a multi-dimensional encoder comprising a two-dimensional encoder (2D encoder) and a three-dimensional encoder (3D encoder). The 2D encoder, consisting of three blocks, takes 2D slices from three different planes (axial,

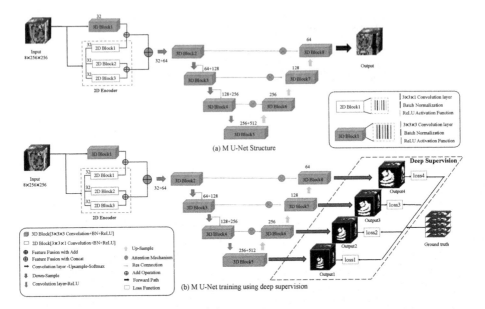

**Fig. 2.** Structure of the M U-Net and training using deep supervision. The network has two encoders to extract features from CT volume. The region enclosed by red dotted lines indicate deep supervision. It is worth noting that deep supervision is just used in training. (Color figure online)

sagittal, and coronal) as input to extract 2D semantic information. The 3D encoder comprises four blocks, each incorporating $3 \times 3 \times 3$ convolution filters, batch normalization, and the ReLU activation function. Rather than Max Pooling, we connect the two blocks through down-sampling. We accomplish this by using $2 \times 2 \times 2$ convolution filters to down-sample the feature maps, adjusting parameters such as stride and padding accordingly. During the encoding phase, the image undergoes three times of down-sampling. The structure of the decoder mirrors that of the encoder. As a result, we perform three up-sampling operations to restore the feature map size to match the input.

The multi-dimensional encoder efficiently utilizes the semantic information from both the slices and patches. The two encoders enhance the model's performance by extracting distinct features from different dimensions.

## 2.2 Compound Loss Function with Deep Supervision

### 2.2.1 Compound Loss Function

The overall loss function includes Dice loss [20] and hausdorff distance loss [21]. The formula of the compound loss function is $L_{overall}(\mathbf{G}, \mathbf{S}) = \lambda \mathrm{L}_{\mathrm{Dice}}(\mathbf{G}, \mathbf{S}) + \omega \mathrm{L}_{\mathrm{HD}}(\mathbf{G}, \mathbf{S})$. In Table 3, we evaluate the influence of different weights $\lambda$ and $\omega$ in compound loss. It is worth noting that we only calculate the loss by labelled slices because of using a sparse label data set.

Dice loss [20] is more sensitive to the internal of the label image and can alleviate data imbalance, which is common in medical image segmentation tasks. The Dice loss can be computed by

$$L_{Dice}(\mathbf{G}, \mathbf{S}) = 1 - 2\frac{\mathbf{G} \cup \mathbf{S}}{\mathbf{G} \cap \mathbf{S}}, \tag{1}$$

where $\mathbf{G}$ denotes the ground truth, $\mathbf{S}$ denotes the segmentation result. $\mathbf{G} \cup \mathbf{S}$ denotes the intersection of the label image and the segmentation result. $\mathbf{G} \cap \mathbf{S}$ denotes the union of the label image and the segmentation result.

HD loss guides the convergence of the network by describing the boundary similarity between the label image and prediction. Since minimizing the hausdorff distance directly is difficult and may lead to unstable training, Karimi et al. [21] showed that the distance between the label image and prediction can replace it. The HD loss can be computed by

$$L_{HD}(\mathbf{G}, \mathbf{S}) = \frac{1}{N} \sum_{i=1}^{N} \left[ (s_i - g_i) \cdot (d_{g_i}^{\alpha} - d_{s_i}^{\alpha}) \right], \tag{2}$$

where $\mathbf{G}$ denotes the ground truth, $\mathbf{S}$ denotes the segmentation result, $N$ denotes the voxel number of ground truth and the segmentation result, $s_i \in \mathbf{S}$ stands for the $i$-th voxel of the segmentation result, $g_i \in \mathbf{G}$ stands for the $i$-th voxel of the label image. $d_{g_i}$, $d_{s_i}$ are the distance transformation results of the label image and segmentation results. $\cdot$ denotes the multiply operation. $\alpha$ determines how strongly we penalize more significant errors. According to the original paper about HD Loss, we use the values of $\alpha = 2$.

### 2.2.2  Deep Supervision

To overcome the under-fitting of training deep neural networks with weak annotation data sets. We incorporated the deep supervision strategy, which uses feature maps from different blocks to calculate the loss. And then, we add all loss values calculated by different blocks as the final loss value. As shown in Fig. 2, we calculate loss1, loss2, loss3 and loss4 for output1, output2, output3 and output4 by using $L_{overall}$ equation. Since we reconstruct outputs for each level of the decoder, we can calculate for $L_{Dice}$ and $L_{HD}$ for each level. Then we add them with different weights. Specifically, we assign a weight of ($\gamma = 1$) to the loss value of the final block (loss4) and a weight of ($\beta = 0.8$) to the loss values from the other block. The weight ($\beta = 0.8$), called the deep supervision coefficient, decays at 0.8 every 30 epochs. The final loss value can be calculated as

$$l_{\text{final}} = \gamma loss_4 + \beta(loss_1 + loss_2 + loss_3), \tag{3}$$

where $l_{\text{final}}$ denotes the final loss value, $loss_4$ denotes the loss value calculated by the output of the final block, $loss_1$, $loss_2$, and $loss_3$ denote the loss values from the other three blocks, $\beta$ denotes the deep supervision coefficient.

**Table 1.** Evaluation results of different methods. We compared the proposed method with different methods. The best performance of each evaluation term is bolded in the table.

| Methods | Dice (%) | Recall (%) | Precision (%) |
|---|---|---|---|
| 3D U-Net [6] | $42.24 \pm 10.55$ | $65.19 \pm 13.65$ | $35.25 \pm 11.57$ |
| 2.5D U-Net [8] | $65.26 \pm 9.25$ | $76.48 \pm 7.53$ | $61.25 \pm 12.23$ |
| RIU-Net [9] | $59.64 \pm 9.84$ | $\mathbf{80.80 \pm 6.80}$ | $50.81 \pm 11.14$ |
| H-DenseU-Net [10] | $67.46 \pm 8.85$ | $78.53 \pm 7.27$ | $62.73 \pm 10.06$ |
| Oda et al. [17] | $73.09 \pm 12.67$ | $69.42 \pm 15.37$ | $\mathbf{80.47 \pm 11.88}$ |
| M U-Net | $\mathbf{73.22 \pm 4.94}$ | $79.89 \pm 6.79$ | $70.61 \pm 6.65$ |

# 3    Experiments and Results

## 3.1    Experiment Detail

In this experiment, we used a private data set consisting of 109 cases of ileus patients' CT volumes with $512 \times 512 \times 198$–$546$ voxels with $(0.549$–$0.904\,\mathrm{mm}) \times (0.549$–$0.904\,\mathrm{mm}) \times (1.0$–$2.0\,\mathrm{mm})$ per voxel resolution. Then these volumetric images were interpolated to isotropic voxel resolution $(1\,\mathrm{mm}^3/\mathrm{voxel})$. Interpolated volume size is $(281 \times 281)$ – $(463 \times 463)$ pixels in axial planes and 396–762 slices. This data set was divided into the training set and testing set according to a ratio of about 3:1.

The CT volumes were labelled several slices (6–15 slices) according to the axial plane by clinicians. 83 CT volumes were randomly selected to generate 3D patches for the training and 27 CT volumes for testing. The proposed M U-Net was implemented with PyTorch and processing was performed on one NVIDIA Tesla V100-PCIE GPU. The initial learning rate was set to 0.00001 and the adaptive learning rate optimization mechanism was used to reduce the learning rate by half every 100 epochs.

Before training, pre-processing was conducted for CT volumes to better leverage the limited labelled data. We normalized the CT value to $[-100, 200]$ to clarify the intestines region in CT images. To trade off the computational efficiency, we cropped many 3D CT patches with sizes $256 \times 256 \times 8$ for training. Data augmentation was utilized to improve the generalization ability of the segmentation model, including cropping, flipping, and non-rigid transformation.

## 3.2    Results

To assess the effectiveness of the M U-Net, we conducted contrast experiments with previous methods. The evaluation criteria utilized for this comparison include Dice score, precision, and recall. And we calculate the standard deviation between each testing sample. Table 1 presents the segmentation performance of these methods on our intestines data set. Figure 3 shows the segmented intestine regions obtained by the M U-Net from three different planes. Furthermore,

Fig. 4 displays the intestine segmentation results obtained using different methods. Figure 5 shows the intestine segmentation results of the proposed method with the compound loss with different weights.

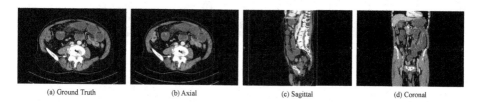

(a) Ground Truth        (b) Axial        (c) Sagittal        (d) Coronal

**Fig. 3.** Intestine segmentation result of the proposed method on three different planes. (a) is the ground truth. (b), (c), and (d) are segmentation results on axial, sagittal, and coronal planes, respectively. Regions with red colour denote the intestine. (Color figure online)

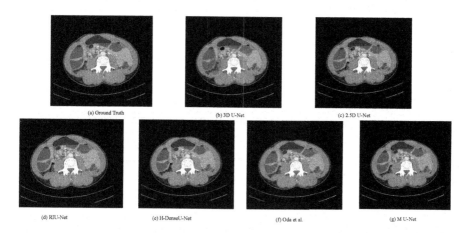

**Fig. 4.** Intestine segmentation results from different methods. (a) is the ground truth; (b)–(f) are the results of five previous methods; (g) is the result of the proposed method. Regions with red colour denote the intestine. (Color figure online)

### 3.2.1 Contribution of Compound Loss Function

The overall loss in our method consists of the Dice loss and the hausdorff distance loss. The Dice loss is particularly sensitive to the internal regions in the segmentation results, while the hausdorff distance loss updates the model weights by measuring the difference between the surfaces of the ground truth and the predicted results. Our proposed method combineS these two loss functions to guide the model's convergence. The experimental results are presented in Table 2. Additionally, we conducted an ablation study to evaluate the influence of different weights assigned to the two loss functions, with the results shown in Table 3.

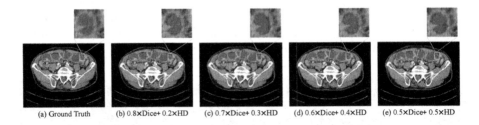

(a) Ground Truth    (b) 0.8×Dice+ 0.2×HD    (c) 0.7×Dice+ 0.3×HD    (d) 0.6×Dice+ 0.4×HD    (e) 0.5×Dice+ 0.5×HD

**Fig. 5.** Segmentation results of compound loss with different weights. (a) is the ground truth; (b)–(e) are the results of compound loss with different weights. The boxes indicated the different segmentation in the boundary part.

**Table 2.** Segmentation results of experiments with and without compound loss. The best performance of each evaluation term with bold font.

| Methods | Dice (%) | Recall (%) | Precision (%) |
|---|---|---|---|
| M U-Net with Dice Loss | $71.99 \pm 6.72$ | $77.68 \pm 7.20$ | $70.28 \pm 8.62$ |
| M U-Net with HD Loss | $69.08 \pm 6.53$ | $\mathbf{76.34 \pm 7.35}$ | $66.74 \pm 8.06$ |
| M U-Net with Compound Loss | $\mathbf{73.22 \pm 4.94}$ | $79.89 \pm 6.79$ | $\mathbf{70.61 \pm 6.65}$ |

**Table 3.** Segmentation results of compound loss with different weights. The best performance of each evaluation term with bold font.

| Methods | Dice (%) | Recall (%) | Precision (%) |
|---|---|---|---|
| M U-Net (0.8×Dice+0.2×HD) | $71.08 \pm 8.12$ | $78.88 \pm 7.53$ | $69.09 \pm 9.89$ |
| M U-Net (0.7×Dice+0.3×HD) | $71.67 \pm 5.74$ | $78.80 \pm 6.81$ | $68.99 \pm 73.30$ |
| M U-Net (0.6×Dice+0.4×HD) | $70.50 \pm 5.52$ | $77.89 \pm 7.21$ | $67.36 \pm 6.78$ |
| M U-Net (0.5×Dice+0.5×HD) | $\mathbf{72.98 \pm 5.41}$ | $\mathbf{80.09 \pm 6.72}$ | $\mathbf{70.20 \pm 7.28}$ |

### 3.2.2 Contribution of Multi-dimensional Encoder

Automatic intestines segmentation plays an important role in clinical diagnosis assistance. Furthermore, intra-slice and inter-slice features are essential for segmentation from CT volumes. However, 2D and 3D segmentation models focus on a single aspect. Thus, we propose a combination of 2D and 3D encoders, effectively extracting features from intra-slice and inter-slice contexts. To validate the effectiveness of the multi-dimensional encoder, we compare it with 3D UNet (only with 3D encoder), 2.5D U-Net, RIU-Net (only with 2D encoder), and H-DenseU-Net based on our data set. The experimental results presented in Table 1 demonstrate the superiority of our method.

## 4    Discussion and Conclusions

We introduce the M U-Net, a novel method specifically developed for improving the low accuracy of intestine segmentation using a sparse label data set. We focus on two critical optimizations of the 3D U-Net, the multi-dimensional encoder and the compound loss function. Compared with H-DenseU-Net, our method has a lower parameter count (around 50Millions), H-DenseU-Net (around 60Millions). Reducing of parameters effectively reduces the risks of overfitting when training with sparse data using a complex network. In Fig. 5, it can be seen that the compound loss with different weights has different effects on boundary segmentation, which can influence the performance of the model. HD loss pays more attention to the boundary part, which can improve the comprehensive performance of the model.

However, our proposed method has segmented more intestine regions there still has more space to improve. In the future, we will further explore the influence of parameters in deep supervision. In addition, the robustness of the proposed model needs to be verified on CT volumes with different layer thicknesses. Furthermore, we will combine some advanced strategies to reduce the influence of the weak annotation data set. Inspired by the widely used pseudo-labels for incorporating unlabelled images in semi-supervised learning, we will explore the pseudo-label strategy to use weak annotation data set in our method effectively.

**Prospect of Application:** The method is important to construct the computer aided diagnosis (CAD) system, which can help doctors to diagnose intestinal diseases (such as ileus). The method also can facilitate more accurate pre-operative preparations.

**Acknowledgments.** Thanks for the help and advice from Mori laboratory. A part of this research was supported by Hori Sciences and Arts Foundation, MEXT/JSPS KAKENHI (17H00867, 22H03203), the JSPS Bilateral International Collaboration Grants, and the JST CREST (JPMJCR20D5). And this work was also financially supported by the JST SPRING, Grant Number JPMJSP2125.

# References

1. Sinicrope, F., Ileus and Bowel Obstruction: Holland-Frei Cancer Medicine, 6th edn. Hamilton BC Decker, Hamilton (2003)
2. Roth, H.R., et al.: Deep learning and its application to medical image segmentation. Med. Imag. Technol. **36**(2), 63–71 (2018)
3. Ronneberger, O., Fischer, P., Brox, T.: U-Net: convolutional networks for biomedical image segmentation. In: Navab, N., Hornegger, J., Wells, W.M., Frangi, A.F. (eds.) MICCAI 2015, Part III. LNCS, vol. 9351, pp. 234–241. Springer, Cham (2015). https://doi.org/10.1007/978-3-319-24574-4_28
4. Xiao, X., Lian, S., Luo, Z., Li, S.: Weighted Res-UNet for high-quality retina vessel segmentation. In: 2018 9th International Conference on Information Technology in Medicine and Education (ITME), pp. 327–331. IEEE (2018)
5. Cai, S., Tian, Y., Lui, H., Zeng, H., Wu, Y., Chen, G.: Dense-UNet: a novel multiphoton in vivo cellular image segmentation model based on a convolutional neural network. Quant. Imag. Med. Surg. **10**(6) (2020). https://qims.amegroups.com/article/view/43519. ISSN 2223–4306

6. Çiçek, Ö., Abdulkadir, A., Lienkamp, S.S., Brox, T., Ronneberger, O.: 3D U-Net: learning dense volumetric segmentation from sparse annotation. In: Ourselin, S., Joskowicz, L., Sabuncu, M.R., Unal, G., Wells, W. (eds.) MICCAI 2016, Part II. LNCS, vol. 9901, pp. 424–432. Springer, Cham (2016). https://doi.org/10.1007/978-3-319-46723-8_49

7. Angermann, C., Haltmeier, M.: Random 2.5 D U-Net for Fully 3D Segmentation, pp. 158–166 (2019)

8. Han, X.: Automatic liver lesion segmentation using a deep convolutional neural network method. arXiv preprint arXiv:1704.07239 (2017)

9. Lv, P., Wang, J., Wang, H.: 2.5D lightweight RIU-Net for automatic liver and tumor segmentation from CT. Biomed. Signal Process. Control **75**, 103567 (2022). https://doi.org/10.1016/j.bspc.2022.103567. https://www.sciencedirect.com/science/article/pii/S1746809422000891. ISSN 1746–8094

10. Li, X., Chen, H., Qi, X., Dou, Q., Chi-Wing, F., Heng, P.-A.: H-DenseUNet: hybrid densely connected UNet for liver and tumor segmentation from CT volumes. IEEE Trans. Med. Imaging **37**(12), 2663–2674 (2018)

11. Rajamani, K., et al.: Segmentation of colon and removal of opacified fluid for virtual colonoscopy. Pattern Anal. Appl. **21**(1), 205–219 (2018)

12. Zhang, W., Kim, H.M.: Fully automatic colon segmentation in computed tomography colonography. In: 2016 IEEE International Conference on Signal and Image Processing (ICSIP), pp. 51–55. IEEE (2016)

13. Sato, Y., et al.: Tissue classification based on 3D local intensity structures for volume rendering. IEEE Trans. Visual Comput. Graphics **6**(2), 160–180 (2000)

14. Frimmel, H., Näppi, J., Yoshida, H.: Centerline-based colon segmentation for CT colonography. Med. Phys. **32**(8), 2665–2672 (2005)

15. Procedures, I.-G., Barr, K., Laframboise, J., Ungi, T., Hookey, L., Fichtinger, G.: Automated segmentation of computed tomography colonography images using a 3D U-Net. In: SPIE Medical Imaging 2020. Robotic Interventions, and Modeling, vol. 1315, pp. 635–641 (2020)

16. Shin, S.Y., Lee, S., Elton, D., Gulley, J.L., Summers, R.M.: Deep small bowel segmentation with cylindrical topological constraints. In: Martel, A.L., et al. (eds.) MICCAI 2020. LNCS, vol. 12264, pp. 207–215. Springer, Cham (2020). https://doi.org/10.1007/978-3-030-59719-1_21

17. Oda, H., et al.: Visualizing intestines for diagnostic assistance of ileus based on intestinal region segmentation from 3D CT images. In: SPIE Medical Imaging 2020: Computer-Aided Diagnosis, vol. 11314, pp. 728–735 (2020)

18. Zeng, Y., Tsui, P.-H., Weiwei, W., Zhou, Z., Shuicai, W.: Fetal ultrasound image segmentation for automatic head circumference biometry using deeply supervised attention-gated V-Net. J. Digit. Imaging **34**(1), 134–148 (2021)

19. Zhou, Y., Xie, L., Fishman, E.K., Yuille, A.L.: Deep supervision for pancreatic cyst segmentation in abdominal CT scans. In: Descoteaux, M., Maier-Hein, L., Franz, A., Jannin, P., Collins, D.L., Duchesne, S. (eds.) MICCAI 2017, Part III. LNCS, vol. 10435, pp. 222–230. Springer, Cham (2017). https://doi.org/10.1007/978-3-319-66179-7_26

20. Milletari, F., Navab, N., Ahmadi., S.-A.: V-Net: fully convolutional neural networks for volumetric medical image segmentation. In: 2016 Fourth International Conference on 3D Vision (3DV), pp. 565–571. IEEE (2016)

21. Karimi, D., Salcudean, S.E.: Reducing the Hausdorff distance in medical image segmentation with convolutional neural networks. IEEE Trans. Med. Imaging **39**(2), 499–513 (2019)

# Enhancing Cardiac MRI Segmentation via Classifier-Guided Two-Stage Network and All-Slice Information Fusion Transformer

Zihao Chen[1,2,3], Xiao Chen[1], Yikang Liu[1], Eric Z. Chen[1], Terrence Chen[1], and Shanhui Sun[1(✉)]

[1] United Imaging Intelligence, Cambridge, MA, USA
shanhui.sun@uii-ai.com
[2] University of California, Los Angeles, Los Angeles, CA, USA
[3] Cedars-Sinai Medical Center, Los Angeles, CA, USA

**Abstract.** Cardiac Magnetic Resonance imaging (CMR) is the gold standard for assessing cardiac function. Segmenting the left ventricle (LV), right ventricle (RV), and LV myocardium (MYO) in CMR images is crucial but time-consuming. Deep learning-based segmentation methods have emerged as effective tools for automating this process. However, CMR images present additional challenges due to irregular and varying heart shapes, particularly in basal and apical slices. In this study, we propose a classifier-guided two-stage network with an all-slice fusion transformer to enhance CMR segmentation accuracy, particularly in basal and apical slices. Our method was evaluated on extensive clinical datasets and demonstrated better performance in terms of Dice score compared to previous CNN-based and transformer-based models. Moreover, our method produces visually appealing segmentation shapes resembling human annotations and avoids common issues like holes or fragments in other models' segmentation.

**Keywords:** CMR segmentation · Classifier-guided · Transformer

## 1 Introduction

Cardiac Magnetic Resonance imaging (CMR) is the gold standard for evaluating cardiac function by capturing heart structure and motion. Image segmentation is a crucial yet time-consuming step in CMR analysis, involving the segmentation of anatomies like the left ventricle (LV), right ventricle (RV), and myocardium (MYO). These segmentations provide clinical metrics such as volumes and volume ratios. However, CMR imaging presents challenges due to slow MRI acquisition and the need for breathholding [19], resulting in multiple 2D image acquisitions with large slice gaps ($\sim$10 mm). This introduces spatial discontinuity across

---

Z. Chen—Contribution from Zihao Chen was carried out during his internship at United Imaging Intelligence, Cambridge, MA.

S. Wu et al. (Eds.): AMAI 2023, LNCS 14313, pp. 145–154, 2024.
https://doi.org/10.1007/978-3-031-47076-9_15

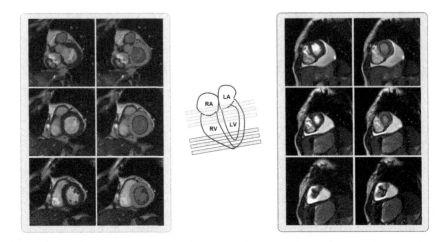

**Fig. 1.** Example of base (yellow) and apex (green) slices of CMR images with corresponding annotations. The red, green, and blue colors represent RV, MYO and LV, respectively. The middle diagram illustrates the locations of the slices. LV: left ventricle; RV: right ventricle; LA: left atrium; RA: right atrium. (Color figure online)

slices, especially at boundaries like basal and apical slices (Fig. 1). Even for experienced radiologists, distinguishing ambiguous anatomies in these slices can be challenging due to the complex appearance variations.

Deep learning segmentation methods, such as [10–12,17,20,23], have demonstrated remarkable ability in automating the medical imaging segmentation process, including CMR. Convolution neural networks (CNNs), particularly U-Net like networks [11,18,21] are a popular backbone in many applications. While 3D networks have the potential to combine information from different slices, previous work using 3D CNNs did not outperform 2D networks due to the challenge of modeling the large discontinuity across slices in CMR data [1,16]. Some approaches adopts a two-stage coarse-to-fine framework [6,15] trying to fine-tune the coarse segmentation results. Several recent works in [3,5,8,9,14,22] have combined the long-distance modeling capability of transformers with CNNs, demonstrating their superiority over pure CNN-based networks. Despite the advancements in CMR segmentation, segmenting the basal and apical slices remains challenging and impedes its broad clinical translation [4]. In Fig. 1, we present a multi-slice CMR image that illustrates the variability in anatomy appearances across slices. The basal slices often include the chamber junction, where right atrium can appear very similar as RV. Determining apical segmentation also requires referring to neighboring slices due to the small region size.

Radiologists typically assess whether the anatomy is present in an image slice before proceeding with the annotation. Moreover, in challenging cases, radiologists may refer to the anatomy structures in the neighboring slices with clear information to aid in the annotation. Building upon these observations, we propose

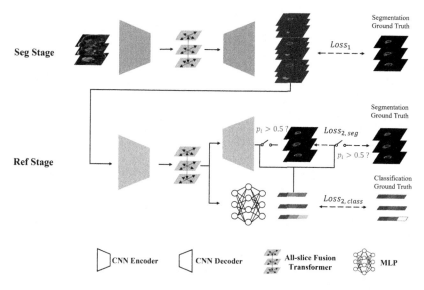

**Fig. 2.** Overview of the proposed two-stage and multi-task model with all-slice fusion transformer for cardiac imaging segmentation. The top and bottom parts are the initial segmentation stage (Seg stage) and segmentation refinement stage (Ref stage), respectively. The switches in Ref stage are turned on only when classification branch's output $p_i > 0.5$.

a framework that emulates the radiologists' annotation process, utilizing a two-stage and multi-task model structure with all-slice fusion transformer.

We conducted a comprehensive evaluation of our methods using both a public dataset (ACDC [2]) and a private clinical CMR dataset. Our proposed method quantitatively outperformed both CNN-based and transformer-based models in terms of Dice coefficients. Notably, our approach produced significantly better results in challenging regions such as basal RV, apical RV, and basal MYO. In addition, qualitative assessments showed that our method generated visually appealing segmentation shapes that closely resembled human annotations without holes or broken fragments.

## 2    Methods

### 2.1    Two-Stage Based Segmentation

The proposed framework comprises two stages (Fig. 2): initial segmentation (Seg stage) and segmentation refinement (Ref stage). During the Seg stage, a CNN + transformer model (detailed in Sect. 2.2) processes all the slices and generates initial segmentation probability maps. In the Ref stage, the probability maps from the Seg stage are inputted to a second CNN + transformer model, with the guidance of a classifier (explained in Sect. 2.3) to further improve the segmentation. Notably, while the first stage uses image information from all slices,

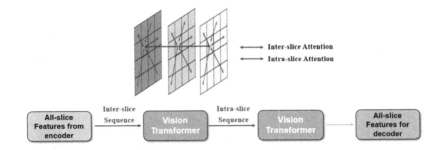

**Fig. 3.** The details of the all-slice fusion transformer bottleneck

the second stage does not require original images, simplifying the task and preventing variations in image intensities from affecting the results.

## 2.2    All-Slice Fusion Transformer

To efficiently fuse different slices' information and long-distance intra-slice information, we propose an all-slice fusion transformer that can take any number of slices as input and performs intra- and inter-slice attentions (Fig. 3). The transformers are placed at the bottlenecks of both Seg stage and Ref stage in Fig. 2. Each stage's network is a hybrid of UNet [18] with selective kernel (SK) convolutions [13,21] and vision transformer [7]. Images from all the slices are first concatenated along the batch dimension and then fed into a CNN encoder. Two consecutive transformers receive the bottleneck features from CNN encoder, and perform inter-slice attention and intra-slice attention respectively (Fig. 3). Lastly a CNN decoder with skip connections from the encoder produces segmentation results. This structure is motivated by AfterUNet [22] but we add additional SK to enhance in-plane global feature extraction and also remove the position encoding in transformer to facilitate the variable input slice length.

## 2.3    Classifier-Guided Segmentation Refinement

The Ref stage is a multitasking (MT) model, consisting of a classification branch and a segmentation refining branch. The classification branch determines the presence or absence of specific anatomies while the segmentation refining branch predicts the final refined segmentation. The classification branch is a multilayer perceptron (MLP) which takes the bottleneck features from the CNN encoder and outputs a vector of $[p_{RV}, p_{LV}, p_{MYO}]$, indicating the probability of the existence of RV, LV or MYO in the slice. The corresponding classification labels are derived from the ground truth segmentation. Note that the proposed classification branch is utilized to guide the segmentation refinement:

1) During training, only if the classification branch determines the presence of one class of anatomy ($p_i > 0.5$), the segmentation output of that class is compared to the segmentation ground truth in loss function.
2) During inference, only if the classification branch determines the presence of one class of anatomy ($p_i > 0.5$), that class will be shown in the final segmentation output.

Under this training and inference scheme, the segmentation branch will only optimize and show high-certainty anatomies, reducing the chances of producing holes or fragments in segmentation.

### 2.4 Loss Functions

In Seg stage of Fig. 2, the loss function $Loss_1$ is the cross-entropy loss between initial segmentation probability map and segmentation ground truth. In Ref stage, the loss function is a combination of both branches' loss:

$$Loss_2 = Loss_{2,seg} + \lambda \, Loss_{2,class} = \sum_{i=1}^{N} \frac{1}{2}[sign(p_i - \frac{1}{2}) + 1] \cdot CE_{seg,i} + \lambda \sum_{i=1}^{N} CE_{class,i}$$

where $CE_{seg}$ is cross entropy loss between segmentation output and segmentation ground truth, $p_i$ is classification probability for a specific class, and $CE_{class}$ is cross entropy loss between classification probability and classification ground truth. $N = 3$ is the number of total segmentation classes (RV, LV and MYO) and $\lambda = 0.1$ was set to balance the loss from the two branches so that the scaling of two branches' losses were similar.

## 3 Experiments

### 3.1 Datasets and Settings

The proposed method was evaluated using the ACDC dataset [2] and a private CMR dataset collected from clinical routine with patient's consent. Both datasets contain multi-slice 2D cine CMR images where images were acquired at multiple slice locations and multiple time points. All slices at one time point is treated as a set for multi-slice experiments. For the ACDC dataset, each patient data has 6~18 slices and 2 time points. For the in-house dataset, each patient data has 4~18 slices and 6~29 time points. The training and testing data were split on the patient level. In total there are 8350/1859 images and 1123/198 multi-slice sets for training/testing. For the private data, each image was annotated LV, RV and MYO by two experienced annotators and was screened by an experienced doctor. The classification labels was calculated from the segmentation labels where an anatomy is present if the corresponding segmentation is present. For evaluation purpose, the stack of multiple slices were divided into base, mid and apex groups according to clinical standard, where in most cases the slices covering the whole heart were evenly divided into the three groups.

All models were trained with an Adam optimizer and a learning rate of 0.0001 for 200 epochs. We trained all the models in PyTorch framework with a NVIDIA Tesla v100 GPU. As a part of the data preprocessing step, all images are resampled to a uniform in-plane spacing of 1.3 mm. Data augmentation techniques such as random rotation, shifting, flipping and cropping are employed. Dice score was used to evaluate segmentation results.

## 3.2   Results

**Table 1.** Comparison of methods in term of the Dice of RV, MYO and LV in different slice level. The bold texts mark the best performance.

| Models | Slice level | RV Dice | MYO Dice | LV Dice | Average Dice |
|---|---|---|---|---|---|
| SS SK-UNet | Base | 0.909 | 0.847 | 0.939 | 0.898 |
| | Mid | 0.927 | 0.896 | 0.950 | 0.924 |
| | Apex | 0.800 | 0.807 | 0.917 | 0.842 |
| AS After-UNet | Base | 0.899 | 0.838 | 0.947 | 0.895 |
| | Mid | **0.932** | **0.904** | **0.953** | **0.930** |
| | Apex | 0.830 | 0.810 | 0.914 | **0.852** |
| Two-stage: | Base | 0.907 | 0.843 | 0.940 | 0.897 |
| Det + Seg | Mid | 0.931 | 0.903 | **0.953** | 0.929 |
| | Apex | 0.789 | **0.820** | **0.922** | 0.844 |
| Proposed | Base | **0.920** | **0.848** | **0.955** | **0.908** |
| | Mid | **0.932** | 0.902 | **0.953** | 0.929 |
| | Apex | **0.836** | 0.810 | 0.911 | **0.852** |

The performance of the proposed method was compared with several state-of-the-art methods (Table. 1). For the single-slice (SS) network, SK-UNet [21] was used for comparison. For the all-slice (AS) network, After-UNet [22] and a two-stage detection (Det) + segmentation (Seg) model [15] were used for comparison. For all the models, the number of CNN blocks, as well as the corresponding convolution hyper-parameters are the same to make a fair comparison.

As is shown in Table 1, the proposed method outperforms all other methods on the average Dice of basal and apical slices. The proposed method's average Dice of mid slices (0.929) is almost the same to the best one (0.930). Regarding the difficult RV segmentation, the proposed method achieves the best RV Dice in all slice levels. The proposed method also achieves the best Dice scores for basal MYO, basal LV and mid LV. Figure 4 shows example segmentation results for two basal slices from adjacent frames and one apical slice. As we can see in the ground truth column, although the two basal images look very similar, one has full RV annotations while the other has no RV annotation. The proposed

| SS SK-UNet | AS After-UNet | Det + Seg | Proposed: Seg (AS) + Ref (AS w/ MT) | Ground Truth |

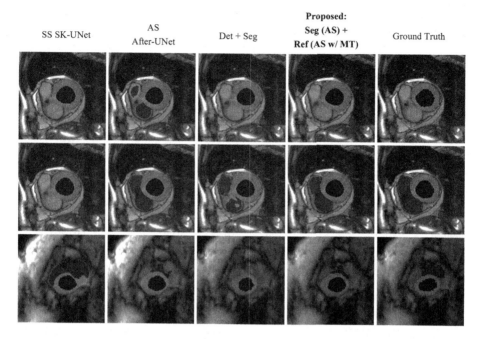

**Fig. 4.** Example segmentation results from state-of-the art methods, the proposed and the ground truth, at base (first and second rows) and apex (third row) slices.

method is the only method that can entirely match ground truth annotations and produce no holes or fragments. For the apical slice, the proposed method produces similar segmentation shape to the ground truth.

### 3.3  Ablation Study

Multiple ablation studies were performed to examine the effectiveness of our specific designs (Table 2). We use SK-UNet as the backbone for SS models and After-UNet as the backbone for AS models, so Seg (SS) is SS SK-UNet, and Seg (AS) is AS After-UNet in Table 1. By incorporating multi-slice information, the AS models show better segmentation performances in mid and apical slices. By adding Ref stage, big improvements can be seen on challenging cases, such as RV, MYO and LV on the base slices and RV on apex slices.

The additional classification branch (Seg(AS)+Ref(AS w/MT)) further improves the very challenging cases such as the RV on the base level, agreeing with the qualitative example (Fig. 4). In addition, by moving the classification branch to the Seg stage which takes the image level features as input (Seg (AS+MT)), we observed degraded quality comparing to Seg (AS). It suggests that the complex image features may deteriorate the classification accuracy and then damage the segmentation results.

**Table 2.** The ablation study results. Seg: Initial segmentation stage; Ref: Segmentation refinement stage; MT: Multitasking model.

| Models | | Slice level | RV Dice | MYO Dice | LV Dice | Average Dice |
|---|---|---|---|---|---|---|
| Single slice (SS) models | Seg (SS) | Base | 0.909 | 0.847 | 0.939 | 0.898 |
| | | Mid | 0.927 | 0.896 | 0.950 | 0.924 |
| | | Apex | 0.800 | 0.807 | 0.917 | 0.842 |
| | Seg (SS) + Ref (SS w/o MT) | Base | 0.915 | 0.849 | 0.941 | 0.902 |
| | | Mid | 0.929 | 0.898 | 0.949 | 0.925 |
| | | Apex | 0.799 | 0.811 | 0.915 | 0.842 |
| | Seg (SS) + Ref (SS w/ MT) | Base | 0.914 | 0.856 | 0.952 | 0.907 |
| | | Mid | 0.928 | 0.897 | 0.950 | 0.925 |
| | | Apex | 0.795 | 0.810 | 0.916 | 0.840 |
| All slice (AS) models | Seg (AS) | Base | 0.899 | 0.838 | 0.947 | 0.895 |
| | | Mid | 0.932 | 0.904 | 0.953 | 0.930 |
| | | Apex | 0.830 | 0.810 | 0.914 | 0.852 |
| | Seg (AS + MT) | Base | 0.893 | 0.839 | 0.945 | 0.892 |
| | | Mid | 0.931 | 0.905 | 0.953 | 0.930 |
| | | Apex | 0.809 | 0.817 | 0.916 | 0.847 |
| | Seg (AS) + Ref (AS w/o MT) | Base | 0.914 | 0.848 | 0.952 | 0.905 |
| | | Mid | 0.932 | 0.904 | 0.953 | 0.930 |
| | | Apex | 0.834 | 0.813 | 0.911 | 0.853 |
| | Seg (AS) + Ref (AS w/ MT) | Base | 0.920 | 0.848 | 0.955 | 0.908 |
| | | Mid | 0.932 | 0.902 | 0.953 | 0.929 |
| | | Apex | 0.836 | 0.810 | 0.911 | 0.852 |

# 4  Discussion and Conclusion

We proposed a two-stage, multi-task, and all-slice fusion transformer to address challenges in deep learning CMR segmentation of basal and apical slices. The two-stage and multi-task structures significantly enhance basal segmentation, while the all-slice fusion structure greatly improves apical and mid segmentation. Our method effectively leverages multi-slice information and the long-distance modeling capabilities of vision transformers, yielding promising results. The Ref stage, coupled with a classification branch, demonstrates notable improvements when incorporating multi-slice information, aligning with expert knowledge of referring to neighboring slices for delineating ambiguous anatomies. Additionally, our classifier-guided segmentation approach proves more effective when applied to coarse segmentation rather than the image itself. By removing intensity variations, artifacts, and adjacent anatomies in the image domain, the classifier-guided segmentation may focus more on the heart's structure and shape.

The classification branch serves as a crucial prior during both training and inference, providing global information to alleviate the limitations of pixel-level losses like cross-entropy and mean square error. The global supervision helps guide the network in handling ambiguous cases, such as the RV on base slices with even inconsistent ground truth labels. In this study, we focused on segmenting multi-slice cine images without leveraging temporal correlations, which could offer further advantages. However, the proposed features can be easily extended to explore temporal and spatiotemporal correlations. Our method is applicable to other multi-slice CMR applications, including Late Gadolinium Enhancement (LGE) images. Additionally, the choice of backbone is not restricted to After-UNet, and other backbones capable of effectively integrating 3D spatial information are worth investigating.

**Prospect of Application:** The proposed study introduces a novel approach that aims to automate the segmentation of CMR images, thereby alleviating the workload burden on radiologists. Notably, the proposed work achieves accurate and visually pleasing segmentation shapes in challenging basal and apical slices, which may represent a significant stride towards the practical implementation of deep learning CMR segmentation in clinical settings.

# References

1. Baumgartner, C.F., Koch, L.M., Pollefeys, M., Konukoglu, E.: An exploration of 2D and 3D deep learning techniques for Cardiac MR image segmentation. In: Pop, M., et al. (eds.) STACOM 2017. LNCS, vol. 10663, pp. 111–119. Springer, Cham (2018). https://doi.org/10.1007/978-3-319-75541-0_12
2. Bernard, O., et al.: Deep learning techniques for automatic MRI cardiac multi-structures segmentation and diagnosis: is the problem solved? IEEE Trans. Med. Imaging **37**(11), 2514–2525 (2018)
3. Cao, H. et al.: Swin-Unet: Unet-like pure transformer for medical image segmentation. In: Karlinsky, L., Michaeli, T., Nishino, K. (eds.) Computer Vision – ECCV 2022 Workshops. ECCV 2022. Lecture Notes in Computer Science, vol. 13803. Springer, Cham (2023). https://doi.org/10.1007/978-3-031-25066-8_9
4. Chen, C., et al.: Deep learning for cardiac image segmentation: a review. Front. Cardiovasc. Med. **7**, 25 (2020)
5. Chen, J., et al.: TransUNet: Transformers make strong encoders for medical image segmentation. arXiv preprint arXiv:2102.04306 (2021)
6. Ding, Y., et al.: ToStaGAN: an end-to-end two-stage generative adversarial network for brain tumor segmentation. Neurocomputing **462**, 141–153 (2021)
7. Dosovitskiy, A., et al.: An image is worth $16 \times 16$ words: Transformers for image recognition at scale. arXiv preprint arXiv:2010.11929 (2020)
8. Gao, Y., Zhou, M., Metaxas, D.N.: UTNet: a hybrid transformer architecture for medical image segmentation. In: de Bruijne, M., et al. (eds.) MICCAI 2021. LNCS, vol. 12903, pp. 61–71. Springer, Cham (2021). https://doi.org/10.1007/978-3-030-87199-4_6
9. Hatamizadeh, A., Nath, V., Tang, Y., Yang, D., Roth, H.R., Xu, D.: Swin UNETR: swin transformers for semantic segmentation of brain tumors in MRI images. In: Crimi, A., Bakas, S. (eds.) Brainlesion: Glioma, Multiple Sclerosis, Stroke and Traumatic Brain Injuries. BrainLes 2021. Lecture Notes in Computer Science, vol. 12962. Springer, Cham (2022). https://doi.org/10.1007/978-3-031-08999-2_22

10. Isensee, F., Jaeger, P.F., Full, P.M., Wolf, I., Engelhardt, S., Maier-Hein, K.H.: Automatic cardiac disease assessment on cine-MRI via time-series segmentation and domain specific features. In: Pop, M., et al. (eds.) STACOM 2017. LNCS, vol. 10663, pp. 120–129. Springer, Cham (2018). https://doi.org/10.1007/978-3-319-75541-0_13

11. Isensee, F., Jaeger, P.F., Kohl, S.A., Petersen, J., Maier-Hein, K.H.: nnU-Net: a self-configuring method for deep learning-based biomedical image segmentation. Nat. Methods **18**(2), 203–211 (2021)

12. Li, C., Chen, M., Zhang, J., Liu, H.: Cardiac MRI segmentation with focal loss constrained deep residual networks. Phys. Med. Biol. **66**(13), 135012 (2021)

13. Li, X., Wang, W., Hu, X., Yang, J.: Selective kernel networks. In: Proceedings of the IEEE/CVF Conference on Computer Vision and Pattern Recognition, pp. 510–519 (2019)

14. Liu, D. et al.: TransFusion: multi-view divergent fusion for medical image segmentation with transformers. In: Wang, L., Dou, Q., Fletcher, P.T., Speidel, S., Li, S. (eds.) Medical Image Computing and Computer Assisted Intervention – MICCAI 2022. MICCAI 2022. Lecture Notes in Computer Science, vol. 13435. Springer, Cham (2022). https://doi.org/10.1007/978-3-031-16443-9_47

15. Liu, Y., Zhang, M., Zhan, Q., Gu, D., Liu, G.: Two-stage method for segmentation of the myocardial scars and edema on multi-sequence cardiac magnetic resonance. In: Zhuang, X., Li, L. (eds.) MyoPS 2020. LNCS, vol. 12554, pp. 26–36. Springer, Cham (2020). https://doi.org/10.1007/978-3-030-65651-5_3

16. Patravali, J., Jain, S., Chilamkurthy, S.: 2D-3D fully convolutional neural networks for cardiac MR segmentation. In: Pop, M., et al. (eds.) STACOM 2017. LNCS, vol. 10663, pp. 130–139. Springer, Cham (2018). https://doi.org/10.1007/978-3-319-75541-0_14

17. Qin, C., et al.: Joint learning of motion estimation and segmentation for cardiac MR image sequences. In: Frangi, A.F., Schnabel, J.A., Davatzikos, C., Alberola-López, C., Fichtinger, G. (eds.) MICCAI 2018. LNCS, vol. 11071, pp. 472–480. Springer, Cham (2018). https://doi.org/10.1007/978-3-030-00934-2_53

18. Ronneberger, O., Fischer, P., Brox, T.: U-Net: convolutional networks for biomedical image segmentation. In: Navab, N., Hornegger, J., Wells, W.M., Frangi, A.F. (eds.) MICCAI 2015. LNCS, vol. 9351, pp. 234–241. Springer, Cham (2015). https://doi.org/10.1007/978-3-319-24574-4_28

19. Slomka, P.J., et al.: Patient motion correction for multiplanar, multi-breath-hold cardiac cine MR imaging. J. Magn. Reson. Imaging. **25**(5), 965–973 (2007). An Official Journal of the International Society for Magnetic Resonance in Medicine

20. Sun, X., Garg, P., Plein, S., van der Geest, R.J.: SAUN: stack attention u-net for left ventricle segmentation from cardiac cine magnetic resonance imaging. Med. Phys. **48**(4), 1750–1763 (2021)

21. Wang, X., et al.: SK-Unet: an improved u-net model with selective kernel for the segmentation of LGE cardiac MR images. IEEE Sens. J. **21**(10), 11643–11653 (2021)

22. Yan, X., Tang, H., Sun, S., Ma, H., Kong, D., Xie, X.: AFTer-UNet: axial fusion transformer UNet for medical image segmentation. In: Proceedings of the IEEE/CVF Winter Conference on Applications of Computer Vision, pp. 3971–3981 (2022)

23. Zotti, C., Luo, Z., Lalande, A., Jodoin, P.M.: Convolutional neural network with shape prior applied to cardiac MRI segmentation. IEEE J. Biomed. Health Inform. **23**(3), 1119–1128 (2018)

# Accessible Otitis Media Screening with a Deep Learning-Powered Mobile Otoscope

Omkar Kovvali and Lakshmi Sritan Motati[✉]

Thomas Jefferson High School for Science and Technology,
Alexandria, VA 22312, USA
{2024okovvali,2024lmotati}@tjhsst.edu

**Abstract.** Otitis media (OM) is the leading cause of hearing loss in children globally, affecting nearly a billion people per year. Impoverished areas typically lack trained ear specialists, which prevents millions from being diagnosed and treated while causing severe complications. Currently, there is no viable diagnostic system for inexpensively and accurately detecting such ear conditions. This research presents OtoScan, a novel pipeline for the detection of middle ear infections using diagnosis networks and a cost-effective mobile otoscope. The physical attachment was developed using custom-designed 3D models, a compact magnification lens, fiber optics, and various electronics for illumination. To develop detection algorithms, public otoscopic images were collected and augmented with realistic perturbations. A dynamic ensemble of Inception-based architectures trained using transfer learning and label smoothing was developed to mitigate class imbalance and overconfidence while improving diagnostic accuracy for acute and chronic suppurative OM. Regions of interest are highlighted as gradient saliency maps in a smartphone application using Grad-CAM++. Evaluation shows that the proposed algorithm surpasses architectures such as CBAM in accuracy and F1 score. Further testing using an industry-standard medical simulator validated the potential viability of this system. With a production cost of $9.50 USD, OtoScan represents a step towards the democratization of ear care and improvement of patient outcomes.

**Keywords:** Telemedicine · Deep learning · Otoscopic imaging

## 1  Introduction

Otitis media (OM) and its acute and chronic variants are one of the most common infections in the world, with over 700 million cases each year [12]. With 51% of these occurring in children under the age of five, OM is truly a global burden. Clinical features of acute OM (AOM) include a bulging tympanic membrane (TM), partial or complete opacification of the TM, and prominently dilated

---

Both authors contributed equally.

S. Wu et al. (Eds.): AMAI 2023, LNCS 14313, pp. 155–164, 2024.
https://doi.org/10.1007/978-3-031-47076-9_16

vessels [11]. OM is frequently misdiagnosed or undiagnosed, leading to serious, or even life-threatening complications [14]. Consequences of undiagnosed or untreated cases of otitis media include hearing loss, delayed speech and/or language development, meningitis, brain abscess, and even death. Additionally, the economic burden of otitis media is about 4 billion dollars annually in the United States alone [19].

Access to doctors and equipment to diagnose OM is severely limited in developing countries, with only 1% of primary care clinics having basic diagnostic capacity in low/middle income areas [8]. In developing countries around the world such as Malawi, there is only one ear, nose, and throat (ENT) specialist for up to twelve million people [18]. Additionally, average physician diagnostic accuracy is also low, ranging from 50–73% [15]. Thus, there exists a massive need to develop rapid and effective diagnostic systems that can enable accurate diagnosis of otitis media in underdeveloped areas of the world.

Traditional OM diagnosis methods include optical coherence tomography (OCT), endoscopy, and medical professional-guided otoscopy. While OCT is useful to observe sections of TM in vivo, the high cost prevents it from being an effective diagnostic tool in a low-resource setting [5]. In recent years, alternative OM diagnosis methods have emerged. Deep learning (DL) algorithms are able to learn patterns in data via epochs, using neural networks. DL algorithms have been applied to OM diagnosis in the past by numerous research groups [1–3,9,20,23]. A common approach has been to capture several hundred tympanic membrane images with otoscopes or endoscopes and train models to characterize disease classifications.

The aim of this study was to develop and validate a novel and inexpensive otoscopic screening system to detect OM via TM images. The constructed algorithm showed promise as a state-of-the-art for otitis media detection in algorithmic evaluation on unseen images from the original dataset used for training.

## 2    Methodology

### 2.1    Mobile Otoscope

The first prototype was inspired by online CAD models. It consisted of a large conical bulb that narrowed into a specula. The lens was fit near flush with the edge of the otoscope, as shown in Fig. 1. The smartphone's flashlight was used as a light source. However, this approach presented numerous limitations. The flashlight reflected intensely off the lens, resulting in extremely poor image quality. To remedy this, LED bulbs connected to resistors and a 9V battery were placed further down the otoscope. This effort proved to be futile, as the bright LED once again obscured the user's field of view. Various other prototype designs were tested; however, all proposed designs had flaws and did not allow for clear TM visualization. The decision was made to shift away from the utilization of the smartphone flashlight and instead develop a self-contained otoscope. The final late-stage prototype, as depicted in Fig. 1, featured a 3D-printed shell that was designed using AutoDesk Fusion 360 and sliced with Cura software. Employing

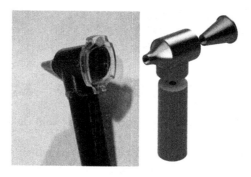

**Fig. 1.** Image of the assembled custom otoscope (left) and 3D render (right).

fusion deposition molding (FDM) with polylactic acid filament (PLA), the shell was successfully 3D printed using an Ender-3 printer. The mobile otoscope was assembled using a custom 3D-printed shell, a 3x magnification lens, a fiber optic piece, a battery holder, copper wire, a halogen otoscopic light, and 3 AAA batteries. Notably, a significant advancement in the new advanced prototype was the integration of fiber optic cables, as illustrated in Fig. 2. These cables operate by guiding the light source through repeated internal reflections within a glass core and cladding, allowing for photon movement along the cable path due to the varying refractive indexes.

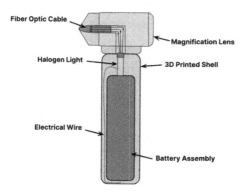

**Fig. 2.** Internal diagram of the otoscope. A sterile specula tip was also added for safety.

## 2.2  Deep Learning

**Data and Preprocessing.** The models used in OtoScan were trained using a publicly available set of 956 otoscopic images collected at the zel Van Akdamar Hospital in Turkey [1]. This dataset contained images of tympanic membranes from normal subjects (n = 535) and patients with acute otitis media (AOM) (n = 119), chronic suppurative otitis media (CSOM) (n = 63), earwax (n = 140),

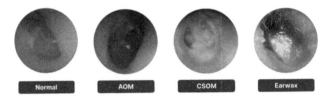

Fig. 3. Examples of preprocessed images from the dataset.

and other middle ear conditions (ex. Otitis externa) which were disregarded due to limited data (n < 50). As such, the class distribution of the training data was extremely imbalanced. To prepare the developed algorithms to be robust to imperfect imaging conditions and perform well on unseen real-world images, realistic image perturbations were used to augment the image diversity of the training data. Specifically, random horizontal and vertical flips, brightness and contrast shifts, rotations (up to 30 °C), and RGB color normalization were applied to training images, most of which were also used in [1]. Example perturbed images are shown in Fig. 3. This was later used to upsample minority class images in the training set to double their original size, which was not utilized in [1].

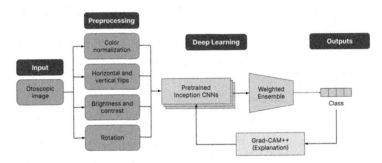

Fig. 4. Developed end-to-end deep learning pipeline for OtoScan.

**Architecture.** This research proposes a novel dynamically-weighted ensemble of multi-class convolutional neural network (CNN) architectures for the detection of otitis media (Fig. 4). Preliminary training of several well-known models including ResNet-50, VGG-19, and EfficientNet were evaluated to determine a final set of models. From such testing, it was found that models stemming from the Inception module or one of its modified variations achieved the highest testing performances. Specifically, the InceptionV3, Inception-ResNet-v2, and Xception architectures were used as sub-networks for the proposed ensemble [6,16,17]. We hypothesize that such models outperformed other similar CNNs due to the ability of the Inception module, or blocks of parallel convolutions of varying filter sizes which are concatenated to create a final feature map, to explore the images at various spatial scales. This is especially important to otitis media diagnosis, as physiological markers of infection can be localized (ex. scarring) or large-scale (ex. effusions).

Each model was trained individually from the other sub-networks in the ensemble. ImageNet-pretrained weights were used to initialize the models before training. After training the voter models, an MLP was trained to generate the optimal ensemble weights using the individual predictions. Ensemble predictions could then be made by using the learned weights to integrate the predictions from each voter model.

**Training.** Models were trained using the standard categorical cross-entropy loss function. Additionally, label smoothing ($\alpha = 0.1$) was utilized to suppress the true labels during training and, in turn, discourage overconfidence, which was done to prevent a model from learning to classify all images as healthy due to sheer probability [13]. With this method of regularization, one-hot encoded target vectors are modified as follows, where is the original target vector, is the smoothing parameter, and is the number of classes in the classification task:

$$y_{LS} = y(1 - \alpha) + \alpha/K \tag{1}$$

Each sub-network was trained for 50 epochs with the Adam optimizer. Learning rates were also optimized using a cosine-annealed warm restart learning schedule [10].

**Saliency Maps.** To extract human-compatible insights from the learned intuition behind predictions from the proposed deep learning solution, the Grad-CAM++ algorithm was employed [4]. The Grad-CAM++ algorithm traces a saliency map of model attention from weighted positive partial gradients, which can be easily interpreted by patients and medical professionals. Grad-CAM++ was used as opposed to Grad-CAM because it has been shown to invoke superior human trust in the explanations.

### 2.3 Smartphone Application

A cross-platform Flask application was developed for the automated analysis of otoscopic images using the developed neural networks (Fig. 5). Images taken with the novel mobile otoscope are uploaded to a web server and subsequently passed to the diagnostic suite to retrieve the model prediction, confidence, and the saliency heatmap. The frontend of the application was developed using HTML, CSS, and JavaScript with Tailwind CSS for interface design.

## 3   Results

### 3.1   Algorithmic Testing

The developed ensemble predictive model was first evaluated on an unseen portion of the original data (15% of the entire available dataset). The VGG-19 and ResNet-50 architectures are trained using ImageNet-pretrained weights to serve

**Fig. 5.** Flowchart of the developed smartphone application.

as general image classification network baselines. Furthermore, the architecture proposed by [1] for the diagnosis of otitis media in their collected data was re-implemented as a task-specific baseline. This model relied on the Convolutional Block Attention Module (CBAM), which is known for being lightweight while providing information on non-local image features through an attention mechanism [21]. A comparison of all resultant metrics is shown in Fig. 6. The developed ensemble surpasses all baseline models with an overall accuracy of 91.5%, an AUROC of 0.968, and an F1 score of 0.868. In these metrics, the ensemble outperforms the highest-performing baseline by 10.9%, 0.072, and 0.206, respectively. Our model also outperforms the baselines in class-wise AUROC scores (Fig. 7). The discrepancy between the ensemble and baseline models is most visible in the diagnosis of CSOM images, where it outperforms the highest-performing baseline, ResNet-50, by 50%. These results serve to validate the unique combination of techniques used to mitigate class imbalance and overconfidence.

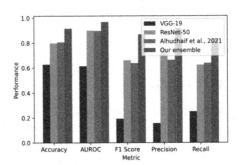

**Fig. 6.** Graph of comparison of key classification metrics of all models.

### 3.2 Validation Testing

In order to test the system in the best capacity possible, OtoScan was tested using the OtoSim Mobile otoscopic simulator (Fig. 8). The simulator modeled the anatomy of the pinna, external auditory canal, and tympanic membrane. In our validation study, 16 images of acute OM and earwax patients' eardrums were captured and automatically diagnosed for evaluation. In simulation testing, the

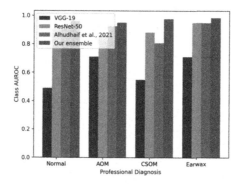

**Fig. 7.** Graphs of comparison of class-wise AUROC scores of all models.

**Fig. 8.** Experimental setup for the OtoSim Mobile simulator [22].

images captured were of good quality, indicating that the mobile otoscope worked as intended. The images were uploaded to the smartphone application and fed to the ensemble ML model, which returned correct predictions for most images and achieved an AUROC score of 0.930, whereas the ResNet-50, VGG-19, and CBAM models achieve AUROC scores of 0.905, 0.520, and 0.835. This validates the potential of the proposed system (Fig. 9). Furthermore, the saliency heatmaps constructed for both images highlight areas with red scarring and/or visible effusion commonly found with AOM, which ensures that the models learned anatomically-relevant features.

Numerous tests were also conducted to verify the otoscope's durability and potential longevity. In preliminary testing, the hardware was able to withstand consecutive 4-feet drops onto concrete with no significant performance delta. The otoscope can be cleaned by preparing a 70% isopropyl alcohol solution and wiping the surface and head. Additionally, the specula is disposable, similar to traditional otoscopes, ensuring a hygiene instrument for examinations.

Across both the digital and OtoSim evaluation datasets, we observed significant changes in AUROC score between models using pairwise statistical analysis (i.e. the two obtained AUROC scores formed pairs for each model). A repeated measures ANOVA test found overall significant differences between the models ($p = 0.005$). More specifically, matched-pair t-tests found significant differences in performance between our ensemble and all baselines ($p < 0.05$) except for ResNet-50 ($p = 0.137$).

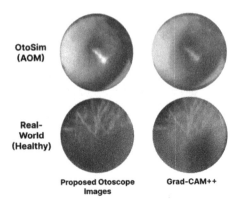

**Fig. 9.** Pictures taken with the developed mobile otoscope with various imaging methods and middle ear conditions and the respective Grad-CAM++ saliency maps.

## 4  Discussion and Conclusions

Early diagnosis of OM prevents severe complications such as hearing loss, meningitis, and death. Current ear imaging technologies such as optical coherence tomography (∼8,000 USD) and endoscopy (∼210 USD) are far too expensive for low-cost usage [7]. With a prototype production cost of only 9.50 USD, OtoScan has the potential to democratize access to proper OM diagnosis with otoscopy. When compared to conventional products, self-fabricated otoscopes have several salient limitations, however, such as sensitivity.

From algorithmic evaluation on the original dataset, it is evident that the developed ensemble achieves superior performance when compared to both general image classification (e.g. ResNet-50) and otitis media-specific baselines (e.g. CBAM-based model). The ensemble achieves the highest overall performance across overall and class-wise metrics. The OtoSim Mobile simular results hint at favorable outcomes if the system where to be validated in a clinical trial setting. The Grad-CAM++ saliency heatmaps showed that the models accurately highlight anatomically relevant features for diagnosis.

The primary limitation of the existing methodology is the lack of data, as the relatively small number of images available publicly prevents the models from becoming more generalized for real-world images. A major secondary limitation includes a small number of classes. The current study only looks into three major middle ear diseases, while previous groups have looked into many more. Future research should involve more diverse datasets, to ensure applicability to all types of patients. It would also be beneficial to gather more data for classes to ensure that all middle ear infections are able to be diagnosed. Further, the research presented does not show conclusive real-world applicability as it has only been tested in a simulated environment thus far.

This research presents a functioning, low-cost otoscope working in conjunction with an artificial intelligence-powered mobile application to detect, classify, and visualize middle ear infections, specifically acute and chronic suppurative otitis media. Furthermore, OtoScan serves as a proof-of-concept prototype device for the democratization of middle ear infection screening by streamlining the entire diagnostic process. Such streamlining also permits the development of future telemedicine software for physicians working remotely with inaccessible areas. Subsequently, OM care becomes far more accessible as industry-wide costs are reduced by millions.

## 4.1 Prospect of Application

OtoScan has the potential to revolutionize otitis media screening by enabling inexpensive and accurate diagnosis of middle ear infections. The mobile otoscope ($9.50), coupled with deep learning algorithms, can be deployed in primary care clinics and underserved communities. OtoScan has the reach to improve patient outcomes, assist nurses, decrease costs, and address the global burden of OM.

# References

1. Alhudhaif, A., Cömert, Z., Polat, K.: Otitis media detection using tympanic membrane images with a novel multi-class machine learning algorithm. PeerJ Comput. Sci. **7**, e405 (2021). https://doi.org/10.7717/peerj-cs.405
2. Camalan, S., et al.: OtoMatch: content-based eardrum image retrieval using deep learning. PLOS ONE **15**(5), e0232776 (2020). https://doi.org/10.1371/journal.pone.0232776
3. Cavalcanti, T.C., Lew, H.M., Lee, K., Lee, S.Y., Park, M.K., Hwang, J.Y.: Intelligent smartphone-based multimode imaging otoscope for the mobile diagnosis of otitis media. Biomed. Opt. Express **12**(12), 7765 (2021). https://doi.org/10.1364/boe.441590
4. Chattopadhyay, A., Sarkar, A., Howlader, P., Balasubramanian, V.N.: Grad-CAM++: generalized gradient-based visual explanations for deep convolutional networks. In: 2018 IEEE Winter Conference on Applications of Computer Vision (WACV), pp. 839–847. IEEE (2018)
5. Cho, N.H., Lee, S.H., Jung, W., Jang, J.H., Kim, J.: Optical coherence tomography for the diagnosis and evaluation of human otitis media. J. Korean Med. Sci. **30**(3), 328 (2015). https://doi.org/10.3346/jkms.2015.30.3.328
6. Chollet, F.: Xception: deep learning with depthwise separable convolutions. In: Proceedings of the IEEE Conference on Computer Vision and Pattern Recognition, pp. 1251–1258 (2017)
7. Ciocîrlan, M.: Low-cost disposable endoscope: pros and cons. Endosc. Int. Open **07**(09), E1184–E1186 (2019). https://doi.org/10.1055/a-0959-6003
8. For Economic Co-operation, O., Development: Physicians (per 1,000 people) (2019). https://data.worldbank.org/indicator/SH.MED.PHYS.ZS
9. Livingstone, D., Talai, A.S., Chau, J., Forkert, N.D.: Building an otoscopic screening prototype tool using deep learning. J. Otolaryngol. Head Neck Surg. **48**(1), 66 (2019). https://doi.org/10.1186/s40463-019-0389-9
10. Loshchilov, I., Hutter, F.: SGDR: Stochastic gradient descent with warm restarts. arXiv preprint arXiv:1608.03983 (2016)

11. Mankowski, N.L., Raggio, B.S.: Otoscope exam - statpearls - NCBI bookshelf (2022). https://www.ncbi.nlm.nih.gov/books/NBK553163/
12. Monasta, L., et al.: Burden of disease caused by otitis media: systematic review and global estimates. PLoS ONE **7**(4), e36226 (2012). https://doi.org/10.1371/journal.pone.0036226
13. Müller, R., Kornblith, S., Hinton, G.E.: When does label smoothing help? In: Advances in Neural Information Processing Systems, vol. 32 (2019)
14. Myburgh, H.C., van Zijl, W.H., Swanepoel, D., Hellström, S., Laurent, C.: Otitis media diagnosis for developing countries using tympanic membrane image-analysis. EBioMedicine **5**, 156–160 (2016). https://doi.org/10.1016/j.ebiom.2016.02.017
15. Pichichero, M.E., Poole, M.D.: Assessing diagnostic accuracy and tympanocentesis skills in the management of otitis media. Arch. Pediatr. Adolesc. Med. **155**(10), 1137 (2001). https://doi.org/10.1001/archpedi.155.10.1137
16. Szegedy, C., Ioffe, S., Vanhoucke, V., Alemi, A.: Inception-v4, inception-ResNet and the impact of residual connections on learning. In: Proceedings of the AAAI Conference on Artificial Intelligence, vol. 31 (2017)
17. Szegedy, C., Vanhoucke, V., Ioffe, S., Shlens, J., Wojna, Z.: Rethinking the inception architecture for computer vision. In: Proceedings of the IEEE Conference on Computer Vision and Pattern Recognition, pp. 2818–2826 (2016)
18. Ta, N.: ENT in the context of global health. Ann. R. Coll. Surg. Engl. **101**(2), 93–96 (2019). https://doi.org/10.1308/rcsann.2018.0138
19. Tong, S., Amand, C., Kieffer, A., Kyaw, M.H.: Trends in healthcare utilization and costs associated with acute otitis media in the united states during 2008–2014. BMC Health Serv. Res. **18**(1), 318 (2018). https://doi.org/10.1186/s12913-018-3139-1
20. Won, J., et al.: Handheld briefcase optical coherence tomography with real-time machine learning classifier for middle ear infections. Biosensors **11**(5), 143 (2021). https://doi.org/10.3390/bios11050143
21. Woo, S., Park, J., Lee, J.Y., Kweon, I.S.: CBAM: convolutional block attention module. In: Proceedings of the European Conference on Computer Vision (ECCV), pp. 3–19 (2018)
22. Xu, J., Campisi, P., Forte, V., Carrillo, B., Vescan, A., Brydges, R.: Effectiveness of discovery learning using a mobile otoscopy simulator on knowledge acquisition and retention in medical students: a randomized controlled trial. J. Otolaryngol. Head Neck Surg. **47**(1), 70 (2018). https://doi.org/10.1186/s40463-018-0317-4
23. Zeng, X., et al.: Efficient and accurate identification of ear diseases using an ensemble deep learning model. Sci. Rep. **11**(1), 10839 (2021). https://doi.org/10.1038/s41598-021-90345-w

# Feature Selection for Malapposition Detection in Intravascular Ultrasound - A Comparative Study

Satyananda Kashyap[1]($\boxtimes$), Neerav Karani[2], Alexander Shang[3],
Niharika D'Souza[1], Neel Dey[2], Lay Jain[2], Ray Wang[2], Hatice Akakin[3],
Qian Li[3], Wenguang Li[3], Corydon Carlson[3], Polina Golland[2],
and Tanveer Syeda-Mahmood[1]

[1] IBM Research, San Jose, CA 95120, USA
satyananda.kashyap@ibm.com
[2] Massachusetts Institute of Technology, Cambridge, MA 02139, USA
[3] Boston Scientific, Maple Grove, MN 55311, USA

**Abstract.** Coronary atherosclerosis is a leading cause of morbidity and mortality worldwide. It is often treated by placing stents in the coronary arteries. Inappropriately placed stents or malappositions can result in post-interventional complications. Intravascular Ultrasound (IVUS) imaging offers a potential solution by providing real-time endovascular guidance for stent placement. The signature of malapposition is very subtle and requires exploring second-order relationships between blood flow patterns, vessel walls, and stents. In this paper, we perform a comparative study of various deep learning methods and their feature extraction capabilities for building a malapposition detector. Our results in the study address the importance of incorporating domain knowledge in performance improvement while still indicating the limitations of current systems for achieving clinically ready performance.

## 1 Introduction

Atherosclerosis is a chronic disease that is a leading cause of mortality and morbidity globally [4]. It is characterized by plaque accumulation in the arterial walls, causing artery narrowing and reduced blood flow to vital organs leading to heart disease, peripheral artery disease, and stroke. A common treatment for atherosclerosis is stenting, a procedure that involves inserting a small mesh tube to widen narrowed or blocked arteries. However, stent placement is challenging and intricate, and improper placement or sizing can lead to post-operative complications. Malapposition, a condition where the stent is incorrectly deployed, can lead to thrombus formation and increased risk of restenosis [23]. Intravascular Ultrasound (IVUS) provides real-time endovascular information on the coronary vasculature, offering a cross-sectional view of the vessel wall [17]. This is

---

This work was funded in part by MIT-IBM Watson AI Lab.

S. Wu et al. (Eds.): AMAI 2023, LNCS 14313, pp. 165–175, 2024.
https://doi.org/10.1007/978-3-031-47076-9_17

valuable for stent sizing and placement and can reduce the need for overlapping stents, which increases thrombosis risk. IVUS can also check stent placement post-intervention and identify malapposed regions.

Despite its benefits, IVUS has not been shown to have a positive clinical impact for percutaneous coronary interventions due to low signal-to-noise ratio (SNR) and numerous imaging artifacts [26,27], making IVUS image interpretation challenging and increasing time training time required for physicians. Manual malapposition detection is especially difficult and time-consuming, requiring an experienced eye to identify subtle cues of blood flow behind a malapposed stent gap (Fig. 1).

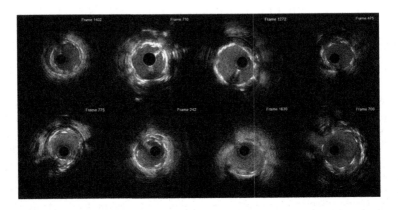

**Fig. 1.** Challenge of identifying malapposed frames: The subtle differences between well-apposed and malapposed stent struts. The top row presents well-apposed frames, while the bottom row displays malapposed frames. Detecting these subtle distinctions requires expertise and a keen eye for detail, as the differences between well-apposed and malapposed stent struts are not immediately apparent and highlights the complexity of the task.

In this paper, we perform a comparative study on incorporating domain knowledge into deep learning models for detecting malapposition. We introduce a stent strut detector and employ temporal flow-based techniques combined with a late fusion-based classification approach. We also address the issue of limited training data by implementing robust augmentations. Our methods leverage domain knowledge to filter out irrelevant information from input data before using powerful machine learning algorithms.

## 2   Related Work

**IVUS Analysis Methods:** Various methods have been developed for automatic IVUS image analysis [10], with a focus on dense prediction tasks like image segmentation and registration. Lumen segmentation [1,5,13,25] has been the primary focus, with methods also been developed for stent segmentation [28] and calcification segmentation [16]. For image classification, frame-level calcification detection has been examined in several studies [18,20]. Only one study [21] has focused on malapposition detection, arguably more challenging due to the subtle cues indicating malapposition. Unlike this study, our method does not require paired pre- and post-stenting IVUS pullbacks either for training or testing, representing a more common clinical scenario.

**Feature Selection Methods:** Before deep learning's widespread use, feature selection was an integral part of most machine learning pipelines [7,15], designed to remove task-irrelevant information in the inputs. For vectorized data, where different dimensions correspond to measurements of different signals, information-theoretic approaches [6] or unsupervised clustering techniques [14,22] have been proposed. For image data, correlations between dimensions are determined by spatial neighborhood information. A key idea here is to extract high-level representations from images before applying feature selection methods designed for vectorized data [8]. Other approaches include retaining all dimensions of the input images and regularizing the classifier learning to base its decision off only a few input dimensions [12], unsupervised feature ranking followed by cross-validation based feature selection [24], or selecting features with the least reconstruction error [29]. Notably, all these approaches rely on statistics of the input dataset for feature selection. *In contrast, our approach leverages domain knowledge to identify regions of input images that contain information relevant to the task and removes irrelevant features based on that information.*

## 3    Methods

We aim to learn a malapposition classifier $f_\theta : \mathcal{R}^{m \times n} \to \{0,1\}$, using a labelled training dataset, with $X \in \mathcal{R}^{m \times n}$ an IVUS image frame, and $Y \in \{0,1\}$ the corresponding malapposition classification label.

Given the challenges of a relatively small training dataset and the difficulty of visually seeing the malapposition area, we hypothesize learning a function on pre-processed images, $h(X)$, may lead to better results than learning the function on raw images, $X$. We design $h(X)$ to either filter out information that is known to be unwanted for malapposition detection or to incorporate potentially helpful information for this task.

In the following, we introduce three modules, which we combine to design $h(X)$ in different ways.

### 3.1    Masking Irrelevant Regions

Malapposed areas are regions between the lumen boundary and the stent so signals that effectively identify malappositions are expected to be located near the stent. We introduce a filter $M : \mathcal{R}^{m \times n} \to \mathcal{R}^{m \times n}$ that selectively masks all image regions except those that surround the stent struts. We use Mask-RCNN [9] to locate stent strut objects in the image. After detecting the stent struts, we

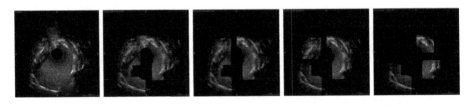

**Fig. 2.** Example patchwork image by assembling the $96 \times 96$ patches containing stent struts and the surrounding regions. The red dots highlight the Mask-RCNN detected bright regions as stent struts. From L-R: Original image $X$ that corresponds to $\tau = 0.0$, followed by masked images, $M(X)$ with $\tau$ set to 0.2, 0.4, 0.6 and 0.8. As $\tau$ increases, the detected struts and retained image information decrease. (Color figure online)

define a filter $M$ the zeros our all the image pixels except for those in patches of size $d \times d$ pixels around the detected struts. $d$ is empirically set to 96. The amount of information retained by $M$ can be optimized by adjusting the threshold $\tau$.

### 3.2 Including Temporal Context

The disease signature of malapposition is characterized by blood flow behind the stent strut, a subtle feature that is difficult to detect. Identifying malapposition requires scrolling through multiple ultrasound image slices to spot the subtle blood flow speckle. To address this challenge, we incorporate temporally adjacent frames to improve the accuracy of malapposition detection. We used multiple frames temporally to capture subtle blood flow movements behind the stent struts by defining a mapping $T : \mathcal{R}^{m \times n} \rightarrow \mathcal{R}^{(2t+1) \times m \times n}$ that concatenates an IVUS frame with $t$ frames acquired before and after it. We set the value of $t$ empirically to 5 based on the speed of typical IVUS pullbacks.

### 3.3 Including Blood Flow Information via Deformation Fields

We capture blood flow information using voxelmorph [2], an unsupervised registration method that can estimate the deformation field between two IVUS frames. This approach combines an image similarity loss (e.g., mean square error) and a regularization loss to ensure plausible and smooth deformations. We use these deformation fields to define a mapping $V : \mathcal{R}^{m \times n} \rightarrow \mathcal{R}^{(2t+1) \times m \times n \times 3}$. The output has three channels in the last dimension, representing the intensity image at the pullback location and the magnitude and direction of the deformation field w.r.t to the central image in the temporal sequence.

### 3.4 Combining the Modules

We combine the three modules in different ways to design $h(X)$ and evaluate the performance of the resulting malapposition classifiers. Specifically, we consider six methods:

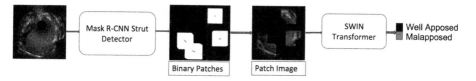

**Fig. 3.** Workflow of the proposed method when $h(X) = M(X)$: the input image is masked according to the strut detection predictions, followed by a Swin Transformer-based $f_\theta$ to classify between well-apposed and malapposed frames.

1. **Full frame 2D (baseline):** This method uses the raw IVUS frames as input to the classifier, i.e., $h(X) = X$.
2. **Patchwise 2D (baseline - irrelevant information):** This method uses the masked IVUS frames as input to the classifier, i.e., $h(X) = M(X)$.
3. **Temporal Full Frame (baseline + temporal info):** This method uses the temporally concatenated IVUS frames as input to the classifier, i.e., $h(X) = T(X)$.
4. **Temporal Patchwise (baseline + temporal info - irrelevant information):** This method uses the temporally concatenated and masked IVUS frames as input to the classifier, i.e., $h(X) = M(T(X))$.
5. **Temporal Full Frame with Voxelmorph (baseline + temporal info + deformation fields):** This method uses the temporally concatenated IVUS frames and the deformation fields as input to the classifier, i.e., $h(X) = V(X)$.
6. **Temporal Patchwise with Voxelmorph (baseline + temporal info + deformation fields - irrelevant information):** This method uses the temporally concatenated, masked IVUS frames and the deformation fields as input to the classifier, i.e., $h(X) = M(V(X))$.

Each method uses a deep learning model for the classifier $f_\theta$ (See Fig. 3). The model is trained on a labeled training dataset and evaluated on a separate test dataset. The performance of the methods is compared in terms of their ability to accurately detect malapposition in IVUS images.

## 4    Experiments and Results

We used a clinical dataset of IVUS pullbacks acquired using 60 MHz Opti-CrossHD catheters to conduct the experiments. Each frame in the pullbacks was labeled for stents and malapposition by domain experts. Some of the stented frames also had pixel-wise stent strut segmentations for exploring segmentation approaches. The dataset consisted of pullbacks from different hospitals, physicians, imaged coronary arteries, and stages within coronary interventions, which had malapposed frames in 8.5% of the dataset, highlighting the scarcity of the disease's prevalence.

Stent struts, identifiable by their distinct appearance, were labeled in limited 2D frames due to resource constraints. In Total, 451 malapposed frames from

37 patients and 72 pullbacks were labeled, along with 53, 404 well-apposed stent frames from 53 patients and 117 pullbacks. Pixel-wise stent strut annotations were available for 456 2D frames from 44 pullbacks (Fig. 4).

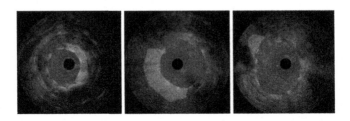

**Fig. 4.** From left to right: typical malapposition within the lesion, malapposition at proximal widening, and stent strut covering side branch. Note that the stent strut covering the side branch isn't considered as malapposition technically; it was labeled to increase the number of examples of blood behind the stent strut.

We present our experiments in the following order: First, in Sect. 4.1, we discuss the details of training the *preprocessing* modules required to define our engineered representations $h(X)$. Specifically, Sect. 4.1 contains the details of training the stent strut detector and the voxelmorph deformation field predictor, respectively. Next, in Sect. 4.2, we study the effect of training a malapposition classifier on raw IVUS frames with either the full context or reduced context due to masking. Finally, in Sect. 4.3, we discuss how our temporal information induces $h(X)$ variants and their masked extensions. All experiments were implemented in PyTorch using NVIDIA-V100 GPU (Fig. 5).

### 4.1   Training Modules Needed for Defining $M$ and $V$

**Stent Strut Detector Required for $M$.** This module aims to identify regions around the *bright spots* in the image, corresponding to the stent struts. To this end, we trained a Mask R-CNN network. The object detection loss was minimized for 20 epochs, using a batch size of 16 and an Adam optimizer for training. Transformations used for augmenting the dataset included Gaussian blurring and random flipping. We used 10-fold cross-validation. Upon averaging the results of the 10-fold cross-validation, the total quantitative performance yielded a Mask-RCNN BBOX-AP @[IoU $= 0.50$] as $0.515 \pm 0.019$.

**Temporal Registration Required for $V$.** In order to capture the subtle blood flow behind the stent struts, we pre-trained a voxelmorph model on temporal frames [2]. The self-supervised pre-training was minimized for 20 epochs on a ten-frame sequence optimized for a weighted combination of the mean square error and a deformation field smoothness consistency loss with a batch size of 1 and an Adam optimizer for training. The UNet in the voxelmorph module for producing the deformation map used an EfficientNet-B4 encoder pre-trained

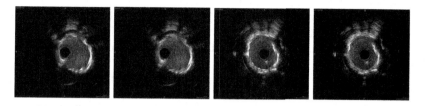

**Fig. 5.** From left to right: Two example frames of images with ground truth stent struts annotated. They characteristically appear as bright spots on the lumen used to train a Mask-RCNN algorithm.

"noisy-student" from the [11] package. We trained on a subset of the DICOM pullbacks on 74 patients and validated on 18 patients. The best model was chosen based on the lowest validation score for further downstream experiments.

**Table 1.** Results of single-frame classification experiments ($h(X) = X, h(X) = M(X)$), with varying $\tau$ of Mask-RCNN based $M(X)$. Average results over all folds are shown. The best-performing setting for each metric is highlighted in bold.

| $h(X)$ | AUC | Precision | Recall | F1 |
|---|---|---|---|---|
| $X$ | **0.770** | 0.478 | **0.227** | **0.308** |
| $M(X), \tau = 0.2$ | 0.747 | 0.494 | 0.189 | 0.273 |
| $M(X), \tau = 0.4$ | 0.739 | **0.591** | 0.174 | 0.269 |
| $M(X), \tau = 0.6$ | 0.756 | 0.567 | 0.177 | 0.270 |
| $M(X), \tau = 0.8$ | 0.712 | 0.510 | 0.129 | 0.206 |
| $M(X), \tau = 0.9$ | 0.670 | 0.519 | 0.106 | 0.176 |

## 4.2   Single-Frame Classification

This set of experiments corresponds to $h(X)$ set as $h(X) = X$ and $h(X) = M(X)$, that is, the two representation choices that do not include temporal information in the classification process. For these settings, experiments were conducted with 5-fold cross-validation, 10 training epochs, batch size set to 16, and using the Adam optimizer. The architecture of the classifier $f_\theta$ was chosen to be the Swin Transformer model [19]. We evaluate classification performance using the four metrics: accuracy, precision, recall, and F1-score.

$h(X) = X$ corresponds to the baseline performance of single-frame classification. This is shown in the first row of Table 1.

For $h(X) = M(X)$, the best-performing Mask-RCNN model was used (at different $\tau$ values) to detect stent strut. Then, $96 \times 96$ patches were retained around the detected struts, and the remaining regions were zeroed out. These masked images were then used as inputs to a classifier to determine frame-wise malapposed and well-apposed stent struts. Results of these experiments are shown in the remaining rows of Table 1. When $\tau$ is low, the strut detector picks out many bright regions, including the false positive bright regions such as calcification, catheter, and other artifacts in the lumen. Higher $\tau$ values lead to lesser patches and lesser information retained in the corresponding masked images. See Fig. 2 for examples of Mask-RCNN generated patches at varying thresholds.

### 4.3   Classification Using Temporal Context

Next, we test our hypothesis that incorporating a temporal context could improve the classification performance, by potentially leveraging subtle temporal blood flow patterns. This corresponds to the settings $h(X) = T(X)$, $h(X) = V(X)$, and their masked variants $h(X) = M(T(X))$, $h(X) = M(V(X))$. These classifiers were trained for 10 epochs with a batch size of 4. As before, classification performance was evaluated using accuracy, precision-recall, and F1-score, as presented in Table 2.

We employed a pre-trained EfficientNet-B0 CNN model and a late fusion method to classify the central frame. To determine whether domain-specific knowledge could provide further improvements, we utilized VoxelMorph to capture flow information. By keeping the central slice in the 10 frame sequence as the fixed image, we generated deformation maps for the remaining 9 moving images and calculated their magnitude and direction. These values were then input into the classifier, along with intensity images.

Further, we used the Mask R-CNN model (trained on stent struts as described earlier) to generate patch-wise temporal images to assess their impact on performance. Based on the results presented in Table 1, we selected the $\tau = 0.6$ Mask R-CNN for defining the mask function $M$.

**Table 2.** Temporal Classification Results: This table presents the outcomes for the Full Frame without Voxelmorph ($T(X)$) and with Voxelmorph ($V(X)$), as well as the patchwise experiments with Mask-RCNN at $\tau = 0.6$ without ($M(T(X))$) and with Voxelmorph ($M(V(X))$). The performance metrics averaged over all five folds are provided. The highest-performing metrics for each fold are emphasized in bold.

| $h(X)$ | AUC | Precision | Recall | F1 |
|---|---|---|---|---|
| $T(X)$ | 0.587 | **0.214** | 0.051 | 0.083 |
| $V(X)$ | 0.551 | 0.122 | 0.064 | 0.084 |
| $M(V(X))$ | 0.631 | 0.159 | 0.064 | 0.092 |
| $M(T(X))$ | **0.676** | 0.170 | **0.095** | **0.122** |

## 5   Conclusion

Malapposition, a significant clinical issue leading to complications like thrombosis and re-stenosis, requires accurate detection for improved patient outcomes.

This study aimed to assess the performance of various domain-specific enhancements to prime deep-learning models for accurate stent strut malapposition detection. We explored methodologies, including 2D frame-by-frame detection, domain-specific feature selection, and temporal techniques. However, the best performance was still using whole 2D frames, achieving an AUC of 0.77 for a challenging problem. The other methods of feature priming did not show improvement, suggesting that current deep learning models may not effectively utilize domain-specific features. While an AUC of 0.77 is acceptable, the overall performance did not meet the required clinical standard of achieving a 90% recall rate with at least 50% precision.

The masking approach did not significantly improve performance, suggesting a delicate balance between minimizing information and preserving detection accuracy. Future research will investigate the impact of the patch size of the Mask R-CNN stent strut on performance. Additionally, we will investigate the heterogeneity of malapposition labels. Recent clinical studies have suggested the existence of various sub-types of malapposed frames [3]. Treating these sub-types as distinct classes may enhance classification performance. Additional exploration of the temporal approach with voxel morph is necessary. We hypothesize that motion artifacts in the ultrasound lumen may overshadow the subtle flow behind the stent strut. Future research could investigate methods for addressing this issue and enhancing the temporal approach's accuracy.

The prospect of application: By meeting the clinical need with greater accuracy and efficiency, the detection of malapposition post-stenting can occur more quickly and effectively, ultimately minimizing the risk of further complications.

# References

1. Arora, P., Singh, P., Girdhar, A., Vijayvergiya, R.: A state-of-the-art review on coronary artery border segmentation algorithms for intravascular ultrasound (IVUS) images. Cardiovasc. Eng. Technol. 14, 1–32 (2023)
2. Balakrishnan, G., Zhao, A., Sabuncu, M.R., Guttag, J., Dalca, A.V.: Voxelmorph: a learning framework for deformable medical image registration. IEEE Trans. Med. Imaging 38(8), 1788–1800 (2019)
3. Banerjee, S., Alaiti, A.: Complications of percutaneous coronary interventions in calcified lesions: causes, recognition, management, and how to avoid. In: Debulking in Cardiovascular Interventions and Revascularization Strategies, pp. 311–319. Elsevier (2022)
4. Benjamin, E.J., et al.: Heart disease and stroke statistics-2018 update: a report from the American heart association. Circulation 137(12), e67–e492 (2018)
5. Blanco, P.J., et al.: Fully automated lumen and vessel contour segmentation in intravascular ultrasound datasets. Med. Image Anal. 75, 102262 (2022)
6. Brown, G., Pocock, A., Zhao, M.J., Luján, M.: Conditional likelihood maximisation: a unifying framework for information theoretic feature selection. J. Mach. Learn. Res. 13, 27–66 (2012)
7. Chandrashekar, G., Sahin, F.: A survey on feature selection methods. Comput. Electr. Eng. 40(1), 16–28 (2014)

8. Cong, Y., Wang, S., Liu, J., Cao, J., Yang, Y., Luo, J.: Deep sparse feature selection for computer aided endoscopy diagnosis. Pattern Recogn. **48**(3), 907–917 (2015)

9. He, K., Gkioxari, G., Dollár, P., Girshick, R.: Mask r-cnn. In: Proceedings of the IEEE International Conference on Computer Vision, pp. 2961–2969 (2017)

10. Huang, C., Wang, J., Xie, Q., Zhang, Y.D.: Analysis methods of coronary artery intravascular images: a review. Neurocomputing **489**, 27–39 (2022)

11. Iakubovskii, P.: Segmentation models pytorch (2019). https://github.com/qubvel/segmentation_models.pytorch

12. Jia, Y., Huang, C., Darrell, T.: Beyond spatial pyramids: receptive field learning for pooled image features. In: 2012 IEEE Conference on Computer Vision and Pattern Recognition, pp. 3370–3377. IEEE (2012)

13. Katouzian, A., Angelini, E.D., Carlier, S.G., Suri, J.S., Navab, N., Laine, A.F.: A state-of-the-art review on segmentation algorithms in intravascular ultrasound (IVUS) images. IEEE Trans. Inf Technol. Biomed. **16**(5), 823–834 (2012)

14. Li, J., Wu, L., Wen, G., Li, Z.: Exclusive feature selection and multi-view learning for Alzheimer's disease. J. Vis. Commun. Image Represent. **64**, 102605 (2019)

15. Li, J., et al.: Feature selection: a data perspective. ACM Comput. Surv. (CSUR) **50**(6), 1–45 (2017)

16. Li, Y.C., Shen, T.Y., Chen, C.C., Chang, W.T., Lee, P.Y., Huang, C.C.J.: Automatic detection of atherosclerotic plaque and calcification from intravascular ultrasound images by using deep convolutional neural networks. IEEE Trans. Ultrason. Ferroelectr. Freq. Control **68**(5), 1762–1772 (2021)

17. Liebson, P.R., Klein, L.W.: Intravascular ultrasound in coronary atherosclerosis: a new approach to clinical assessment. Am. Heart J. **123**(6), 1643–1660 (1992)

18. Liu, S., et al.: Automated quantitative assessment of coronary calcification using intravascular ultrasound. Ultrasound Med. Biol. **46**(10), 2801–2809 (2020)

19. Liu, Z., et al.: Swin transformer: hierarchical vision transformer using shifted windows. In: Proceedings of the IEEE/CVF International Conference on Computer Vision, pp. 10012–10022 (2021)

20. Masuda, T., et al.: Deep learning with convolutional neural network for estimation of the characterisation of coronary plaques: validation using IB-IVUS. Radiography **28**(1), 61–67 (2022)

21. Min, H.S., et al.: Prediction of coronary stent underexpansion by pre-procedural intravascular ultrasound-based deep learning. Cardiovasc. Intervent. **14**(9), 1021–1029 (2021)

22. Mitra, P., Murthy, C., Pal, S.K.: Unsupervised feature selection using feature similarity. IEEE Trans. Pattern Anal. Mach. Intell. **24**(3), 301–312 (2002)

23. Ng, J.C.K., Shaoliang, S.L., Zhong, L., Collet, C., Foin, N., Ang, H.Y.: Stent malapposition generates stent thrombosis: insights from a thrombosis model. Int. J. Cardiol. **353**, 43–45 (2022)

24. Roffo, G., Melzi, S., Cristani, M.: Infinite feature selection. In: Proceedings of the IEEE International Conference on Computer Vision, pp. 4202–4210 (2015)

25. Shinohara, H., et al.: Automatic detection of vessel structure by deep learning using intravascular ultrasound images of the coronary arteries. PLoS ONE **16**(8), e0255577 (2021)

26. Song, H.G., et al.: Intravascular ultrasound assessment of optimal stent area to prevent in-stent restenosis after zotarolimus-, everolimus-, and sirolimus-eluting stent implantation. Catheter. Cardiovasc. Interv. **83**(6), 873–878 (2014)

27. Truesdell, A.G., et al.: Intravascular imaging during percutaneous coronary intervention: JACC state-of-the-art review. J. Am. Coll. Cardiol. **81**(6), 590–605 (2023)
28. Wissel, T., et al.: Cascaded learning in intravascular ultrasound: coronary stent delineation in manual pullbacks. J. Med. Imaging **9**(2), 025001–025001 (2022)
29. Zou, Q., Ni, L., Zhang, T., Wang, Q.: Deep learning based feature selection for remote sensing scene classification. IEEE Geosci. Remote Sens. Lett. **12**(11), 2321–2325 (2015)

# Author Index

**A**

Abdalla, Amira Mahmoud  104
Abi-Nader, Clément  42
Akakin, Hatice  165
An, Qin  135
Attieh, Elham  1

**B**

Bauchet, Anne-Laure  1
Benitez, Benito K.  94
Bergman, Jacques J.  21, 32
Boers, Tim G. W.  21, 32
Bône, Alexandre  42

**C**

Carlson, Corydon  165
Chen, Eric Z.  145
Chen, Terrence  145
Chen, Xiao  145
Chen, Zihao  145

**D**

D'Souza, Niharika  165
de Groof, Albert J.  21, 32
de With, Peter H. N.  21, 32, 52
Debs, Noëlie  42
Dey, Neel  165
Drira, Hassen  72

**E**

El-Gendy, Hosam  104

**F**

Flanagan, Nic  83
Fockens, Kiki N.  21

**G**

Gershov, Sapir  11
Golland, Polina  165

Gözcü, Baran  94
Gross, Markus  94
Gunraj, Hayden  83

**H**

Hamdi, Ibraheem  104
Hashmi, Shahrukh K.  104
Hayashi, Yuichiro  135
Hellström, Terese A. E.  52
Hinoki, Akinari  135
Hodzic, Nedim  83
Hussain, Shakir  104

**J**

Jacobs, Igor  52
Jain, Lay  165
Jang, Jinhyeok  72
Jaspers, Tim J. M.  21, 32
Jha, Abhishek  62
Jiang, Yuming  114, 125
Jong, Martijn R.  21, 32
Jukema, Jelmer B.  21, 32

**K**

Karani, Neerav  165
Kashyap, Satyananda  165
Kitasaka, Takayuki  135
Kovvali, Omkar  155
Kusters, Carolus H. J.  21, 32

**L**

Laufer, Shlomi  11
Li, Qian  165
Li, Ruijiang  114, 125
Li, Wenguang  165
Li, Yichen  1
Li, Zhe  114
Lill, Yoriko  94
Lingens, Lasse  94

S. Wu et al. (Eds.): AMAI 2023, LNCS 14313, pp. 177–178, 2024.
https://doi.org/10.1007/978-3-031-47076-9

Liu, Leon   114
Liu, Yikang   145
Luyer, Misha   52

**M**
Mahameed, Fadi   11
Marcoux, Arnaud   42
Mavroeidis, Dimitrios   52
Mirza, Imran   104
Mori, Kensaku   135
Motati, Lakshmi Sritan   155
Mueller, Andreas A.   94
Mukherjee, Pritam   62

**N**
Nalabothu, Prasad   94

**O**
Oda, Hirohisa   135
Oda, Masahiro   135
Okel, Sanne E.   52

**P**
Pacak, Karel   62
Patel, Mayank   62
Pluyter, Jon   52
Pochet, Etienne   1

**Q**
Qi, Bozhao   1

**R**
Ramaekers, Mark   52
Raz, Aeyal   11
Ridzuan, Muhammad   104
Rohé, Marc-Michel   42
Routier, Alexandre   42

**S**
Sabri, Ali   83
Saeed, Mohamed   104
Santra, Bikash   62

Schnabel, Till   94
Seo, Hyewon   72
Shang, Alexander   165
Sharshar, Ahmed   104
Solenthaler, Barbara   94
Summers, Ronald M.   62
Sun, Shanhui   145
Suzuki, Kojiro   135
Syed, Naveed   104
Syeda-Mahmood, Tanveer   165

**T**
Tai, Chi-en Amy   83
Takimoto, Aitaro   135
Tang, Qi   1
Tasios, Nick   52
Trullo, Roger   1

**U**
Uchida, Hiroo   135

**V**
van der Sommen, Fons   21, 32, 52
Viviers, Christiaan G. A.   52

**W**
Wang, Diwei   72
Wang, Ray   165
Wong, Alexander   83

**X**
Xia, Yong   114
Xing, Lei   125

**Y**
Yaqub, Mohammad   104

**Z**
Zhao, Wei   1
Zhou, Zixia   125
Zouaoui, Chaima   72

Printed in the United States
by Baker & Taylor Publisher Services